D1526556

HISPANIC
MEDAL OF HONOR
RECIPIENTS

WILLIAMS-FORD

TEXAS A&M UNIVERSITY

MILITARY HISTORY

SERIES

HISPANIC MEDAL OF HONOR RECIPIENTS

American Heroes

MICHAEL LEE LANNING

Texas A&M University Press

COLLEGE STATION

This paper meets the requirements of ANSI/NISO Z39.48–1992 (Permanence of Paper).
Binding materials have been chosen for durability.

Manufactured in the United States of America

Library of Congress Cataloging-in-Publication Data

Names: Lanning, Michael Lee, author.
Title: Hispanic Medal of Honor recipients:
American heroes / Michael Lee Lanning.
Other titles: Williams-Ford Texas A&M University military history series.
Description: First edition. | College Station: Texas A&M University Press,
[2022] | Series: Williams-Ford Texas A&M University military history
series | Includes bibliographical references and index.
Identifiers: LCCN 2021050035 (print) | LCCN 2021050036 (ebook) | ISBN
9781648430329 (hardcover) | ISBN 9781648430336 (ebook)
Subjects: LCSH: Medal of Honor—Biography. | Hispanic American
soldiers—Biography. | United States—Armed Forces—Hispanic
Americans—Biography. | BISAC: HISTORY / Military / United States |
HISTORY / Reference | LCGFT: Biographies.
Classification: LCC UB433 .L37 2022 (print) | LCC UB433 (ebook) | DDC
355.1/3420922—dc23/eng/20211028
LC record available at https://lccn.loc.gov/2021050035
LC ebook record available at https://lccn.loc.gov/2021050036

*To archivist Laura S. Jowdy and the entire staff
of the Congressional Medal of Honor Society
at their national headquarters, located in
Mount Pleasant, South Carolina*

CONTENTS

KOREA

VIETNAM

HISPANIC
MEDAL OF HONOR
RECIPIENTS

Introduction

THE FIRST CHALLENGE in properly recognizing the valor of Hispanics in the armed forces of the United States of America is to define the basic term *Hispanic* itself. Hispanic is not a race. Rather, it is an ethnic term derived to designate descendants of Hispania, an area on the European Iberian Peninsula that today includes Spain and Portugal. Although the area is still called Hispania by those in surrounding countries, neither Spanish nor Portuguese nor other Europeans use the term *Hispanic* for its residents.

The evolution of the term has taken many turns. Prior to the mid-nineteenth century, those whom we now refer to as Hispanics were called Spanish, Mexican, Cubans, or other nationalities based on their country of origin. The defining moment for the racial status of Hispanics came with the signing of the Treaty of Guadalupe Hidalgo, which ended the US-Mexican War in 1848. This document gave the United States the ownership of California and a large portion of what is now Arizona, Nevada, and Utah as well as smaller parts of current-day Wyoming and Colorado. Residents in those annexed areas who traced their ancestors to Mexico had the choice of relocating to within Mexico's new boundaries or receiving American citizenship with full civil rights. At the time, only "white" Americans could be citizens; therefore, the Mexicans who stayed were classified as "whites," creating the term "white Hispanic."

In 1917, the US Congress passed the Jones Act, which made residents of the Commonwealth of Puerto Rico American citizens. Except for those who had obvious Negroid color and features, Puerto Ricans were considered "white" and eligible for conscription into the US Armed Forces.

It was not until the 1930 census that Mexicans received their own category. The Civil Rights Act of 1964 addressed treatment and discrimination based on color and race, but it did not include Hispanics, as they were officially considered "white." At this time, the terms "Latino" and "Chicano" also were used interchangeably with "Hispanic," but the former was considered to be more of an activist or political term while the latter was looked upon as a militant designation by many.

In 1976 the US Congress passed Public Law 94-311, which required the monitoring of the welfare and progress of "Americans of Spanish descent." Finally, in 1977, the Office of Management and Budget of the Executive Branch issued Directive 15, titled "Race and Ethnic Standards for Federal Statistics and Administrative Reporting." Directive 15 introduced officially the term "Hispanic" and defined it as "a person of Mexican, Puerto Rican, Cuban, Central or South American or other Spanish culture or origin, regardless of race."

From that time, the Congressional Medal of Honor Society and the Hispanic Medal of Honor Society have used these definition guidelines. Both have also broadened the term to include Medal of Honor recipients of Portuguese descent.

Hispanics in the Armed Forces of the United States

HISPANIC SETTLEMENTS in North America predate those of English-speaking Europeans by more than a century. By the time the Pilgrims landed on Plymouth Rock, the Spanish had already conquered, civilized, and colonized much of Mexico and Central and South America as well as the portion of what would later become the southwestern United States.

Few Hispanics were involved in the colonization along the North American Atlantic Seaboard. Those who were had immigrated not from Mexico or Central or South America but rather directly from the Iberian Peninsula, the Canary Islands, or the island of Minorca. They came to work in the fishing and shipping industries, and likely some of these men served in their state militias or in the Continental Army upon the outbreak of the American War of Independence.

Although the number of Hispanics in the emerging American army is not documented, the support of Spain played an important role in the move toward independence. Having been at war off and on for much of the eighteenth century and having suffered great losses in territory and manpower during the Seven Years War (1756 to 1763), Spain supported the Americans, seeing them as allies against a common enemy, Great Britain. On the June 21, 1779, Spain declared war against England, hoping that the British defeat in North America would result in their own recovery of territories lost to the English, particularly Florida. They also hoped that the longstanding threat that the British posed to their territories in the Western Hemisphere would be removed.

King Charles III of Spain dispatched Juan de Miralles Trayllon as an observer of and messenger to the new American army of George Washington early in the war. Miralles, who had been born to French parents on July 23, 1713, in Petrel, Spain, but had spent much of his youth in Cuba, met and became friends with Washington and many of the leaders of the revolution. Until his death in Morristown, New Jersey, on April 30, 1780, Miralles arranged monetary loans to the newly declared United States as well as arranging for the importation of arms and supplies and the gathering of intelligence on the British.

More direct assistance came from Bernardo de Galvez y Madrid, who was the Spanish governor of Louisiana. Galvez, born in the Spanish province of Malaga and the future namesake of Galveston Island, favored the Americans and allowed the smuggling of arms and ammunition through the Port of New Orleans and on north up the Mississippi River. When Spain formally declared war against the British in 1779, Galvez assembled a multiracial, multiethnic army that included locals as well as recruits from Mexico, Cuba, and Puerto Rico.

Galvez initially defeated British garrisons at forts at Baton Rouge and Natchez along the Mississippi River and then began a campaign along the Gulf Coast that captured Mobile and Pensacola—actions that took away British troops that might otherwise have been fighting the Continental Army on the East Coast. The Spanish king was so pleased with Galvez's performance that he gave permission for the soldier to add the words "Yo solo" (I alone) to his family coat of arms.

Although Mexicans are usually considered "the enemy" of Texans in the war for Texas independence, many Hispanics, known as Tejanos, fought for their liberty as Texans because that's what they considered themselves to be. Eight of the 189 who died at the Alamo were Tejanos. Another Tejano, Capt. Juan Nepomuceno Seguín, led a cavalry company at the Battle of San Jacinto.

It was not until the Civil War, however, that Hispanics played a significant role in the history of the American armed forces. The conclusion of the Mexican-American War in 1848 left many Hispanics in the lands ceded to the United States, and they were granted American citizenship. At the outbreak of the Civil War, about 27,500 Hispanics lived in the United States. Some 2,550 joined the Confederacy, and 1,000 enlisted in the Union army. Hispanics played a significant role in defending New Mexico from an invasion by the Southern rebels. Four companies of Hispanics from California were raised because of their "extraordinary horsemanship" to guard supply trains in their native state and to deter Confederate raiders. Hispanics also served in Confederate gray as members of infantry and cavalry regiments from Texas, Missouri, and Florida.

Two Hispanic Union sailors and one soldier earned the Medal of Honor in the war: John Ortega, born in Spain, Phillip Bazaar, a native of Chile, and Joseph de Castro, born to a Spanish father in Boston.

David Glasgow Farragut (1801–1870) is the best-known Hispanic veteran of the Civil War. His father, Jordi, was a native of Minorca, Spain, and came to the United States in 1776. David Farragut entered the navy at age nine and served until his death sixty years later. He was the first rear admiral, vice admiral, and admiral in the US Navy, being best known, however, for his order at the Battle of Mobile Bay: "Damn the torpedoes, full speed ahead."

The Hispanic population in the United States remained small in the latter decades of the nineteenth century, but France Silva of Portuguese descent earned a Medal of Honor in the Boxer Rebellion in 1900. At that time there were about 500,000 Hispanics in the United States. This number increased to nearly 800,000 in 1910 and to 1.3 million in 1920. Much of this growth was the result of Hispanics looking for work and opportunity. The largest numbers came from Mexico, many of whom were refugees from the dangers and hardships of the Mexican Revolution (1910–1920). It is estimated that 200,000 Hispanics, the majority being Mexican Americans, volunteered or were drafted into the armed services during World War I. David Barkley, whose mother was Mexican American, earned the Medal of Honor in the war's final days.

By the 1940s, the Hispanic population of the United States, especially Mexican Americans, was changing from immigrants to native born. Twice as many were born and raised in the United States, often by immigrant families, as those born outside the country. These native-born Hispanics identified with and loved their country, resulting in about 500,000 serving in the US Armed Forces during World War II. Seventeen earned the Medal of Honor.

Hispanics served throughout the military in World War II but were concentrated in state units nationalized for the conflict. Many of those who defended Bataan and Corregidor in the Philippines in the early days of the conflict were from New Mexico National Guard air defense units activated and deployed to the islands shortly before the attack by Japan. The Arizona National Guard's

158th Infantry Regiment, made up largely of Mexican and Native Americans, earned the praise of Gen. Douglas MacArthur, who said they were "one of the greatest fighting combat teams ever deployed for battle."

In an article published in the June 1950 edition of *Pageant*, Gen. Jonathan M. Wainwright said, "I can't forget the Latin-American boys shed their blood fabulously during World War II; 80 percent of the names on San Antonio's casualty lists were names of Latin Americans."

Famed war correspondent Ernie Pyle wrote about the 45th Infantry Division in his best-selling book *Brave Men*:

> A large percentage of the battalion spoke Spanish and occasionally I heard some of the officers talking Spanish among themselves, just to keep in practice I suppose. That New Mexico bunch missed more than anything, I believe, the Spanish dishes they were accustomed to back home. Their folks occasionally sent them cans of chili and peppers, and then they had a minor feast.
>
> They were part of the old New Mexico outfit, most of which were lost in Bataan. It was good to get back to those slow talking, wise, and easy people of the desert, and good to speak of places like Las Cruces, Socorro, and Santa Rosa.

More than 148,000 Hispanics served in the US military during the Korean War, with 14 receiving the Medal of Honor. This included 61,000 Puerto Ricans, 18,000 of whom were from the Continental United States. The segregated 65th Infantry Regiment was one of the first to arrive on the Korean Peninsula and fought in every major campaign of the conflict. It was finally integrated in March 1953.

Approximately 80,000 of the 2.1 million Americans who served in the ten-year-long Vietnam War were Hispanics, 22 of whom received the Medal of Honor. Another 20,000 took part in Operation Desert Shield/Desert Storm to liberate Kuwait. About 13.5 percent of today's military personnel are Hispanic, with many serving in Iraq and Afghanistan. One has earned the Medal of Honor.

In 2002, the US Congress, through the Defense Authorization Act, required that "[t]he Secretary of each military department shall review the service records of each Jewish American war veteran or Hispanic American war veteran to determine whether that veteran should be awarded the Medal of Honor." Over the next twelve years, Pentagon officials reviewed more than

6,500 records of Jewish and Hispanic recipients of the Distinguished Service Cross (the second-highest medal for valor) to see if they had been denied the Medal of Honor because of prejudice or discrimination. The review yielded 17 Hispanics whose Distinguished Service Crosses during World War II, Korea, and Vietnam were upgraded to the Medal of Honor. At the presentation ceremony at the White House on March 18, 2014, Pres. Barack Obama said, "This ceremony reminds us of one of the enduring qualities that makes America great, that makes us exceptional. No nation is perfect. But here in America, we confront our imperfections and face a sometimes painful past, including the truth that some of these soldiers fought and died for a country that did not always see them as equal."

Over the centuries of American military history, Hispanic service members have suffered much of the same discrimination, prejudice, and mistreatment as those in the civilian sector. This book is not, however, about that abuse and racism. Rather it is about the valor of a group of Americans whose most common characteristic is the Spanish language—and a willful desire to serve their country and their fellow service members. A total of sixty Hispanic Americans have exhibited the bravery that earned them the highest combat award in the US Armed Forces.

The Medal of Honor

THE MEDAL OF HONOR is the highest award that the United States Armed Forces presents for bravery displayed in combat against an enemy force. It is awarded to those who distinguish themselves by gallantry and intrepidity beyond the call of duty at the risk of their own lives. Generally presented by the president in the name of Congress, it is often called the Congressional Medal of Honor. More than 40 million men and women have served in the US Armed Forces since the formation of the Continental Army in 1775. Fewer than 3,500 Medals of Honor have been awarded in its 150-year history. Sixty of the recipients have been Hispanic.

Armed forces around the world have presented medals or other decorations for valor since the beginnings of recorded history. Acts of bravery or other distinguished services have also been "mentioned in the dispatches" of battlefield commanders. Medals for bravery have been viewed not only as recognition of valorous acts but also as incentives for battlefield bravery. French emperor Napoleon Bonaparte said, "Give me enough medals and I'll win you any war." He added, "A soldier will fight long and hard for a bit of colored ribbon."

The first effort to recognize valor on the part of Americans came from Gen. George Washington when he established the Badge of Military Merit on August 7, 1782. Intended to be granted for "any singularly meritorious action," it was awarded to only three persons before it fell into disuse after the conclusion of the American Revolution. The original Badge of Military Merit was a purple-shaped heart of cloth with an embroidered "Merit" on the face. It was revived in 1932 as the Purple Heart to be awarded to wounded veterans of World War I.

For the next fifty years the US military had no formal way of recognizing valor on the battlefield. The expansion of the army in the Mexican-American War (1846–1848) brought new demands for honoring the brave. On March 23, 1847, the US Congress authorized the Certificate of Merit "to any private soldier who had distinguished himself by gallantry performed in the presence of the enemy." The certificates were discontinued after the war but were reintroduced in 1876 after the Battle of the Little Bighorn. On January 11, 1905, the Certificate of Merit was changed to the Certificate of Merit Medal. This remained the decoration for bravery until World War I, when the Merit Medal was replaced by the Army Distinguished Service Medal on January 2, 1918, and the Navy Distinguished Service Medal the following year. These medals were changed to the Distinguished Service Cross and the Navy Cross in 1934. The 1918 act also authorized the Citation Star, which was replaced by the Silver Star in 1932.

The mass mobilization, huge battles, and general carnage of the American Civil War brought new interests from members of the US Congress and the military in creating a new medal for valor. There were objections that such an award was "too European"; that it smacked of Old World vanity, elitism, and snobbery and had no place in democratic America. Still, most Americans believed it was time for a national medal to recognize military bravery. On December 9, 1861, Sen. James W. Grimes of Iowa introduced a bill that authorized the distribution of "medals of honor" to be awarded sailors and marines who distinguished themselves in battle. Sen. Henry Wilson of Massachusetts introduced a similar bill on February 17, 1862, authorizing the Medal of Honor to be awarded to army personnel. Pres. Abraham Lincoln signed both bills, and the most prominent and honored military medal became a permanent part of US history.

On June 22, 2000, US Army Chief of Staff Gen. Eric S. Shinseki spoke at an induction ceremony of recent recipients of the Medal of Honor into the Pentagon Hall of Heroes. He said then what has remained true about the men who have received the award since its authorization more than a century and a half ago. General Shinseki said, "The Medal of Honor is not something soldiers seek. No one can train for it. In fact, no one expects people to make the kinds of sacrifice required in order to receive it."

Although initially authorized only for Civil War heroes, the Medal of Honor was made permanent by Congress on March 3, 1863. The legislation also extended eligibility to officers in addition to enlisted personnel. It placed

no restrictions on when a medal could be approved, and applications continued for decades after the war concluded. Because there were no specific cri-
teria or time limits for awarding the medal, it was liberally presented—some
to individuals and even entire units who had performed few acts of bravery
or none.

In 1876 a new standard for eligibility for the Medal of Honor stated, "The
[individual's] conduct which deserves such recognition should not be the
simple discharge of duty, but such acts beyond this if omitted or refused to
be done, should not justly subject the person to censure as a shortcoming or
failure."

The US Congress passed legislation in 1897 stating that the Medal of Honor
could only be awarded for "gallantry and intrepidity." In 1905, Pres. Theodore Roosevelt, by executive order, outlined the basic policy and procedures
for awarding the medal. It stated that, whenever possible, award ceremonies
would be held in Washington, DC, with the president or his designated representative making the presentation.

Later, in 1916, Congress established the Medal of Honor Review Board "for
the purpose of investigating and reporting upon past awards or issue of the
so-called Congressional Medal of Honor by or through the War Department;
this with a view to ascertain what Medals of Honor, if any, had been awarded
or issued for any cause other than distinguished conduct by an officer or enlisted man in action involving actual conflict with an enemy."

A panel of five former generals was formed to review each of the 2,625
recipients who had been honored since the medal's creation, including 1,520
recipients from the Civil War, 443 from the Indian Wars, and 662 from the
Spanish-American War. The board's final report came out in 1917, striking 911
names from the list of Medal of Honor recipients. Most of these were from the
Civil War and included members of the regiment who had received the medal
for extending their enlistment dates and six civilian who were not deemed
eligible for the military award.

In 1944 a light blue moiré neck ribbon was added to display the medal.
The center of the ribbon displays thirteen white stars in the form of three
chevrons. Both the top and middle chevrons are made up of five stars, with
the bottom chevron made of three stars.

The US Coast Guard, organized in 1915, serves as part of the navy in wartime, and its members are eligible for the Navy Medal of Honor. One member
has been so honored. Marines also receive the Navy Medal of Honor. The US

Air Force, formerly part of the Army Air Corps, became a separate service in 1947. It continued to award the army version of the Medal of Honor until Congress authorized the Air Force Medal of Honor in 1956.

On July 25, 1963, the US Congress amended previous Medal of Honor legislation. The new version states that the medal is to be awarded to those who distinguish themselves "conspicuously by gallantry and intrepidity at the risk of his life above and beyond the call of duty while engaged in an action against an enemy of the United States; while engaged in military operations involving conflict with an opposing foreign force; or while serving with friendly foreign forces engaged in an armed conflict against an opposing armed force in which the United States is not a belligerent party. The deed performed must have been one of personal bravery or self-sacrifice so conspicuous as to clearly distinguish the individual above his comrades and must have involved risk of life. Incontestable proof of the performance of the service will be exacted and each recommendation for the award of this decoration will be considered on the standard of extraordinary merit. Eligibility is limited to members of the Army of the United States in active Federal military service."

Since the 1980s, a few Medals of Honor for actions dating all the way back to the Civil War have been awarded to correct past oversights and administrative errors. The records of African Americans, Asian Americans, Jewish Americans, and Hispanic Americans were reviewed to see if racial discrimination denied them their country's highest medal for valor.

Designs of the Medals of Honor have changed over the years, but they still closely resemble that of the original Civil War awards. The Institute of Heraldry, as authorized by Public Law 85-263, approved in September 1957, delineates the authority of the secretary of the army to furnish heraldic services to the military departments and other branches of the federal government. It describes the army version of the Medal of Honor as "a five-pointed star, each point tipped with trefoils, 1½ inches wide, surrounded by a green laurel wreath and suspended from a gold bar inscribed *VALOR*, surmounted by an eagle. In the center of the star, Minerva's (the Roman goddess of war) head surrounded by the words *UNITED STATES OF AMERICA*. On each ray of the star is a green oak leaf. On the reverse is a bar engraved *THE CONGRESS TO* with a space for engraving the name of the recipient." The pendant and suspension bar are made of gilding metal, with the eye, jump rings, and suspension ring made of red brass. The finish on the pendant and suspension bar is hard enameled, gold-plated, and rose gold–plated, with polished highlights. It is suspended from an eagle holding cannons and cannonballs in its talons.

The institute describes the navy version as "a five-pointed bronze star, tipped with trefoils containing a crown of laurel and oak. In the center is Minerva, personifying the United States, standing with left hand resting on fasces and right hand holding a shield blazoned with the shield from the coat of arms of the United States. She repulses Discord, represented by snakes. The medal is suspended from the flukes of an anchor." It is made of solid red brass, oxidized and buffed.

According to the institute, the Air Force Medal of Honor is "within a wreath of green laurel, a gold five-pointed star, one point down, tipped with trefoils and each point containing a crown of laurel and oak on a green background. Centered on the star, an annulet of 34 stars is a representation of the head of the Statue of Liberty. The star is suspended from a bar inscribed with the word *VALOR* above an adaptation of the thunderbolt from the Air Force Coat of Arms." The pendant is made of gilding metal. The connecting bar, hinge, and pin are made of bronze. The finish on the pendant and suspension bar is hard enameled, gold-plated, and rose gold–plated, with buffed relief.

Privileges and courtesies of those who have received the Medal of Honor include a pension of $1,406.72 per month, as of 2020, which is subject to cost-of-living increases. Retired recipients receive a 10 percent increase in their retirement pay. Recipients receive a Medal of Honor Flag; they can wear the uniform anytime as long as the standard restrictions are observed; they are authorized burial in Arlington National Cemetery; and their qualified children are admitted to the US military academies without nomination and quota requirements. Although not required by law or military regulation, members of the armed forces are encouraged to render hand salutes to recipients of the Medal of Honor as a matter of respect and courtesy regardless of rank or status.

According to the Medal of Honor Society, the Medal of Honor was awarded to 3,499 recipients between March 25, 1863, and July 31, 2017. This number includes the following:

Civil War, 1861–1865: 1,522 (3 Hispanics)
Indian War Campaigns, 1865–1891: 423
Interim, 1866–1870: 11

Korean Campaign, 1871: 15
Interim, 1871–1898: 100
War with Spain, 1898: 110
Boxer Rebellion, 1899–1901: 58 (1 Hispanic)
Philippine Insurrection, 1899–1902: 84
Interim, 1901–1911: 50
Actions against Philippine Outlaws, 1911: 6
Mexican Campaign—Vera Cruz, 1914: 55
Haiti, 1915: 6
Interim, 1915–1916: 8
Dominican Campaign, 1916: 3
World War I, 1917–1918: 127 (1 Hispanic)
Haiti Campaign, 1919–1920: 2
Interim, 1920–1940: 18
Second Nicaraguan Campaign, 1926–1933: 2
World War II, 1941–1945: 472 (17 Hispanics)
Korean War, 1950–1953: 146 (15 Hispanics)
Vietnam War, 1955–1975: 261 (22 Hispanics)
Somalia Campaign, 1993: 2
War in Afghanistan, 2001–present: 14 (1 Hispanic)
War in Iraq, 2003–2013: 4

CIVIL WAR

★★★

1

Joseph H. De Castro,
US Army

Company I, 19th Massachusetts Volunteer Infantry

Gettysburg, Pennsylvania, July 3, 1863

Date Presented: December 1, 1864

CITATION:
For capture of flag of 19th Virginia Regiment (Confederate States of America).

JOSEPH H. DE CASTRO was the first Hispanic American to be awarded the Medal of Honor. He was born in Boston, Massachusetts, on November 14, 1844, to Domingo (born in Spain) and Dorothea Haley (born in Maine) De Castro. Joseph joined the all-volunteer 19th Massachusetts Infantry as a private on August 12, 1861, at Camp Schouler, Lynnfield, Massachusetts, shortly after the outbreak of the American Civil War. A regiment roster shows that De Castro was a waiter prior to his enlistment.

The 19th Massachusetts participated in the Peninsula Campaign and the battles of Antietam, Fredericksburg, and Chancellorsville before arriving at Gettysburg under the command of Col. Arthur Forrester Devereux on July 2, 1863. The following day the unit was assigned a position behind a stone wall on Cemetery Ridge near what was known as the Copse of Trees—the center of attack of Pickett's Charge. At the height of the battle, when the Confederates were threatening to break the Union line, De Castro, who was carrying his state's flag, engaged the color bearer of the 19th Virginia Infantry Regiment. De Castro prevailed, seized the rebel flag, and handed it over to his brigade commander, Brig. Gen. Alexander S. Webb.

Webb later wrote, "At the instant a man broke through my lines and thrust a rebel flag into my hands. He never said a word and darted back. It was Corporal Joseph H. De Castro, one of my color bearers. He had knocked down a color bearer in the enemy's line with the staff of the Massachusetts State colors, seized the falling flag and dashed it to me."

Gen. George G. Meade, commander of the Army of the Potomac, awarded De Castro the Medal of Honor on December 1, 1864, for his actions at Gettysburg. His regiment then fought at Spotsylvania and Petersburg, was present at Appomattox Court House for the surrender of Gen. Robert E. Lee, and participated in the Grand Review of the Armies victory parade in Washington, DC, on May 23, 1865.

De Castro, now a sergeant, mustered out of the 19th Regiment on June 30, 1865, at Readville, Massachusetts. On July 19, 1870, he enlisted in the 6th Cavalry of the regular army and served until April 16, 1874. Upon his honorable discharge, he returned to Boston and married Rosalia Rodriguez, whose parents had immigrated to America from the Canary Islands. They divorced in 1882. De Castro and his second wife, Emma, moved to New York City, where he worked at the New York Barge Office at Battery Park. On May 8, 1892, De Castro died at his home at 244 West 22nd Street of a cerebral hemorrhage. His funeral was held at the Eighteenth Street Methodist Church before his burial across the river in the Fairmount Cemetery in Newark, New Jersey. His grave is in Section 2, Lot 300, Site 1.

There are no known photographs or images of De Castro. Other than his grave maker, no memorials to the first Hispanic to earn the Medal of Honor exist. Although he remains obscure in history, an occasional mention of his accomplishment does appear. In the eighth episode of the second season (chapter 21) of the Netflix political drama *House of Cards*, the White House chief of staff, who is Hispanic, presents what is supposed to be De Castro's medal to the vice president as a departure gift. The scene is rather confusing and occurs with little explanation other than to show the vice president's interest in the American Civil War.

★★★

2

John Ortega,
US Navy

USS *Saratoga*

USS *Saratoga*, August–September 1864

Date Presented: December 31, 1864

CITATION:

Served as seaman on board the USS Saratoga *during actions of that vessel on two occasions. Carrying out his duties courageously during these actions, Ortega conducted himself gallantly through both periods. Promoted to acting master's mate.*

SEAMAN JOHN ORTEGA was the first Hispanic member of the US Navy to be awarded the Medal of Honor. Born on November 30, 1839, in Spain, Ortega immigrated to Philadelphia, Pennsylvania, in 1856. On October 2, 1863, he successfully filed a petition to the Pennsylvania Supreme Court to become a naturalized citizen.

A short time later, Ortega enlisted in the US Navy and was assigned to the USS *Saratoga*, a sail-driven sloop of war commanded by Cmdr. George Musalas Colvocoresses. The 146-foot-long *Saratoga*, armed with four eight-inch and eighteen thirty-two-pound guns, had a crew of 210 officers and men. On January 13, 1864, the *Saratoga* joined the South Atlantic Blockading Squadron off the South Carolina coast with the mission of interdicting supplies and trade goods from reaching or departing the Confederate states.

The *Saratoga* not only blockaded ship traffic, but also its commander dispatched landing parties onto the mainland to capture prisoners, to destroy ammunition and other military supplies, and to wreck salt works, bridges,

19

and other rebel infrastructure. Ortega participated in two of these raids, the actions for which he earned his Medal of Honor.

Despite the decoration and a promotion to acting master's mate, Ortega, for unknown reasons, deserted his ship and the navy in June 1865. Perhaps it was because the war was over and he was bored with sea duty. Whatever the reason, he dropped from sight and there is no record of his later life, death, or grave site. The only monument to him is his name and ship on the Pennsylvania Medal of Honor Memorial, located on the east side of the Pennsylvania State Capitol in Harrisburg.

There are no known photographs or other images of Ortega. However, pictures of his Medal of Honor, without the suspension ribbon as displayed above, are often included in stories about the decoration. Ortega's medal was apparently never presented. Many Civil War medals were forwarded to a sailor's ship but were returned when it was discovered that he had transferred to another vessel, left the service, or, as in the case of Ortega, deserted. In the early years of the twentieth century, the Department of the Navy posted newspaper and other periodical notices in an attempt to track down lost recipients.

Ortega's medal was among these, but it remained unclaimed. It stayed in the possession of the Department of the Navy Personnel Office until 1957, when it was transferred to the Naval Historical Center at the Washington Navy Yard in Washington, DC, where it remains today.

***

3

Philip Bazaar,
US Navy

USS *Santiago de Cuba*
USS *Santiago de Cuba*, January 15, 1865
Date Presented: June 22, 1865

CITATION:
On board the USS Santiago de Cuba *during the assault on Fort Fisher on 15 January 1865. As one of a boat crew detailed to one of the generals on shore, Ordinary Seaman Bazaar bravely entered the fort in the assault and accompanied his party in carrying dispatches at the height of the battle. He was 1 of 6 men who entered the fort in the assault from the fleet.*

PHILIP BAZAAR (also spelled Phillip in some documents) was born in Valparaiso, Chile, South America, in 1844 or 1845 (the exact date is not known). As a boy he immigrated to New Bedford, Massachusetts, where he joined the US Navy on May 18, 1864, as an ordinary seaman. His enlisted documents describe him as "blue eyed, black hair, dark complexion." After a brief duty aboard the USS *Ohio*, he joined the crew of the USS *Santiago de Cuba*. This wooden, brigantine-rigged, side-wheel steamship participated in the Union blockade of the Confederate states initially in the Gulf of Mexico and then along the western Atlantic. The ship was successful in capturing several rebel blockade runners.

By the fall of 1864, the blockade had proven so successful that Wilmington, North Carolina, was the only port open to Confederate shipping on the Atlantic Coast. Fort Fisher stood as the guardian of the harbor. US Navy forces, including the *Santiago de Cuba*—commanded by R. Adm. David D. Porter with US Army troops led by Maj. Gen. Benjamin Butler—unsuccessfully assaulted the fort on December 24–27, 1864. Maj. Gen. Alfred Terry replaced Butler and again advanced on the fort along with Porter's naval support on January 13, 1865. The fort fell on January 15, and on February 22 the combined Union forces occupied Wilmington, concluding the last significant naval action of the Civil War.

During the battle, Bazaar and five fellow sailors served directly under Admiral Porter as message carriers—often under heavy fire—to and from the army commanders. All six were awarded the Medal of Honor.

Five months after the battle and two months following the conclusion of the war, Bazaar officially received his medal. Records state that Bazaar was transferred to the USS *Princeton* effective June 17, 1865, but "never reported."

Little is known of Bazaar's life after he deserted. From what can be determined, he apparently journeyed to New York City, where he remained the rest of his life living under the name of Philip Bazan. The 1900 census records Bazaar/Bazan as living in the city with a family named Wade. Apparently, he still worked aboard ships, as his occupation is listed as "seaman." The 1910 census has Bazaar/Bazan at the same address but now listed as "retired" for his occupation.

It is believed that Bazaar/Bazan married a woman named Bridget, who died on December 7, 1916. According to "New York, New York City Municipal Deaths, 1795–1949," Philip Bazan died at his home at 149 East 90th Street on December 28, 1923, at age seventy-eight. He was buried two days later in the city's Cavalry Cemetery in the Wade family lot. His grave is unmarked. Cemetery records list his name as Bogan—either a further attempt to hide his real identity or perhaps just poor handwriting on the part of the burial ground's director.

BOXER REBELLION

★★★

4

France George Silva,
US Marine Corps

US Marine Detachment, USS *Newark*

Peking, China, June 28–August 17, 1900

Date Presented: July 19, 1901

CITATION:

In the presence of the enemy during the action at Peking, China, 28 June to 17 August 1900. Throughout this period, Silva distinguished himself by meritorious conduct.

FRANCE SILVA was born in Haywards (changed to Hayward in 1894), California, on May 8, 1876, to Joseph and Mary Silva. He is the first Hispanic marine to earn the Medal of Honor. Some sources claim that Silva was of Mexican heritage, but his death certificate states that his parents were both born in France. Although born French, Silva's parents are believed to have been Portuguese and have come to Haywards, largely a Portuguese community at the time, from Portugal or the Azores. Their naming their son France was likely in honor of their birthplace.

Silva joined the US Marine Corps in San Francisco on September 12, 1899, and underwent his basic training at the Mare Island Naval Shipyard in nearby Vallejo. Upon completion of his training he was assigned to the marine detachment on the navy cruiser USS *Newark*.

Aboard the *Newark*, he became good friends with fellow marine Daniel J. Daly, one of only nineteen men who have twice received the Medal of

Honor—for his actions in the Boxer Rebellion in 1900 and again fifteen years later in the Haitian Rebellion.

In early 1900, the *Newark* sailed for China to protect the US legation and those of other countries in Peking that were threatened by rebels. Calling themselves the Society of Righteous and Harmonious Fists—better known as Boxers—these rebels opposed imperialist expansion in their country and its associated Christian missionary efforts. The *Newark* arrived at the port of Tientsin, where the marines unsuccessfully attempted to secure the city and the route to Peking on June 19. They were successful in their second effort on June 23, forcing the Boxers to withdraw to Peking. The marines followed and entered the foreign legation compound to take up the defense of the diplomats on June 28. They were welcomed by the senior US diplomat, Edwin Conger, who said to the marines, "Thank God you are here. Now we are safe."

Silva and his fellow marines defended the ligations' walled compound against vastly superior numbers from the time of his arrival until an allied relief force arrived on August 17. During the battle on July 1, Silva received a wound to his left elbow and sternum. Despite his wounds, he continued to fight. When ordered to the medical sick bay, Silva refused and traded his rifle, which he could no longer operate because of his wounds, for his captain's pistol and returned to the defenses. Silva's departing response to his commander was, "I can take care of myself."

His commander would later write that Silva was the "most interesting" of his marines. In the List of Casualties for the battle dated August 26, 1900, the commander of the First Regiment US Marines stated that Silva "has been in the English hospital under care of civilian physician. At this date the wound entirely healed. Affected elbow somewhat stiff, complete extension being impossible. Wasting of muscles of hand and partial loss of sensation."

Following the victory over the Boxers, Silva returned to the Mare Island Naval Shipyard, where he was medically discharged on January 6, 1901. His last commander wrote in Silva's efficiency report that he was "cool and reliable." Silva was formally awarded his Medal of Honor at Mare Island on July 19. He remained in the San Francisco area after his discharge. Following the 1906 earthquake that destroyed much of the city, Silva notified the Marine Corps that he had lost all of his personal papers and his Medal of Honor in the earthquake and resulting fire. A replacement medal was sent to him via the US Mail. There is no evidence that the replacement medal was formally presented.

Silva later lived in Oregon, Washington, and Idaho before returning to California, where he resided in the olive and fruit orchard center of Corning for the last twelve years of his life. His occupation on census records is listed as "nursery man." There are records that he married and divorced several times during this period. Silva died on April 10, 1951, of cardiac failure in nearby Red Bluff. He is buried in the Corning Sunset Hill Cemetery, where his grave is marked by a simple Veterans Affairs flat marker. Each year on November 10, the Marine Corps Birthday, Detachment 1140 of the Marine Corps League conducts a memorial service at Silva's grave.

WORLD WAR I

★★★

5

David Bennes Cantu Barkley,
US Army

Company A, 356th Infantry Regiment, 89th Infantry Division

Pouilly-sur-Meuse, France, November 9, 1918

Date Presented: February 17, 1919

CITATION:

When information was desired as to the enemy's position on the opposite side of the Meuse River, Pvt. Barkley, with another soldier, volunteered without hesitation and swam the river to reconnoiter the exact location. He succeeded in reaching the opposite bank, despite the evident determination of the enemy to prevent a crossing. Having obtained his information, he again entered the water for his return, but before his goal was reached, he was seized with cramps and drowned.

DAVID BENNES CANTU BARKLEY was the first Mexican American and the final American to earn the Medal of Honor in World War I. He was born in Laredo, Texas, on March 31, 1899, to Antonia Cantu, a Mexican born in Matamoros, and Josef Barkley, an American career soldier from Pennsylvania stationed with the 5th US Cavalry at Fort Ringgold. Antonia's death certificate, dated November 5, 1956, reflects that both of her parents were born in Mexico.

In 1904 Barkley's family relocated to San Antonio, where he attended Brackenridge Elementary School and worked as a newsboy. He won contests in both swimming and singing. Sometime during this period Josef Barkley moved with the 5th Cavalry to Fort Grant, Arizona Territory, and left his family behind. He was honorably discharged on October 13, 1904, and returned to his native state, where he died in 1922 in a Philadelphia veterans hospital.

Antonia and her son moved in with her sister. At age thirteen David dropped out of school to work as a delivery boy for a local merchant in order to help his family. At the outbreak of World War I, Barkley joined the Texas Guard and trained at Camps Travis and Bowie. Barkley made no mention of his racial heritage when he enlisted. He initially had difficulty adjusting to army life and spent three months in the stockade for an unnamed offense. Barkley distrusted his officers to the point that he feared they might read his mail, so he wrote his mother requesting that she not use her Spanish maiden name in correspondence. The young soldier was concerned that if he were labeled Hispanic or Mexican, he might be assigned to a labor battalion rather than the combat unit he desired. He maintained his secret even as he joined the 89th Infantry Division in France, where he participated in the action in the Argonne near Pouilly-sur-Meuse during the war's final days.

On November 9, 1918, two days before the war ended, Barkley and another soldier volunteered to swim across the icy Meuse River to reconnoiter enemy positions. They penetrated 400 meters behind the German lines and then attempted to recross the river. Barkley developed cramps and drowned in the cold waters, but his companion made it back with the much-needed intelligence that assisted in the Allies' final attacks against the Germans in the Meuse-Argonne Offensive.

Barkley's bravery was the last of the war's heroism to be recognized with the Medal of Honor. France also recognized his valor with the Croix de Guerre, and Italy awarded him the Croce al Merito di Guerra. Maj. Gen. DeRosey C. Cabell, commander of the US Army Southern Department, presented Barkley's Medal of Honor to his mother on February 17, 1919, in a ceremony at San Antonio's Gunter Hotel.

At the request of his mother in 1921, Barkley's remains were removed from their place of interment in France and returned to San Antonio. His body was met by an honor guard and his casket lay in state, first at his mother's home on Belvin Street, then at the Alamo, and finally at San Fernando Cathedral before burial in the San Antonio National Cemetery (Section G, Grave 921). He was only the second person ever to receive such honors at the Alamo—the first being Gen. Frederick Funston, veteran of the Spanish-American War and the Philippine-American War and a recipient of his own Medal of Honor. That same year San Antonio Public School No. 32 was renamed the David Barkley Elementary School. Camp Barkeley (a misspelling based on several that appear on Barkley's service documents and his mother's correspondence with the Veterans Administration for a pension claim, an error that was never cor-rected), a training center for World War II soldiers near Abilene, Texas, was named in his honor in 1941. When the camp closed at the end of the war, its flagpole was salvaged and placed in storage. When the Texas State Veterans Cemetery in Abilene opened in 2009, the Camp Barkeley flagpole was erected at the facility.

During World War II, Antonia became active in war bond drives, to which she wore her son's medal and his army hat covered with a traditional Mexican mourning veil. Despite her Hispanic features and Mexican mourning veil, no one made mention of her or her son's ethnic heritage. It was not until 1989, when Barkley's grandnephew contacted a San Antonio newspaper, that his Mexican American background became widely recognized. In 2003 the city of Laredo erected a monument to Hispanic Medal of Honor recipients that in-cludes a bronze statue of Barkley. At the center of the monument is a 308-foot-tall flagpole—the tallest in the United States. A group of Purple Heart recipi-ents in Laredo honored him by naming their organization the Military Order of the Purple Heart David Barkley Cantu Chapter No. 766 on October 1, 2004. On November 8, 2006, the campus chapel of Laredo Community College was renamed the Pvt. David Barkley Cantu Veterans Memorial Chapel. In both instances Barkley's name was rearranged to place his father's name first, and his mother's last, in accordance with Hispanic traditions.

WORLD WAR II

6

Joe Pantillion Martinez,
US Army

Company K, 32nd Infantry Regiment, 7th Infantry Division

Attu, Alaska, May 26, 1943

Date Presented: October 27, 1943

CITATION:

For conspicuous gallantry and intrepidity above and beyond the call of duty in action with the enemy. Over a period of several days, repeated efforts to drive the enemy from a key defensive position high in the snow-covered precipitous mountains between East Arm Holtz Bay and Chichagof Harbor had failed. On 26 May 1943, troop dispositions were readjusted and a trial coordinated attack on this position by a reinforced battalion was launched. Initially successful, the attack hesitated. In the face of severe hostile machine gun, rifle, and mortar fire, Pvt. Martinez, an automatic rifleman, rose to his feet and resumed his advance. Occasionally he stopped to urge his comrades on. His example inspired others to follow. After a most difficult climb, Pvt. Martinez eliminated resistance from part of the enemy position by BAR fire and hand grenades, thus assisting the advance of other attacking elements. This success only partially completed the action. The main Holtz-Chichagof Pass rose about 150 feet higher, flanked by steep rocky ridges and reached by a snow-filled defile. Passage was barred by enemy fire from either flank and from tiers of snow trenches in front. Despite these obstacles, and knowing of their existence, Pvt. Martinez again led the troops on and up, personally silencing several trenches with BAR fire and ultimately reaching the pass itself. Here, just below the knifelike rim of the pass, Pvt. Martinez encountered a final enemy-

occupied trench and as he was engaged in firing into it he was mortally wounded.
The pass, however, was taken, and its capture was an important preliminary to
the end of organized hostile resistance.

PVT. JOE MARTINEZ (also known as Joseph and Jose) was the first Hispanic American to earn the Medal of Honor in World War II. Born on July 27, 1920, as the youngest of nine children to Manuel V. and Maria Eduvigen Tafoya—both New Mexico natives—Joe moved from Taos at the age of seven with his family to Ault in northern Colorado. He attended primary and secondary school before dropping out of Ault High School to join his father in the fields as a farm laborer. His older brother Delfino, who survived the Invasion of Normandy and the Battle of the Bulge, remembers their boyhoods, saying, "Our mother raised us as Catholics. We went to church all the time and worked hard in the sugar beet and cabbage fields."

Joe's niece, Josie Brito, said about Martinez, "He was a very helpful person. He helped my dad on our farm, cooked for my mom, and took care of his nieces and nephews. He enjoyed fishing, hunting, and riding his motorcycle when he wasn't working on the farm."

Martinez was drafted into the army on August 17, 1942. His enlistment papers list "farm laborer" as his civilian occupation. Martinez trained at Camp Roberts, California, and Camp Butler, North Carolina, before joining Company K, 32nd Infantry Regiment, 7th Infantry Division at Fort Ord.

On May 7, 1943, the 7th Division went ashore on the tiny island of Attu at the far western end of the Alaskan Aleutian Islands. Japanese forces had occupied the island, as well as nearby Kiska, the previous June. US officials feared that the Japanese would use the islands to mount air attacks against the West Coast. Americans were also incensed that a foreign enemy was occupying US soil for the first time since the War of 1812.

From Holtz Bay, the 7th Division pushed the Japanese back inland onto the snowy high ground known as Fish Hook Ridge. On May 26, 1943—a day that was reasonably warm with clear skies—Martinez's company spearheaded the attack against the high ground. With machine-gun and small-arms fire as well as hand grenades rolled down the hill, the Japanese halted the Americans' advance. That is when Martinez, picking up his Browning Automatic Rifle (BAR) and a sack of hand grenades, charged forward, neutralizing one Japanese position after another. His fellow soldiers followed only to again be pinned down by enemy fire. For the second time, Martinez took the lead and again single-handedly knocked out more Japanese foxholes and bunkers. Again his fellow soldiers followed and successfully captured the ridge line. Martinez did not live to appreciate the victory. As he fired his BAR into one of the final enemy defenses, a bullet struck him in the head. He died in a medical tent back on the beach the next day. A detailed, mostly accurate story about Martinez's heroics appeared in the April 1959 issue of the magazine *Battle Cry*.

The battle of Attu ended with a final, bloody Banzai attack by the surviving Japanese on May 29. During the night, what was left of the foreign force withdrew from Kiska.

Martinez's Medal of Honor and Purple Heart, dated October 27, 1943, were presented to his parents by Maj. Gen. Frederick E. Ulio, commander of the Seventh Service Command, in Ault's Liberty Park on November 16, 1943, at a very difficult time in the war when Americans were desperately seeking heroes. Martinez was initially buried in the hastily constructed Attu Military Cemetery and was later reinterred in Ault Cemetery with full military honors. On April 13, 1945, the navy launched a troop transport, the USNS *Private Joe P. Martinez*, named in his honor. Three statues of Martinez were erected to him: one in Liberty Park, another in Weld County Veterans Memorial Park in Greeley, and the third in Lincoln Park on the capitol grounds in Denver. The Denver statue has an inscription stating, "Dedicated to Private Joe P. Martinez, Colorado's first Congressional Medal of Honor recipient of World War II."

A street in Pueblo, Colorado, was renamed in his honor, as was Denver's American Legion Post 204 and the city's US Army Reserve Center. The post headquarters at Fort Ord was also named for this Hispanic hero, and it maintained his name after the building became the fort's welcome center and later an officers' club. The building was renamed Martinez Hall in 1977, and after Fort Ord closed in 1994, it became the local Veterans Transition Service Center.

Today the Attu Battlefield is a designated National Historic Landmark. The island is part of the Alaska Maritime National Wildlife Refuge, administered by the US Department of the Interior's Fish and Wildlife Service. A plaque was placed on battlefield in 2013 honoring Martinez.

★ ★ ★

7

Lucian Adams,
US Army

Company I, 1st Battalion, 30th Infantry Regiment, 3rd Infantry Division
St. Die, France, October 28, 1944
Date Presented: April 22, 1945

CITATION:

For conspicuous gallantry and intrepidity at risk of life above and beyond the call of duty on 28 October 1944 near St. Die, France. When his company was stopped in its effort to drive through the Mortagne Forest to reopen the supply line to the isolated third battalion, S/Sgt. Adams braved the concentrated fire of machineguns in a lone assault on a force of German troops. Although his company had progressed less than 10 yards and had lost 3 killed and 6 wounded, S/Sgt. Adams charged forward dodging from tree to tree firing a borrowed BAR from the hip. Despite intense machinegun fire which the enemy directed at him and rifle grenades which struck the trees over his head showering him with broken twigs and branches, S/Sgt. Adams made his way to within 10 yards of the closest machinegun and killed the gunner with a hand grenade. An enemy soldier threw hand grenades at him from a position only 10 yards distant; however, S/Sgt. Adams dispatched him with a single burst of BAR fire. Charging into the vortex of the enemy fire, he killed another machine gunner at 15 yards range with a hand grenade and forced the surrender of two supporting infantrymen. Although the remainder of the German group concentrated the full force of its automatic weapons fire in a desperate effort to knock him out, he proceeded through the woods to find and exterminate five more of the enemy. Finally, when the third

German machinegun opened up on him at a range of 20 yards, S/Sgt. Adams killed the gunner with BAR fire. In the course of the action, he personally killed nine Germans, eliminated three enemy machineguns, vanquished a specialized force which was armed with automatic weapons and grenade launchers, cleared the woods of hostile elements, and reopened the severed supply lines to the assault companies of his battalion.

LUCIAN ADAMS was the second Hispanic recipient of the Medal of Honor in World War II and the first to survive the conflict. He was born in Port Arthur, Texas, on October 26, 1922, to Lucian Adams Sr. and Rosa Ramirez Adams, a family consisting of three daughters and nine sons—eight of whom served in World War II and survived. Lucien attended Franklin and Webster elementary schools as well as Thomas Jefferson Junior High School before dropping out of Port Arthur High School to help support his large family. At the outbreak of World War II in 1941, he was working at the Consolidated Iron Works in nearby Orange, where, for eighteen months, he helped build landing craft, the same type of vessels that he and his unit would later use in the invasions of Italy and France.

Adams was drafted into the US Army at Fort Sam Houston, Texas, in February 1943 and trained at Camp Butner, North Carolina, before joining the 30th Infantry Regiment of the 3rd Infantry Division for the assault on Anzio Beach in Italy in January 1944. On May 23, 1944, Adams earned a Bronze Star for destroying a German machine gun position and a Purple Heart for wounds received in the fight.

The young soldier, promoted to staff sergeant, recovered from his wounds and went ashore on August 15, 1944, on the Riviera in southern France as a part of Operation Dragoon. In October, his 30th Infantry Regiment faced stiff resistance from the Germans defending the Vosges Mountains in eastern France. German reinforcements counterattacked, cutting the regiment's supply route and isolating two companies from the rest of the battalion.

On October 28, Adams's company was ordered to clear the supply line and reconnect with the two isolated companies. The Americans advanced under heavy fire by machine guns and grenades. Three of Adams's fellow soldiers were killed and six, including his company commander, wounded. With his company pinned down, Adams took action on his own. Armed with a Browning Automatic Rifle (BAR), he charged the nearest German machine gun position. Using his BAR and hand grenades, he continued his advance until the surviving Germans retreated. Along Adams's path of attack lay three destroyed machine gun positions and nine dead Germans. He also captured two enemy soldiers.

The 3rd Infantry Division continued its advance across France and into Germany before the Nazis finally surrendered. On April 22, 1945, Lt. Gen. Alexander Patch, commander of the Seventh Army, presented the Medal of Honor to Adams at a ceremony in the Zeppelin Stadium in Nuremburg, Germany, the site of many of Hitler's huge rallies; a swastika monument, still atop the structure, was now covered by an American flag. Combat engineers blew up the Nazi symbol shortly after the ceremony.

Adams returned to Port Arthur after his discharge on September 7, 1945. On January 4, 1946, he went to work as a benefits counselor at the San Antonio Veterans Administration, where he remained until his retirement in 1986. He also served as a veterans affairs consultant to Rep. Frank Tejeda (D-TX), a decorated marine veteran of the Vietnam War. Adams often joked about his Anglo last name, but he never claimed to be anything other than a Mexican American.

In an interview with the *Dallas Morning News* in 1993, Adams reflected on the day he earned his medal. He said, "I'd seen all my buddies go down and calling for medics, and I didn't want to go down with any ammunition still on me, so I just kept firing and lucky for me that I got them before they got me." He also later credited his mother's prayers for his survival. In an interview with the *San Antonio Express* in 2002, he said, "In combat, I had no fear. None, until the events were over, and then I began to realize how serious and how dangerous the situations were."

Adams died in San Antonio on March 31, 2003, and is buried in Sam Houston National Cemetery (Section A1, Grave 555). He was survived by his three children. Staff Sergeant Lucian Adams Elementary School on 9th Avenue in Port Arthur is named in his honor. Aurora Park in the city was also renamed for him, as is a stretch of Interstate 17 in San Antonio. A bust of the soldier was dedicated in 1988 in Port Arthur's Gulf Coast Museum.

A modest man, Adam rarely talked about his combat experiences or his medal. He often said, "I'm no hero, I'm just an ex-soldier."

8

José Mendoza Lopez,
US Army

Company K, 23rd Infantry Regiment, 2nd Infantry Division

Krinkelt, Belgium, December 17, 1944

Date Presented: June 18, 1945

CITATION:

On his own initiative, he carried his heavy machine gun from Company K's right flank to its left, in order to protect that flank which was in danger of being over-run by advancing enemy infantry supported by tanks. Occupying a shallow hole offering no protection above his waist, he cut down a group of 10 Germans. Ignoring enemy fire from an advancing tank, he held his position and cut down 25 more enemy infantry attempting to turn his flank. Glancing to his right, he saw a large number of infantry swarming in from the front. Although dazed and shaken from enemy artillery fire which had crashed into the ground only a few yards away, he realized that his position soon would be outflanked. Again, alone, he carried his machine gun to a position to the right rear of the sector; enemy tanks and infantry were forcing a withdrawal. Blown over backward by the concussion of enemy fire, he immediately reset his gun and continued his fire. Single-handed he held off the German horde until he was satisfied his company had effected its retirement. Again he loaded his gun on his back, and in a hail of small arms fire he ran to a point where a few of his comrades were attempting to set up another defense against the onrushing enemy. He fired from this position until his ammunition was exhausted. Still carrying his gun, he fell back with his small group to Krinkelt. Sgt. Lopez's gallantry and intrepidity, on seemingly suicidal missions in which he killed

at least 100 of the enemy, were almost solely responsible for allowing Company K
to avoid being enveloped, to withdraw successfully and to give other forces coming
up in support time to build a line which repelled the enemy drive.

JOSÉ LOPEZ, at ninety-four years of age, was the oldest living Hispanic recipient of the Medal of Honor when he died in 2005. He was born on July 10, 1910, in Santiago Ihuitlian, Oaxaca, Mexico, to Cayetano and Candida Mendoza de Lopez, though he never knew his father. Conflicting stories claim he either drowned or died fighting in the Mexican Revolution while José was still a baby. As a small boy, Lopez rarely attended school as he helped his seamstress mother, who had moved to Veracruz, sell the clothes she made. He was only eight when she died of tuberculosis. Lopez lived with relatives and friends until he hitchhiked to Brownsville, Texas, in his early teens to live with his maternal uncle, Constancio Mendoza.

Lopez worked harvesting cotton and fruit in the Rio Grande Valley until he began to hop freight trains to see the country and follow the harvests. In 1927 the teen caught the attention of a boxing promoter when he won a street fight in Atlanta. For a brief time, he fought as an amateur before turning professional because, as he recalled later, "I needed money for new shoes." Over the next seven years, the five-feet-five, 130-pound Mexican fought professionally as "Kid Mendoza" in the lightweight class across the United States and around the world. Lopez would later say that the highlight of his boxing career was meeting Babe Ruth before a bout in Atlanta.

After earning a recorded fifty-two wins with only three losses, Lopez was fighting in Melbourne, Australia, when he met a group of merchant marines. Just off a rare loss to British fighter Jacque Burgess, Lopez put boxing behind him and signed aboard their vessel. He later explained, "I just didn't want to fight anymore."

Lopez needed a birth certificate to join the US Merchant Marines, so he secured false documents that listed his place of birth as Mission, Texas, a town still carried on his official military records as his birthplace. In 1936, Lopez was accepted into the merchant marine union, and for five years he sailed around the world. In December 1941, while working on the Honolulu docks between ship berths, he decided to return to Texas. Three days out of Hawaii aboard a passenger ship, he learned of the Japanese attack on Pearl Harbor. When Lopez arrived at the Port of Los Angeles, officials held Lopez because they thought he might be Japanese. Only after he showed his papers was he released to make his way home.

In 1942, Lopez married Emilia Herrera in Brownsville; they would eventually have five children. Despite being over thirty years of age and married, Lopez was drafted later that year. After induction at Fort Sam Houston and basic training at Camp Roberts, California, he joined K Company, 23nd Infantry Regiment, 2nd Infantry Division, as it moved to various camps in the United States before sailing for Belfast, Northern Ireland. There Lopez and his unit continued training before going ashore on Omaha Beach on D+1, June 7, 1944, of the Normandy Invasion.

Lopez was wounded soon after going ashore but refused medical evacuation and earned the Bronze Star and Purple Heart. He then participated in the hedgerow fights near Saint-Lo, the battle for Breast, and the regular combat across France and into Belgium for the remainder of 1944.

On December 17, 1944, Lopez and K Company were occupying defensive positions in the Ardennes Forest near Krinkelt, Belgium, when the Germans launched their final great offensive of the war that resulted in the Battle of the Bulge. Tanks and infantry swept into and across the American lines, killing or capturing many Americans. When German infantry and tanks, accompanied by artillery fire, approached K Company, Lopez moved his machine gun to protect the unit's most vulnerable flank. With little or no cover and knocked down several times by artillery concussions, Lopez moved to protect his company. He is credited with killing more than 100 Germans during the battle and holding the line until reinforcements arrived.

Lt. Gen. James A. Van Fleet, commander of III Corps, presented Lopez the Medal of Honor at Nuremberg on June 18, 1945. He was soon on a troop ship on the way back home where legendary New York City mayor Fiorello La Guardia personally gave Lopez a hero's welcome.

Throughout the war and his life, Lopez prayed for protection to the Virgin de Guadalupe, the patron saint of Mexico. Shortly after his return home to Brownsville, the town held a welcome ceremony and then paid for his expenses to make a pilgrimage to Mexico City to pay his respects to the virgin at the Basilica of Our Lady of Guadalupe. While he was there, Mexican president Manuel Avila Camacho presented him with the country's highest military honor, La Medalla al Mérito Militar.

Back in Texas, Lopez moved to San Antonio, where he went to work for the Veterans Administration. In 1948 he again went to Mexico City, where the current president, Miguel Aleman Valdez, honored him with the Order of the Aztec Eagle.

Lopez reenlisted in the US Army in 1949 and was assigned once again to the 2nd Infantry Division. In July 1950 the division deployed to Korea, where Lopez returned to combat. When his commander discovered that they had a Medal of Honor recipient in the front lines, he moved him to a more secure job in the rear area. After a period of working with Graves Registration, processing the bodies for burial, he was transferred to Japan. Lopez remained in the army after the Korean War and served as a recruiter and motor sergeant until his retirement as a master sergeant in 1973.

In his retirement Lopez remained very active. He jogged and worked out at a fitness center until a few months before his death. In 1990, Lopez was one of ten veterans who accompanied Bill Moyers of PBS to return to their battlefields of World War II to film the documentary *From D-Day to the Rhine*. In discussing his actions in the war with Moyers, he said, "I believe any man would do the same thing."

Over the years Lopez has been honored by the towns in which he lived. Mission recognized Lopez with a park and street named after him. San Antonio has the Jose M. Lopez Middle School, and a statue of the soldier stands in Brownsville's Veterans Park. A portion of US Highway 90 in San Antonio is named in his honor. As a Medal of Honor recipient, Lopez was invited to and attended the inaugurations of five US presidents—John F. Kennedy, Richard M. Nixon, George H.W. Bush, and George W. Bush.

Lopez's wife of sixty-two years died in 2004. He died of cancer a year later on May 16, 2005, and is buried in Fort Sam Houston National Cemetery (Section A1, Site 542).

9

Macario Garcia,
US Army

Company B, 1st Battalion, 22nd Infantry Regiment, 4th Infantry Division

Grosshau, Germany, November 27, 1944

Date Presented: August 23, 1945

CITATION:

Staff Sergeant Macario Garcia, Company B, 22nd Infantry, in action involving actual conflict with the enemy in the vicinity of Grosshau, Germany, 27 November 1944. While an acting squad leader, he single-handedly assaulted two enemy machine gun emplacements. Attacking prepared positions on a wooded hill, which could be approached only through meager cover. His company was pinned down by intense machine-gun fire and subjected to a concentrated artillery and mortar barrage. Although painfully wounded, he refused to be evacuated and on his own initiative crawled forward alone until he reached a position near an enemy emplacement. Hurling grenades, he boldly assaulted the position, destroyed the gun, and with his rifle killed three of the enemy who attempted to escape. When he rejoined his company, a second machine-gun opened fire and again the intrepid soldier went forward, utterly disregarding his own safety. He stormed the position and destroyed the gun, killed three more Germans, and captured four prisoners. He fought on with his unit until the objective was taken and only then did he permit himself to be removed for medical care. S/Sgt. (then Pvt.) Garcia's conspicuous heroism, his inspiring, courageous conduct, and his complete disregard for his personal safety wiped out two enemy emplacements and enabled his company to advance and secure its objective.

WHEN PRES. HARRY TRUMAN, a veteran of World War I, awarded the Medal of Honor to S. Sgt. Macario Garcia at the White House on September 1, 1945, he made the now famous statement, "I would rather earn this than be President."

Macario (also spelled Marcario in many documents, including some Medal of Honor citations) Garcia was born on January 20, 1920, in Villa de Castano, Coahuila, Mexico, to Luciano and Josefa Garcia. In October 1923 the family immigrated to Texas and initially settled in Waelder. The Garcias moved to Sugar Land in 1935 to work on the Paul Schumann Ranch as farm laborers. Because of the work in the fields and migrant trips farther north to follow the various harvests, Garcia received only a third-grade education. Despite his lack of formal schooling, according to his military records, he was bilingual in English and Spanish and could read and write in both languages.

Although only five-feet-five in height, Garcia easily passed his draft physical and was inducted into the army at Fort Sam Houston, Texas, on November 11, 1942. He was then reassigned on November 21 to B Company of the 51st Training Brigade at Camp Robinson, Arkansas. In June 1944 he went ashore with B Company, 1st Battalion, 22nd Infantry Regiment of the 4th Infantry Division at Utah Beach in the Normandy Invasion. Garcia was wounded in the advance into France and spent four months recovering from his injuries before rejoining his unit in October.

On November 27, Garcia, now a sergeant and squad leader, and his company were advancing in the Hurtgen Forest near Grosshau, Germany, when his company came under an artillery and mortar attack. A German machine gun nest blocked the Americans' advance out of the aerial kill zone. Garcia crawled forward to knock out the German position with his rifle and hand grenades. When another machine gun opened up on his fellow soldiers, Garcia, despite wounds to his shoulder and foot, refused medical evacuation and again advanced on the enemy. At the end of the fight, six Germans were dead, four captured, and their two machine guns destroyed. In an interview with the *Houston Chronicle* several years later, Garcia said, "I did not know the wound was so serious. I was numb, I think, and besides, we were moving forward, and it was not the time to stop."

In the same article, the B Company commander, Capt. Tony Bizzarro, stated that Garcia was nothing less than the best soldier in the army and that "he was always willing to do anything he was asked to do." Garcia was always modest about his accomplishments in battle. In several interviews he said that he "was just an average soldier and was always scared."

On August 23, 1945, President Truman awarded the Medal of Honor to Garcia and made the famous quote about his own desire for the medal, one he would repeat in various forms at other award ceremonies. The citizens of Garcia's hometown of Sugar Land and Fort Bend County welcomed him back as a hero—at least, most did.

After a reception honoring him in the Richmond City Hall, a few miles south of Houston, Garcia, in full uniform complete with decorations—including the Medal of Honor, the Bronze Star with "V" device with Oak Leaf Cluster, two Purple Hearts, the Combat Infantryman Badge, and other awards—stopped at the Oasis Café for a meal. The owner refused to serve him because he was Mexican. Garcia argued, some sailors in the facility took his side, and a few locals backed the owner, who was now armed with a baseball bat. No one was seriously injured in the melee, but Garcia was ultimately charged with assault. Garcia reportedly told the café owner, "I've been fighting for you, and now you mistreat me."

The Oasis Café incident soon became a national issue when popular radio commentator and newspaper columnist Walter Winchell criticized the locals for their treatment of a war hero. Members of the League of United Latin American Citizens (LULAC) Council No. 60 in Houston, which had recently honored Garcia at a ceremony at the Harris County Courthouse, took up his defense. After much negative national publicity and several court postponements, the charge against Garcia was dropped.

Garcia was employed as a salesman in a downtown Houston department store for several months before accepting a position as a counselor with the Veterans Administration, where he worked for twenty-five years. Mexico honored Garcia with its highest decoration, the Condecoracion del Mérito Militar, in a ceremony held in Mexico City on January 8, 1946. Garcia finally became an American citizen on June 25, 1947. In 1951, he earned his GED, and on May 18, 1952, he married Alicia Reyes, with whom he would have three children.

On November 21, 1963, Garcia joined other dignitaries at a reception at Houston's Rice Hotel, where he was personally introduced to Pres. John F. Kennedy and the first lady. The president spoke of US and Latin American relations, noting the importance of Hispanic organizations such as LULAC.

Mrs. Kennedy, speaking in Spanish, enthusiastically offered words of hope for the future. The next day, Kennedy was struck down by an assassin's bullets in Dallas.

"Mac," as he was known to his friends, Garcia joined the 75th Infantry Regiment of the US Army Reserve in Houston on June 13, 1953, and in 1967 advanced to the highest enlisted rank of sergeant major. In 1968, he volunteered for active duty in Vietnam and served for six months in the 22nd Replacement Battalion at Cam Ranh Bay providing advice to military personnel on their benefits as veterans once they returned home.

In 1970, Garcia and his family moved to Alief, a suburb southeast of Houston. On December 24, 1972, he was in an automobile crash that resulted in his death at age fifty-two. He is buried in Houston National Cemetery (Section HA, Site 1).

A field house at Fort Carson, Colorado, the 665th American Legion post in Galveston, and a city park in Rosenberg are all named in his honor. The Houston City Council changed the name of 69th Street in 1981 to Macario Garcia Drive. It runs for one and half miles through the city's east side, primarily a Mexican American community. A painting of Garcia and a plaque bearing his Medal of Honor citation hangs in the Fort Bend County Courthouse in Richmond. In 1983, Vice Pres. George Bush dedicated the new Macario Garcia US Army Reserve Center in Houston. An elementary school in Houston and a middle school in Sugar Land are also named in his honor, as is the headquarters building at Fort Drum, New York. There is a historical marker erected by the Texas Historical Commission in the Macario Garcia City Park at 716 Blume Road in Rosenberg.

★★★

10

Silvestre Santana Herrera,
US Army

Company E, 142nd Infantry Regiment, 36th Infantry Division

Mertzwiller, France, March 15, 1945

Date Presented: August 23, 1945

CITATION:

He advanced with a platoon along a wooded road until stopped by heavy enemy machinegun fire. As the rest of the unit took cover, he made a 1-man frontal assault on a strongpoint and captured 8 enemy soldiers. When the platoon resumed its advance and was subjected to fire from a second emplacement beyond an extensive minefield, Pvt. Herrera again moved forward, disregarding the danger of explod-ing mines, to attack the position. He stepped on a mine and had both feet severed but, despite intense pain and unchecked loss of blood, he pinned down the enemy with accurate rifle fire while a friendly squad captured the enemy gun by skirting the minefield and rushing in from the flank. The magnificent courage, extraordi-nary heroism, and willing self-sacrifice displayed by Pvt. Herrera resulted in the capture of 2 enemy strongpoints and the taking of 8 prisoners.

SILVESTRE HERRERA was the first person who entered the armed forces from Arizona to earn the Medal of Honor in World War II. Born on July 17, 1917, in Camargo, Chihuahua, Mexico, Herrera was left an orphan when his mother and father both died of influenza when he was eighteen months old. His uncle took Silvestre in and raised him as his own, not revealing to Silvestre until he was in his twenties that he was not his real father. Shortly after his parents' deaths, Herrera moved with his uncle to El Paso and then in 1928 to Arizona. In Phoenix he lived with his maternal aunt until he married his American-born wife, Ramona. By 1944, Silvestre and Ramona were the parents of three children with another on the way. His family status had exempted him from the draft to that point, but the US offensives and resulting casualties in Europe and the Pacific called for more and more men.

It was only when Herrera received his draft notice that his uncle told him that he was not a US citizen and not eligible for the draft. At the same time, the uncle revealed that he was not Herrera's father. Herrera accepted the news while also realizing that he had responsibilities beyond questions of birth and citizenship. He later said, "I thought, I'm going anyway. I didn't want anybody to die in my place . . . I felt that I had my adopted country that had been so nice to me. Besides, I didn't want someone else dying in my place." Herrera added, "I am a Mexican-American and we have a tradition. We're supposed to be men, not sissies."

After basic training, Herrera joined the 36th Infantry Division, a Texas National Guard unit activated for the war. The 36th Division was a veteran unit that had fought its way across Italy before landing in France for the push toward Germany. On March 15, 1945, Herrera's platoon was advancing down a road near Mertzwiller on the French-German border when they encountered heavy enemy fire. As his fellow infantrymen took cover, Herrera charged forward, neutralizing the German positions and capturing eight soldiers. Shortly after the platoon resumed its advance, it was again taken under heavy fire. This time, however, the German positions were protected by a minefield.

Despite the hazards, Herrera again charged forward to engage the enemy and to draw fire away from his comrades. A mine suddenly exploded, blowing off one of Herrera's feet. He propped himself up on his sound leg and continued his advance. Another explosion blew off his other foot. Despite his horrific wounds, Herrera was not yet out of the fight. He rose to his knees and continued to fire at the German positions. His actions enabled the rest of his platoon to flank and destroy the enemy fortifications.

When Herrera reached an evacuation aid station, he said to the examining physician, "Just try to save my knees, Doc." They did so, and two months later evacuated him to the Army Amputation Center in Utah for further recovery. While recuperating, Herrera was able to study for his citizenship exam, which he passed. During a ninety-day furlough to Phoenix, Herrera was welcomed home with a parade and a proclamation by Arizona governor Sidney P. Osborn that declared August 14, 1945, as "Herrera Day."

While on home leave, he was notified of the approval of his Medal of Honor. Herrera had not yet been fitted with prosthetic feet, so he went in a wheelchair to Washington, DC, for the presentation ceremony. In the White House Rose Garden ceremony for three Medal of Honor recipients on August 23, 1945, Pres. Harry Truman leaned over Herrera's wheelchair to place the medal around his neck. Truman then said, "These are wonderful citations. They show just exactly what the fiber of the American people is made of. They show exactly how the young men feel toward their government. They show the sacrifices that they are willing to make to support and keep that Government a free one from now on."

A year after the White House ceremony, the government of Mexico awarded the Order of Military Merit to Herrera. Shortly after his medical disability discharge from the army, the City of Phoenix presented Herrera and his family a new home on April 6, 1947. He adapted so well to his prosthesis that he frequently took his wife out dancing. Despite his disability, he established a successful leather-working and silversmith business. Herrera often said, "I felt that I didn't want anybody to be sorry for me. I have lived a very happy life." He also said that he did not consider himself a particularly brave man, just one of the lucky ones to have survived.

Unlike many of his fellow Medal of Honor recipients, Herrera lived to see several honors for his service. The Silvestre S. Herrera Elementary School was built and named in his honor in 1956. In 1994, Valle Del Sol, Inc., a mental and other health care provider, presented him a Special Recognition Award and added him to its Hall of Fame in 1999. On October 24, 1998, the Silvestre S. Herrera United States Army Reserve Center in Mesa, Arizona, was dedicated.

Herrera died at home in the Phoenix suburb of Glendale on November 26, 2007. At age ninety, he was the oldest American to have received the highest military decoration of both the United States and Mexico. He is buried in Glendale's Resthaven Park Cemetery (Section 26, Block 16, Lot 1).

Prisco Hernandez, writing in *America's Heroes: Medal of Honor Recipients from the Civil War to Afghanistan*, edited by Jim Willbanks, states, "In many ways, Silvestre Herrera's life story is the quintessential Mexican-American immigrant story carried to heroic proportions. His illegal immigration status, work ethic, love for both his Mexican heritage and his chosen country, and life centered on traditional values such as family and faith are all central to the Mexican American defining narrative and its members' self-identity."

★★★

11

Cleto Luna Rodriguez,
US Army

Company B, 148th Infantry Regiment, 37th Infantry Division
Manila, Philippines, February 9, 1945
Date Presented: October 12, 1945

CITATION:

The President of the United States of America, in the name of Congress, takes pleasure in presenting the Medal of Honor to Technical Sergeant Cleto L. Rodriguez, United States Army, for conspicuous gallantry and intrepidity in action above and beyond the call of duty on 9 February 1945, while serving with Company B, 148th Infantry Regiment, 37th Infantry Division. Technical Sergeant Rodriguez (then private) was an automatic rifleman when his unit attacked the strongly defended Paco Railroad Station during the battle for Manila, Philippine Islands. While making a frontal assault across an open field, his platoon was halted 100 yards from the station by intense enemy fire. On his own initiative, he left the platoon, accompanied by a comrade, and continued forward to a house 60 yards from the objective. Although under constant enemy observation, the two men remained in this position for an hour, firing at targets of opportunity, killing more than 35 hostile soldiers and wounding many more. Moving closer to the station and discovering a group of Japanese replacements attempting to reach pillboxes, they opened heavy fire, killed more than 40 and stopped all subsequent attempts to man the emplacements. Enemy fire became more intense as they advanced to within 20 yards of the station. Then, covered by his companion, Private Rodriguez boldly moved up to the building and threw five grenades through a doorway, killing 7 Japanese, destroying a 20-mm gun, and wrecking a heavy machinegun. With their ammuni-

*tion running low, the two men started to return to the American lines, alternately
providing covering fire for each other's withdrawal. During this movement, Private
Rodriguez' companion was killed. In 2½ hours of fierce fighting the intrepid team
killed more than 82 Japanese, completely disorganized their defense, and paved
the way for the subsequent overwhelming defeat of the enemy at this strongpoint.
Two days later, Private Rodriguez again enabled his comrades to advance when he
single-handedly killed six Japanese and destroyed a well-placed 20-mm gun. By his
outstanding skill with his weapons, gallant determination to destroy the enemy,
and heroic courage in the face of tremendous odds, Private Rodriguez, on two
occasions, materially aided the advance of our troops in Manila.*

CLETO RODRIGUEZ was born on April 26, 1923, into the large Hispanic
community in and around San Marcos, Texas, that had fled the Mexican
Revolution (1910–1920) and immigrated to the United States. Both of his
parents had died by the time he was nine years old, and he grew up with relatives in San Antonio.

As a boy, Rodriguez attended Washington Irving and Ivanhoe elementary
schools while shining shoes on the streets of San Antonio in his free time.
He later sold newspapers in the lobby of the historic Gunter Hotel near the
Alamo. In early 1944 Rodriguez enlisted in the army and, after completing
his training, joined the 37th Infantry Division in the Pacific Theater to participate in the division's final battles to secure the island of Bougainville in
Papua New Guinea.

On January 9, 1945, the 37th Division went ashore from the Lingayen Gulf
in the invasion to retake the Philippine Islands. Rodriguez's company fought
their way to Manila, where on February 9, 1945, his platoon was ordered to
attack the Japanese-held Paco Railroad Station. Intense fire from the Japanese
stopped the platoon about 100 meters from their objective. Rodriguez, armed
with a Browning Automatic Rifle that he affectionately called his Senorita,
and Pfc. John Reese Jr., a Cherokee Native American from Pryor, Oklahoma,
charged the enemy positions, killing thirty-five and wounding many more.
Reese provided covering fire while Rodriguez launched five grenades into a
station doorway. His accuracy knocked out a heavy machine gun and killed
more Japanese.

The pair of soldiers continued to fight for more than two hours before they
ran low on ammunition and had to attempt to withdraw back to their platoon.
Reese was mortally wounded during their retreat, but his partner made it

back. Upon Rodriguez's return, his platoon renewed the attack and neutral-ized the railroad station. Two days later the Texas soldier again showed his bravery when he single-handedly destroyed a 20-mm machine gun and killed its crew of six.

On October 12, 1945, Pres. Harry Truman presented Rodriquez and four-teen other members of the US Armed Forces their Medals of Honor. Reese's parents accepted his Medal of Honor posthumously. After presenting the awards, Truman said,

> Once again I have had a very great privilege. I would rather do what I have been doing this morning than any other one of my arduous duties. This one is a pleasure.
>
> When you look at these young men, you see the United States of America, the greatest republic on earth, the country that can meet any situation when it becomes necessary.
>
> These young men were doing their duty. They didn't think they were be-ing heroes. They didn't think they were doing anything unusual. They were just doing what the situation called for.
>
> As I have told the rest of these young men who have been here before me, I would much rather have that Medal around my neck than to be President of the United States. It is the greatest honor that can come to a man. It is an honor that all of us strive for, but very few of us ever achieve.
>
> Now these young men will go back and become citizens of this great country, and they will make good citizens; and you won't find any of them bragging about what they have done or what they propose to do. They are just going to be good citizens of the United States, and they are going to help us take this Republic to its leadership in the world, where it belongs, and where it has belonged for the past 25 years.

Rodriguez returned to San Antonio after the war and was presented a key to the city and a new house for him and his bride, Flora Muniz. In 1952 he joined the US Air Force and after three years transferred back to the army, where he remained until his retirement as a master sergeant in 1970. In addi-tion to his World War II service, Rodriguez also served in Korea and Vietnam.

Despite his more than twenty years in uniform and earning his nation's highest military award for valor, Rodriguez found that jobs were hard to come by in the early 1970s in San Antonio—especially for Mexican Americans. Ro-driquez was parking cars at a hotel in 1970 when George H.W. Bush, then a US senator and the future forty-first president of the United States, recognized him and secured him a position at the Veterans Administration as a contact representative.

In a 1975 interview with the *San Antonio Express News*, Rodriguez reflected on his attack against the Manila railroad station. He said, "I just saw what had to be done and did it."

Rodriquez was always vocal in his appreciation for the support of the city of San Antonio and that of George Bush. In the same interview with the *Express News*, however, he also detailed some of the difficulties of being a Medal of Honor recipient. He said, "The medal really brought me more problems than glory. Everyone expected perfection. There were endless guys wanting to whip the Medal of Honor winner."

Rodriquez died of a heart attack on December 7, 1990—Pearl Harbor Day. In its obituary the *Express News* declared Rodriquez, with his Medal of Honor, Silver Star, two Bronze Stars, and a Purple Heart, to be "San Antonio's most decorated World War II veteran." He is buried in Fort Sam Houston National Cemetery (Section A-1, Site 700). Fellow recipients of the Medal of Honor— Jose Lopez and Lucian Adams of San Antonio and Joseph Rodriguez of El Paso—served as honorary pallbearers.

Shortly after his return to San Antonio the government of Mexico presented Rodriquez with its highest award, the Medal of Military Merit. In 1975 his boyhood school, Ivanhoe Elementary, was renamed Cleto Rodriguez Elementary. The March 1977 edition of *Man's Magazine* featured on its cover a drawing of Rodriguez assaulting the train station with his BAR and presented an in-depth article about the battle.

On the first anniversary of his death, December 7, 1971, a stretch of US Highway 90 between Interstates 410 and 35 in southwest San Antonio was named the Cleto Rodriguez Freeway. A small arms firing range at Camp Perry, Ohio, home of the National Rifle and Pistol Championships, is also named in his honor.

★ ★ ★

12

Ysmael R. Villegas,
US *Army*

Company F, 127th Infantry Regiment, 32nd Infantry Division
Villa Verde Trail, Luzon, Philippines, March 20, 1945
Date Presented: October 19, 1945

CITATION:

He was a squad leader when his unit, in a forward position, clashed with an enemy strongly entrenched in connected caves and foxholes on commanding ground. He moved boldly from man to man, in the face of bursting grenades and demolition charges, through heavy machinegun and rifle fire, to bolster the spirit of his comrades. Inspired by his gallantry, his men pressed forward to the crest of the hill. Numerous enemy riflemen, refusing to flee, continued firing from their foxholes. S/Sgt. Villegas, with complete disregard for his own safety and the bullets which kicked up the dirt at his feet, charged an enemy position, and, firing at point-blank range killed the Japanese in a foxhole. He rushed a second foxhole while bullets missed him by inches, and killed 1 more of the enemy. In rapid succession he charged a third, a fourth, a fifth foxhole, each time destroying the enemy within. The fire against him increased in intensity, but he pressed onward to attack a sixth position. As he neared his goal, he was hit and killed by enemy fire. Through his heroism and indomitable fighting spirit, S/Sgt. Villegas, at the cost of his life, inspired his men to a determined attack in which they swept the enemy from the field.

YSMAEL R. VILLEGAS was born in the Riverside, California, barrio known as Casa Blanca on March 21, 1924, as the oldest of thirteen children to Mexican American parents. Known as "Smiley" to his family and friends for his happy attitude, he was a big fan of dancing the jitterbug to the music of the era's big bands. According to an article in the *Riverside Press-Enterprise* on March 15, 2014, he enjoyed reading the daily comic strips, was an immaculate dresser, often wore a flower in his lapel when he went dancing, and was well liked by the ladies. His prize possession was a lime-green 1937 Buick that he called "The Green Hornet."

Villegas attended schools in Riverside before leaving after one year of high school to support his family by working in the orange groves. When he received his initial draft notice in 1943, he requested and was granted a deferment to further take care of his family. Villegas reported for active duty at the Los Angeles reception station on July 11, 1944. After basic training at Camp Roberts, California, he joined the 32nd Infantry Division, a former Michigan and Wisconsin National Guard unit that had been in the Pacific Theater since 1942, as a replacement.

On March 1, 1945, Villegas's company was advancing along the Villa Verde Trail on the Philippine Island of Luzon when his squad was engaged by a Japanese machine gun. Villegas, now a staff sergeant, charged forward with his M-1 rifle and destroyed the position while killing its occupants. For this action he received the Silver Star, the third-highest decoration for bravery.

Less than three weeks later, on March 20, Villegas's company advanced toward a hill on the same trail that was defended by multiple bunkers and caves. When the fight began, Villegas charged forward using his rifle and hand grenades to neutralize one Japanese position after another. He destroyed five enemy fortifications before he fell to the fire from the sixth. Pres. Harry Truman presented the Medal of Honor to Villegas's family on October 19, 1945.

Following the war, Villegas's remains were returned to Riverside and buried in its Olivewood Cemetery. On November 11, 1978, he was reinterred as the first burial in the newly dedicated and opened Riverside National Cemetery. He is buried in Section 5, Grave 1178.

The Veterans of Foreign Wars Post 184 in Riverside is named the Yamael R. Villegas Memorial Casas Blanca Post in his honor. Also named for him is a Riverside middle school. A statue of the soldier stands in the courtyard of the Riverside Main Street Civic Center.

On March 14, 2014, the Riverside County Mexican American Historical Society held a ceremony at Riverside National Cemetery to honor the upcoming ninetieth anniversary of the birth of their hometown hero. At the gathering, Riverside parks director Ralph Nunez said, "He was an ordinary man from Casa Blanca who on March 20, 1945, demonstrated extraordinary valor in protecting and inspiring his unit in the most difficult of circumstances. He continues to serve as an inspiration to the residents of Riverside, primarily to the youth."

Martha Villegas Diaz, his youngest sister, said, "He belongs to America."

★★★

13

David Maldonado Gonzales,
US Army

Company A, 127th Infantry Regiment, 32nd Infantry Division

Villa Verde Trail, Luzon, Philippines, April 25, 1945

Date Presented: December 8, 1945

CITATION:

He was pinned down with his company. As enemy fire swept the area, making any movement extremely hazardous, a 500-pound bomb smashed into the company's perimeter, burying 5 men with its explosion. Pfc. Gonzales, without hesitation, seized an entrenching tool and under a hail of fire crawled 15 yards to his entombed comrades, where his commanding officer, who had also rushed forward, was beginning to dig the men out. Nearing his goal, he saw the officer struck and instantly killed by machinegun fire. Undismayed, he set to work swiftly and surely with his hands and the entrenching tool while enemy sniper and machinegun bullets struck all about him. He succeeded in digging one of the men out of the pile of rock and sand. To dig faster he stood up regardless of the greater danger from so exposing himself. He extricated a second man, and then another. As he completed the liberation of the third, he was hit and mortally wounded, but the comrades for whom he so gallantly gave his life were safely evacuated. Pfc. Gonzales' valiant and intrepid conduct exemplifies the highest tradition of the military service.

PFC. DAVID MALDONADO GONZALES is the only resident of Los Angeles County to receive the Medal of Honor in World War II. Gonzales was born on June 9, 1923, to Mexican American parents in Pacoima, California, just north of the city of Los Angeles. As a boy he enjoyed playing baseball in an empty lot near his parents' home. The oldest of fourteen children, he completed four years of high school before going to work in a machine shop as a drill press operator. He was married when he was inducted into the US Army on March 31, 1944, at Fort MacArthur, California.

Gonzales completed basic training at Camp Roberts, California, in September. He then had a brief home leave before reporting for shipment overseas. Gonzales left behind his wife and baby son, David V., who would never again see his father. In an article in the *Los Angeles Daily News* on November 8, 2002, David said, "He was home on leave, and I wasn't even a year old yet. My Aunt Carmen told me my father said to her and my mother to take good care of me because he wasn't coming home."

In the Philippines, Gonzales joined the veteran 32nd Division that had departed the United States for the Pacific Theater on April 22, 1942. After additional training in Australia, the division landed in New Guinea on September 15, 1942, and became the first US division to fight an offensive action against the Japanese in the southwest Pacific. By February 1, 1945, Gonzales was also a battle veteran, having earned the coveted Combat Infantryman Badge in the Battle of Luzon.

On April 25, Gonzales's company was fighting along the Villa Verde Trail— a location near where Ysmael Villegas had earned his Medal of Honor a month earlier. When Gonzales's unit became heavily engaged with Japanese protected by bunkers and caves on Hill 507, they called in tactical air support from the Army Air Corps. The planes dropped "skip bombs" that had delayed action fuses so that they would explode underground and destroy caves and tunnels. Unfortunately, one of the bombs fell short, causing a landslide that buried Americans in their foxholes.

Despite heavy enemy fire, Gonzales and his company commander grabbed entrenching tools and rushed forward to rescue the buried soldiers. The company commander was immediately killed, but Gonzales continued to expose himself as he dug into the dirt and rocks. He pulled one soldier, then a second, and finally a third from the debris to safety before he too was mortally wounded. An eyewitness to the action, Sgt. Frank M. Reehoff, later said, "It was the bravest thing I have ever seen a man do."

Pres. Harry Truman presented Gonzales's posthumous Medal of Honor to his widow, Steffanie, on December 8, 1945. Gonzales was initially buried on Luzon before being brought back home on February 2, 1949. A Requiem High Mass was said at the Church of the Guardian Angel in Pacoima, which

Gonzales had attended before the war. His casket was then escorted by police motorcycles to Our Lady of Talpa Church in downtown Los Angeles, where he was honored by the city's mayor and other officials. His widow and son were presented a special citation. Gonzales was then buried in the city's Cavalry Cemetery (Section H, Lot 151, Grave 12).

In 1950 a plaque was placed in the Pacoima Recreation Center honoring Gonzales. It was not until 1997, however, that it was officially renamed the David M. Gonzales Pacoima Recreation Center. The US Army recruiting station in Los Angeles and a county probation camp are also named in his honor. In 1999, David V. Gonzales discovered that the picture used in the Pentagon's Hall of Heroes and in some US Army publications was incorrect and not his father. With the assistance of Rep. Howard Berman (D-CA), the error was corrected. On November 7, 2002, Berman also presented Gonzales's medals, the originals having been lost, to his son. David V. Gonzales said at the ceremony, "My father was extremely proud to serve this great country, and he deserves to be remembered with honor and respect."

★★★

14

Manuel Perez Jr.,
US Army

Company A, 511th Parachute Infantry, 11th Airborne Division

Santo Tomas, Luzon, Philippines, March 14, 1945

Date Presented: December 27, 1945

CITATION:

He was lead scout for Company A, which had destroyed 11 of 12 pillboxes in a strongly fortified sector defending the approach to enemy-held Fort William McKinley on Luzon, Philippine Islands. In the reduction of these pillboxes, he killed 5 Japanese in the open and blasted others in pillboxes with grenades. Realizing the urgent need for taking the last emplacement, which contained 2 twin-mount .50-caliber dual-purpose machineguns, he took a circuitous route to within 20 yards of the position, killing 4 of the enemy in his advance. He threw a grenade into the pillbox, and, as the crew started withdrawing through a tunnel just to the rear of the emplacement, shot and killed 4 before exhausting his clip. He had reloaded and killed 4 more when an escaping Japanese threw his rifle with fixed bayonet at him. In warding off this thrust, his own rifle was knocked to the ground. Seizing the Jap rifle, he continued firing, killing 2 more of the enemy. He rushed the remaining Japanese, killed 3 of them with the butt of the rifle and entered the pillbox, where he bayoneted the 1 surviving hostile soldier. Single-handedly, he killed 18 of the enemy in neutralizing the position that had held up the advance of his entire company. Through his courageous determination and heroic disregard of grave danger, Pfc. Perez made possible the successful advance of his unit toward a valuable objective and provided a lasting inspiration for his comrades.

MANUEL PEREZ was born on March 3, 1923, to Mexican American parents in Oklahoma City, Oklahoma. While a young boy, he moved to Chicago, where he was raised by his father and paternal grandmother, Tiburcia Moncada Perez. Manuel attended Goodrich and Jackson elementary schools and Crane Technical High School on Chicago's west side. He then worked as a warehouseman for Best Foods before being drafted on January 9, 1943.

Known as "Toots" to his family and friends and "Bullet" for his restless behavior by others, Perez had a normal childhood. An article in the February 1991 edition of *American Legion Magazine* stated, "Before Perez's induction, he had led a completely ordinary life. In some ways, he had been a model youth growing up in Chicago's west side. He was always polite and deferential, particularly to the grandmother who raised him."

Upon completion of his basic training, Perez volunteered to become a paratrooper in the 11th Airborne Division. There he participated in maneuvers that tested and refined the new concept of delivery of infantrymen by parachute onto the battlefield. The 11th Airborne continued training and remained in Camp Mackall, North Carolina, before moving to Camp Polk, Louisiana, and on to Camp Stoneman, California, before deploying to the Pacific Theater in May 1944.

Initially stationed in Papua New Guinea for acclimatization and more training, the division went ashore on Leyte Island in Gen. Douglas MacArthur's return to the Philippines in November 1944. The paratroopers of the 11th Airborne honed their skills as conventional infantrymen as they moved northward to participate in the Battle of Luzon.

On February 13, 1945, Perez's unit was ordered to retake Fort William McKinley, the prewar headquarters for US forces in the Philippines. The Japanese had twelve fortified concrete .50-caliber machine-gun positions defending the fort. Eleven fell to the paratroopers before the twelfth stopped their attack. When Perez realized that the pillbox blocked his entire unit's advance, he flanked the fortification and attacked with his bayonet-fixed rifle and hand grenades. With grenade blasts, rifle fire, and finally hand-to-hand bayonet thrusts, Perez killed at least eighteen Japanese soldiers and neutralized the enemy's position.

The battle had been won, but there was still much fighting to be accomplished by Perez and the 11th Airborne before the Philippine Islands were secure. Two weeks after his bravery at Fort McKinley, the young paratrooper sent a letter on February 28, 1945, to his uncle, Pvt. Jesse Perez, who was also serving in the Pacific. He wrote," Dear Uncle . . . they are putting me in for a medal and it's not the Purple Heart, you will be surprised how big it's going to be."

Perez did not live to receive his medal. On March 14 his platoon was fighting near Santo Tomas when a sniper's bullet struck Perez in the chest, killing him. He was initially buried in the Philippines, but his remains were returned to the United States four years later. A memorial service was held at the Manuel Perez Jr. American Legion Post 1017—formed by Mexican American veterans after the war and named in his honor. His body was then moved to Fairlawn Cemetery in Oklahoma City and reinterred in the Catholic Section (Block 12, Lot 4) on February 15, 1949. In addition to a flat VA Medal of Honor marker, Perez's grave has a civilian headstone with his name, dates of birth and death, and the inscription *En Paz Descance*—Spanish for "Rest in Peace."

Perez's father, Manuel Perez Sr., had relocated to Nuevo Laredo, Tamaulipas, Mexico, during the war but returned to the United States to receive his son's Medal of Honor on December 27, 1945. In addition to family members, Perez left behind his fiancée, Mary Torres. Perez had sent her a silk parachute to use to make her gown for the wedding they planned upon his return.

A city park and the US Army Reserve Center in Oklahoma City are named in his honor. In addition to American Legion Post 1017, the City of Chicago named the area at 26th and Kolin Streets Perez Plaza in 1981. The new Manuel Perez Jr. Elementary School at 1241 West 19th Street was dedicated in 1991. On the anniversary of his death in 2013, the Illinois state legislature declared March 14 as Manuel Perez Jr. Day to "honor and remember his selfless acts of bravery during World War II."

★★★

15

Jose F. Valdez,
US Army

Company B, 7th Infantry Regiment, 3rd Infantry Division

Rosenkranz, France, January 25, 1945

Date Presented: February 8, 1946

CITATION:

Private First Class Valdez was on outpost duty with five others when the enemy counterattacked with overwhelming strength. From his position near some woods 500 yards beyond the American lines he observed a hostile tank about 75 yards away, and raked it with automatic rifle fire until it withdrew. Soon afterward he saw three Germans stealthily approaching through the woods. Scorning cover as the enemy soldiers opened up with heavy automatic weapons fire from a range of 30 yards, he engaged in a fire fight with the attackers until he had killed all three. The enemy quickly launched an attack with two full companies of infantrymen, blasting the patrol with murderous concentrations of automatic and rifle fire and beginning an encircling movement which forced the patrol leader to order a withdrawal. Despite the terrible odds, Pfc. Valdez immediately volunteered to cover the maneuver, and as the patrol one by one plunged through a hail of bullets toward the American lines, he fired burst after burst into the swarming enemy. Three of his companions were wounded in their dash for safety and he was struck by a bullet that entered his stomach and, passing through his body, emerged from his back. Overcoming agonizing pain, he regained control of himself and resumed his firing position, delivering a protective screen of bullets until all others of the patrol were safe. By field telephone he called for artillery and mortar fire on the Germans and corrected the range until he had shells falling within 50 yards of his position. For 15 minutes he refused to be dislodged by more than 200 of the enemy; then, seeing that the barrage had broken the counter attack, he dragged himself back to his own lines. He died later as a result of his wounds. Through his valiant, intrepid stand and at the cost of his own life, PFC Valdez made it possible for his comrades to escape, and was directly responsible for repulsing an attack by vastly superior enemy forces.

JOSE VALDEZ, at only a month past his twentieth birthday, was the youngest Hispanic recipient of the Medal of Honor in World War II. Born on January 3, 1945, in what is today the all but abandoned ghost town of Gobernador in northwestern New Mexico, he joined the "old line" New Mexican Valdez family who had lived in the area since territorial days. Valdez worked on his father's ranch and also hired out as a day laborer on nearby ranches before receiving his draft notice in June 1944. He reported for induction at Pleasant Grove just south of Salt Lake City. Although he never lived in Utah, that state, as well as New Mexico, claims him as a native son. He is Utah's only Hispanic Medal of Honor recipient.

After basic training, Valdez joined the 3rd Infantry Division in Alsace in northeastern France to assist in the fight against the Germans to collapse the Colmar Pocket. Valdez was part of a six-man patrol near Rosenkranz on January 25, 1945, that encountered an enemy counterattack. He turned back the lead German tank with his automatic rifle and killed three enemy infantrymen. When two full companies of German foot soldiers joined the attack, Valdez volunteered to stay behind to cover the withdrawal of his fellow soldiers, allowing their safe return to American lines. Although seriously wounded, Valdez managed to drag himself back to his company's positions. However, he died three weeks later from his wounds. His family was presented his medal on February 8, 1946. He is buried in Santa Fe National Cemetery (Section Q, Grave 29).

There were other acts of uncommon valor in the Battle for the Colmar Pocket. Second Lt. Audie Murphy, also of the 3rd Infantry Division—the most decorated soldier of World War II and future Hollywood star—earned his Medal of Honor just one day later a few kilometers north of where Valdez made his stand.

More than a half century after his death, his fellow soldiers clearly remembered Valdez and his valor. In an interview with the *Farmington Daily Times*, Abundio Castro said Valdez was a "quiet individual." Castro added, "He was the type of fellow to stay awake all night, guarding and guarding. He was always alert and quiet. That keeps up the morale of the rest of the troops in the front lines. Your life is at stake."

Personal recollections were not the only tributes to this soldier. The *Private Jose F. Valdez* was launched as a US Army transport vessel before being transferred to the navy in 1950 and renamed the USNS *Private Jose F. Valdez*. During the 1960s it operated as a technical research vessel before being decommissioned in 1976. Valdez Elementary School in Denver, Colorado, and the U.S Army Reserve Center in Pleasant Grove are named in his honor. A 106-mile stretch of US Highway 64 from Bloomfield to Tierra Amarilla in northwestern New Mexico also bears his name. Memorials to Valdez are in nearby Gobernador and Farmington.

On February 17, 2015, Utah Veterans of Foreign War members gathered at the state capitol to honor the seventieth anniversary of Valdez's death and to dedicate a portrait of him to hang in the hall of Pleasant Grove High School. At the ceremony, Utah attorney general Sean Reyes said, "There's so many in the Latino community today that worry that our kids don't have proper role models. This is a beacon of light that they can look to and say, 'He looks like me. His last name sounds like me. He's a hero, and I'd like to be like that.'"

16

Alejandro Renteria Ruiz,
US Army

Company A, 1st Battalion, 165th Infantry Regiment, 27th Infantry Division
Okinawa, Japan, April 28, 1945
Date Presented: June 14, 1946

CITATION:

*When his unit was stopped by a skillfully camouflaged enemy pillbox, he displayed
conspicuous gallantry and intrepidity above and beyond the call of duty. His squad,
suddenly brought under a hail of machinegun fire and a vicious grenade attack,
was pinned down. Jumping to his feet, Pfc. Ruiz seized an automatic rifle and
lunged through the flying grenades and rifle and automatic fire for the top of the
emplacement. When an enemy soldier charged him, his rifle jammed. Undaunted,
Pfc. Ruiz whirled on his assailant and clubbed him down. Then he ran back
through bullets and grenades, seized more ammunition and another automatic
rifle, and again made for the pillbox. Enemy fire now was concentrated on him, but
he charged on, miraculously reaching the position, and in plain view he climbed
to the top. Leaping from one opening to another, he sent burst after burst into the
pillbox, killing 12 of the enemy and completely destroying the position. Pfc. Ruiz's
heroic conduct, in the face of overwhelming odds, saved the lives of many comrades
and eliminated an obstacle that long would have checked his unit's advance.*

WHEN ALEJANDRO RUIZ received his Medal of Honor from Pres. Harry
Truman on June 14, 1946, congressmen from both Texas and New Mexico
attended the White House ceremony, each claiming the Hispanic soldier as
their state's native son. Gen. Dwight D. Eisenhower, a guest at the ceremony,

overheard the dispute when he went to congratulate Ruiz. The general joked, "This ought to be a real scrap."

The claims of both congressmen had some validity. Ruiz was born on April 26, 1924 (several sources erroneously claim 1923), in Loving, New Mexico, to Eujio Ruiz and his wife, Adela. His father had emigrated from Mexico to become a farmer after serving with Pancho Villa in the Border Wars. His mother was born in Pecos, Texas, the daughter of parents born in Mexico. Ruiz grew up working in his father's fields as well as on neighboring cotton and alfalfa farms. He dropped out of elementary school after the third grade to work full time when his father died.

In his early teens Ruiz moved to Barstow in far West Texas. In September 1943 he was back in New Mexico working odd jobs for a rancher near Carlsbad. The rancher told him to take a cow to market, which he set out to do—only he decided to visit a girlfriend back in Barstow, 122 miles away. On his way, Ruiz was stopped by the police and accused of stealing the cow. A judge told him he could volunteer for the army or go to jail. Ruiz's military career began the next day when he enlisted at Carlsbad.

After three weeks of "reading and writing school" at Fort Bliss, Ruiz completed basic training at Camp Roberts, California, and advanced infantry training at Fort Ord, California. On August 18, 1944, he shipped out to join the 165th Infantry Regiment of the 27th Infantry Division in the Pacific Theater. Ruiz and the 27th, a former New York National Guard unit and veteran of the battles for Makin, Eniwetok, and Saipan, stormed ashore on the island of Okinawa on April 9, 1945.

On April 28, 1945, Ruiz's platoon advanced up a ridgeline near the village of Gasukuma, where they were ambushed by Japanese firing from well-camouflaged pillboxes. Every soldier except Ruiz and his squad leader were killed or wounded early in the fight. Ruiz exchanged his M-1 rifle for one of the wounded's Browning Automatic Rifle and ran through machine-gun fire and hand grenade explosions for thirty-five meters to the nearest bunker. When he reached the fortification, his BAR jammed. A Japanese soldier charged out of hiding, only to be killed by Ruiz wielding his broken weapon as a club. He then ran back through the maelstrom of bullets and explosions to retrieve another BAR and more ammunition. A bullet struck Ruiz in the leg as he once again charged the pillboxes. The wound did not stop the Hispanic soldier. He ran from bunker to bunker, pouring fire into the apertures until all were silenced. Twelve dead Japanese lay in his wake.

In a 1976 oral history interview for the University of Texas at El Paso, Ruiz recalled that he did not really feel fear until after the fight. He said, "It happened so fast that actually I don't know what happened. I know that I was pinned down, I was cut off, and I thought I was going to get killed that day. I made up my mind that if I was going to get killed, I wasn't going to go by myself, I was going to take as many as I could with me."

Ruiz returned to Fort Bliss after the war ended while waiting for his Medal of Honor ceremony. He had no interest in returning to farm or ranch work, so he reenlisted in the army. Over the next eighteen years he served in infantry, artillery, armor, and quartermaster units as well as the senior NCO in a training battalion. His assignments included another combat tour in the Korean War. He retired from active duty as a master sergeant in 1964.

While he was in the army, Ruiz's family moved to Visalia, California. He joined them upon his retirement. In the early 1990s, Ruiz was in an automobile accident that left his face slightly disfigured and made talking difficult. In 1996 he moved to the Veterans Home of California in Yountville, where he died of congestive heart failure on November 19, 2009, at age eighty-five. He is buried in Yountville's Veterans Memorial Grove Cemetery (Section J, Row 8, Grave 31).

As a military retiree with a monthly income, Ruiz paid about $3,000 per month for his room and care at the Veterans Home. Upon his death, the California Department of Veterans Affairs billed his estate for $262,500 for additional medical services he had received in his final years. This was done to collect $60,000 from Ruiz's estate under provisions of the California Military and Veterans Code, which stated that any personal property or funds outside the Veterans Home "shall upon the death of the veteran, first be paid to the administrator for payment of funeral expenses or any obligation owed to the home remaining unpaid."

Despite the debate by the congressmen from Texas and New Mexico as to just who had the legitimate claim to Ruiz's residence, neither took any measures to honor the Mexican American hero. It was not until he retired to California that the town of Visalia honored him with the Alejandro R. Ruiz Park. City officials in Carlsbad, New Mexico, dedicated the Alejandro Ruiz Medal of Honor Plaza in 1995, and in 2012 the Veterans Home Post Office in Yountville was renamed the Private First Class Alejandro R. Ruiz Post Office Building.

★★★

17

Charles Harold Gonsalves,
US Marine Corps

Battery L, 4th Battalion, 15th Marine Regiment, 6th Marine Division

Motobu Peninsula, Okinawa, Japan, April 15, 1945

Date Presented: June 19, 1946

CITATION:

For conspicuous gallantry and intrepidity at the risk of his life above and beyond the call of duty as Acting Scout Sergeant of a Forward Observer Team, serving with Battery L, Fourth Battalion, Fifteenth Marines, Sixth Marine Division, during action against enemy Japanese forces in Okinawa Shima in the Ryukyu Cham on 15 April 1945. Undaunted by the powerfully organized opposition encountered on Motobu Peninsula during a fierce assault waged by a Marine infantry battalion against a Japanese strong-hold, Private First Class Gonsalves repeatedly braved the terrific hostile bombardment to aid his Forward Observation Team in directing well-placed artillery fire and, when his commanding officer determined to move into the front lines in order to register a more effective bombardment in the enemy's defensive position, unhesitatingly advanced uphill with the officer and another Marine despite a slashing barrage of enemy mortar and rifle fire. As they reached the front, a Japanese grenade fell close within the group. Instantly Private First Class Gonsalves dived on the deadly missile, absorbing the exploding charge in his own body and thereby protecting the others from serious and perhaps fatal wounds. Stouthearted and indomitable, Private First Class Gonsalves readily yielded his own chances of survival that his fellow Marines might carry on the relentless battle against the fanatic Japanese and his cool decision, prompt action and valiant spirit of self-sacrifice in the face of certain death reflect the highest credit upon himself and the United States Naval Service. He gallantly gave his life in the service of his country.

CHARLES HAROLD GONSALVES was born on January 18, 1926, in Alameda, California, to his Hispanic father John and his Hawaiian mother Annie. Gonsalves rarely used Charles—neither his Medal of Honor citation nor his headstone includes his first name. As a student in the Alameda public school system, he was known for his athletic abilities in baseball, football, track, and swimming. He also had a strong tenor voice that led him to become a member of his school glee club.

After two and a half years of high school, Gonsalves dropped out to work as a stock clerk in the Montgomery Ward department store in Oakland to assist his family financially. On May 27, 1943, at the age of only seventeen, he joined the US Marine Corps Reserves and was called to active duty the following June 17. His enlistment papers state that he stood five feet nine and weighed 178 pounds. Gonsalves completed boot camp at the San Diego Marine Corps Recruit Depot and then volunteered for the elite Marine Raider training at nearby Camp Pendleton. After only three weeks, he was transferred to artillery training at the same camp.

Whether Gonsalves voluntarily dropped from the Raider training or failed to meet their training standards in all likelihood influenced his actions in combat. This failure to become one of the elites may very well have served as later motivation for the young marine to "prove himself" on the battlefield. In artillery school he successfully trained on the 75-mm and 105-mm guns and then reported in the fall of 1943 to the 30th Replacement Battalion.

On November 8, Gonsalves joined the Second Pack Howitzer Battalion in Hawaii. In March 1944 he earned a promotion to private 1st class, and he and his battalion joined the 22nd Marine Regiment the following May. Gonsalves saw his first combat in the successful amphibious assault and capture of Engebi and Parry Islands in the Eniwetok Atoll of the Marshall Islands. From Eniwetok the 22nd went to Kwajalein, to Guadalcanal, back to Kwajalein, and finally again to Eniwetok as they trained for their next mission. In July, Gonzales participated in the invasion and occupation of the island of Guam.

After the Battle of Guam, the 22nd returned to Guadalcanal from where, in November, Gonzales was detached to Battery L, 4th Battalion, 15th Marine Regiment, of the 6th Marine Division. Gonzales, now an "old salt" veteran of several campaigns at only nineteen years of age, went ashore with the 15th in the invasion of Okinawa on April 1, 1945. For two weeks Gonzales acted as a forward observer with an eight-man team to direct artillery fire on Japanese positions on the Motobu Peninsula.

On April 15, 1945, Gonzales joined a lieutenant and another private 1st class on a mission to connect the infantry front line with telephone wires back to the artillery battery. When the trio reached the infantry positions, they came under small arms, machine gun, and mortar fire. Suddenly a Japanese hand grenade fell in the midst of the three marine artillerymen. With no hesitation, Gonsalves threw himself on the grenade just as it exploded. Gonsalves absorbed the full impact of the grenade, leaving the other two untouched and able to complete the wire-laying mission.

On June 19, 1946, Maj. Gen. Henry Louis Larsen presented Gonsalves's Medal of Honor to his sister and parents at the headquarters of the Department of the Pacific in San Francisco. Gonsalves was initially buried in the 6th Marine Division Cemetery on Okinawa. His remains were returned home, and he was buried with full honors on March 20, 1949, in Golden Gate National Cemetery in San Bruno, California, in Section B, Site 61.

The Northern Training Area, later changed to the Marine Corps Jungle Warfare Training Center, on Okinawa was named Camp Gonsalves in 1958. In 1997, Gonsalves Avenue on California's Marine Corp Air Station Miramar also was named in his honor.

★★★

18

Rudolph B. Davila,
US Army

Company H, 7th Infantry Regiment, 3rd Infantry Division
Artena, Italy, May 28, 1944
Date Presented: June 21, 2000

CITATION:

*Staff Sergeant Rudolph B. Davila distinguished himself by extraordinary heroism
in action, on 28 May 1944, near Artena, Italy. During the offensive which broke
through the German mountain strongholds surrounding the Anzio beachhead,
Staff Sergeant Davila risked death to provide heavy weapons support for a beleaguered rifle company. Caught on an exposed hillside by heavy, grazing fire from
a well-entrenched German force, his machine gunners were reluctant to risk putting their guns into action. Crawling fifty yards to the nearest machine gun, Staff
Sergeant Davila set it up alone and opened fire on the enemy. In order to observe
the effect of his fire, Sergeant Davila fired from the kneeling position, ignoring the
enemy fire that struck the tripod and passed between his legs. Ordering a gunner
to take over, he crawled forward to a vantage point and directed the firefight with
hand and arm signals until both hostile machine guns were silenced. Bringing his
three remaining machine guns into action, he drove the enemy to a reserve position two hundred yards to the rear. When he received a painful wound in the leg,
he dashed to a burned tank and, despite the crash of bullets on the hull, engaged a
second enemy force from the tank's turret. Dismounting, he advanced 130 yards in
short rushes, crawled 20 yards and charged into an enemy-held house to eliminate
the defending force of five with a hand grenade and rifle fire. Climbing to the attic,*

he straddled a large shell hole in the wall and opened fire on the enemy. Although the walls of the house were crumbling, he continued to fire until he had destroyed two more machine guns. His intrepid actions brought desperately needed heavy weapons support to a hard-pressed rifle company and silenced four machine gunners, which forced the enemy to abandon their prepared positions. Staff Sergeant Davila's extraordinary heroism and devotion to duty are in keeping with the highest traditions of military service and reflect great credit on him, his unit, and the United States Army.

RUDOLPH DAVILA exhibited extraordinary bravery in protecting his infantry company from a German ambush in Italy in 1944, but he had to wait fifty-six years before he was awarded his Medal of Honor.

According to his enlistment records, Davila was born in El Paso, Texas, on April 27, 1916, to a Filipino mother and a Spanish father. His father died before he was born, and the remaining family moved to Watts, California, a short time later. Rudolph, or Rudy as he was known, had a brother who was ten years older and whom he looked up to as a father figure. After he graduated from high school in Watts, Davila worked as a carpenter and a laborer in the nearby vineyards before joining the Civilian Conservation Corps, which helped restore historic California missions.

Davila enlisted in the army in March 6, 1941, and after his basic training joined the 3rd Infantry Division, one of the army's most decorated units, at Fort Lewis, Washington. The 3rd Division moved to Camp Pickett, Virginia, in September 1942 in preparation for the invasion of North Africa. By the time the division deployed to the European Theater, Davila had advanced to the rank of sergeant. He was soon a hardened veteran of North Africa and Sicily and had advanced in rank to staff sergeant in charge of his company's machine gun section when they went ashore at Anzio in the invasion of mainland Italy in January 1944.

On May 28, Davila's 130-infantryman company was advancing toward Rome when they were ambushed by Germans dug in on high ground to their front. Davila rushed forward, ordering his machine gun crews to join him. The soldiers, scared and pinned down by the enemy fire, were unable to advance. Davila ordered a machine gun passed up to him and, in the midst of heavy incoming fire, began firing back at the Germans, knocking out two of their positions and forcing them to retreat.

Then the sergeant pursued the Germans, despite suffering a leg wound, and killed two snipers in a stone farmhouse. He then assaulted the house ruins and killed five more with a rifle and hand grenades. Using the house as cover, he engaged and neutralized two more German machine gun positions, sending the remainder of the enemy in full retreat.

In the aftermath of the battle, Davila's company commander said that he was recommending him for the Medal of Honor. He added, "If you hadn't done this, I think we all would have been slaughtered."

Davila was awarded the Distinguished Service Cross, the second-highest medal for valor. He heard rumors that his division and the army thought that too many minorities were receiving the Medal of Honor, but Davila had no time to be concerned with past battles. There were still many to be fought and to be survived.

Davila was rewarded with a battlefield commission to second lieutenant. In late 1944, Davila, now a first lieutenant, and the 3rd Infantry Division were in France in the drive toward Germany. In the Vosges Mountains near Strasbourg, a German tank blocked his company's advance. Davila ordered an attack, but fragments from the tank's main gun shell tore into his right shoulder, paralyzing his arm and ending his war.

Evacuated back to the United States, Davila spent six years in and out of a military hospital in Modesto, California, as he endured thirteen operations on his shoulder and arm. While in the hospital, he met a nurse named Harriet, whom he married three months later. A disabled arm did not slow down the former infantryman. Using the GI Bill, he enrolled in the University of Southern California and earned bachelor's and master's degrees in sociology. For the next thirty years, he served as a teacher and counselor in the Los Angeles City School District. Despite his disability of a nonfunctioning right arm, he hand-built his family home in Harbor City and later their retirement home in Vista.

Over the years, Harriet and other family members wrote various government officials seeking an upgrade of Davila's award from DSC to the Medal of Honor. They failed to achieve their goal. Finally, in 1996, Sen. Daniel K. Akaka (D-HI) introduced an amendment, which Congress passed, that waived the regulation of a three-year limit on reassessing valor awards. The bill also recommended that the files of Asian Americans be reviewed to see if those who deserved the Medal of Honor had been denied because of prejudice.

Because his mother was Filipino, Davila was included in the Asian American review. In a White House ceremony on June 21, 2000—fifty-six years after the battle in Italy—Davila and twenty-one other Americans of Asian ancestry were awarded the Medal of Honor by Pres. Bill Clinton. Only seven of the twenty-two recipients were still alive to receive their medals. Harriet Davila did not live to see her husband decorated, having died on December 25 of the previous year.

In interviews Davila said about the action that led to his medal, "I don't remember being afraid or timid. It just happened. I wasn't that kind of person. I wasn't violent. In fact, I was kind of a passive kind of guy. I just wanted to be a good soldier."

After the White House ceremony, Davila said, "I didn't want to think my country would deny me something because I'm not an Anglo." But he added, "The conscience of America went to sleep, in my case, for 56 years."

The City of Vista honored Davila at its Veterans of Foreign Wars Memorial Day ceremony in 2001. In 2012 a portion of the Gardena Freeway (State Highway 91) in Carson was renamed the Rudolph B. Davila Memorial Freeway.

Davila died of complications of cancer on January 26, 2002, and is buried in Arlington National Cemetery (Section 67, Site 3457).

★★★

19

Pedro Cano,
US Army

Company C, 8th Infantry Regiment, 4th Infantry Division
Schevenhutte, Germany, December 2–3, 1944
Date Presented: March 18, 2014

CITATION:

Private Pedro Cano distinguished himself by acts of gallantry and intrepidity above and beyond the call of duty while serving with Company C, 8th Infantry Regiment, 4th Infantry Division during combat operations against an armed enemy in Schevenhutte, Germany on December 2 and 3, 1944. On the afternoon of the 2nd, American infantrymen launched an attack against German emplacements but were repulsed by enemy machinegun fire. Armed with a rocket launcher, Private Cano crawled through a densely mined area under heavy enemy fire and successfully reached a point within ten yards of the nearest emplacement. He quickly fired a rocket into the position, killing the two gunners and five supporting riflemen. Without hesitating, he fired into a second position, killing two more gunners, and proceeded to assault the position with hand grenades, killing several others and dispersing the rest. Then, when an adjacent company encountered heavy fire, Private Cano crossed his company front, crept to within fifteen yards of the nearest enemy emplacement and killed the two machine gunners with a rocket. With another round he killed two more gunners and destroyed a second gun. On the following day, his company renewed the attack and again encountered heavy machinegun fire. Private Cano, armed with his rocket launcher, again moved across fire-swept terrain and destroyed three enemy machineguns in succession,

killing the six gunners. Private Cano's extraordinary heroism and selflessness
above and beyond the call of duty are in keeping with the highest traditions of mili-
tary service and reflect great credit upon himself, his unit and the United States
Army.

PEDRO (no middle name or initial) CANO was born on June 19, 1920, in La
Morita, Nuevo Leon, Mexico, to Secundino and Nicolasa Gonzales Cano.
When he was only two months old, Cano's family crossed the river into Texas
to reside in Edinburg, where, as a boy and young man, he worked as a farm
laborer in the fields and orchards surrounding the town. He enjoyed working
on radios and playing the accordion.

Despite being only five feet three, married with a daughter, and having little
education and a limited ability to speak English, Cano was drafted into the
army in 1943. After training in Louisiana, he joined the 8th Infantry Regiment
of the 4th Infantry Division in Europe in 1944. On December 2, during the
Battle of the Hurtgen Forest, near Schevenhutte, Germany, Cano's infantry
company came under heavy fire from German machine guns and small arms.
Using a rocket launcher and hand grenades, Cano repeatedly assaulted the
enemy positions. The next day he again took the lead in attacking the enemy.
At the end of the two days, he had destroyed six German machine gun positions and killed more than thirty enemy soldiers.

A short time later Cano was on a patrol when he was seriously wounded and
evacuated to the Veterans Hospital in Waco, Texas. Upon his recovery, he was
discharged with a disability and returned to his family in Edinburg. After his
arrival home, the Distinguished Service Cross, our country's second-highest
valor medal, arrived via the US Mail. Cano showed it to a few friends and then
put it in his closet. His friends recognized the significance of the medal and
began to lobby the military officials in San Antonio and at the War Department for an appropriate ceremony. The local newspaper and elected officials
joined the effort.

On April 26, 1946, more than 4,000 people gathered in Edinburg for Pedro
Cano Day. Schools were dismissed for the event, and a parade took place from
the Missouri-Pacific Railroad Station on the east side of town to the ceremonial stage at the Hidalgo County Courthouse. Attendees for the occasion
were Gen. Jonathan M. Wainwright IV, the commander of Corregidor; Adm.
Joseph J. Clark, commander of aircraft carriers in the Pacific and the first Native American graduate of the US Naval Academy; and two senior Mexican

army officers. After the citation for the DSC was read, Wainwright remarked that Cano deserved the Medal of Honor.

The grateful citizens of Hidalgo County also presented Cano with forty acres of land and necessary farm equipment. Cano worked the fields and repaired electrical appliances for the rest of his life.

Many believed at the time and in the years afterward that Cano had not received the Medal of Honor because of prejudice against Hispanics or because at the time he was not a US citizen. Cano, as a US resident, had been eligible for the draft, but citizenship did not come as easily as a draft notice. While in combat in France, he had requested citizenship, but the pressing matters of the battlefield took precedence. Only after the war and the presentation of his DSC, along with the support of his local state senator, did he finally achieve citizenship in May 1946.

Many individuals and groups in Hidalgo County took up efforts for Cano's DSC to be upgraded to the Medal of Honor. Cano did not seem all that concerned about the medal as he continued to battle the memories and demons of combat. He had difficulty sleeping, seemed nervous, and began to drink heavily. His family described him as moody and quiet. This behavior, what is now known as posttraumatic stress disorder, at the time was described as "shell shock."

Over the years, an elementary school in Edinburg was named in his honor. Kruttschnutt Street, the parade route prior to his DSC ceremony, was also changed to Cano Street. Residents of Hidalgo County continued their efforts to recognize Cano's valor by writing to military and civilian officials.

It would be decades before they were successful, so long in fact that Cano would not live to see the day. On June 24, 1952, at the age of only thirty-one, Cano died in an accident that fractured his skull when his truck collided with a car driven by a drunken driver near Pharr, Texas. He left behind three children by his first wife, Hermina, and two children by Estala Garcia, whom he was in the process of arranging to marry. He is buried in Edinburg's Hillcrest Memorial Park.

On April 25, 2009, the State of Texas awarded its Legislative Medal of Honor to Cano. Ongoing efforts continued to secure the Medal of Honor for the Mexican American soldier but were unsuccessful until December 28, 2001, when the US Congress, as a part of the Defense Authorization Act, directed the secretaries of the military departments to review the service records of each Jewish American war veteran or Hispanic American war veteran described in subsection b to determine whether that veteran should be awarded the Medal of Honor. Subsection b stated that the records of those minorities who had received the Distinguished Service Cross, the Navy Cross, or the Air Force Cross should be reviewed. It took more than a decade for the review to be completed and to upgrade the awards to the Medal of Honor. On March 18, 2014, Pres. Barack Obama presented Cano's medal to his daughter Dominga Perez in a White House ceremony—seventy years after his bravery in the Hurtgen Forest and sixty-two years after his death.

★★

20

Joe Gandara,
US Army

Company D, 2nd Battalion, 507th Parachute Infantry Regiment, 17th
Airborne Division
Amfreville, France, June 9, 1944
Date Presented: March 18, 2014

CITATION:

*Private Joe Gandara distinguished himself by acts of gallantry and intrepidity
above and beyond the call of duty while serving with Company D, 2d Battalion,
507th Parachute Infantry Regiment, 17th Airborne Division during combat operations against an armed enemy in Amfreville, France on June 9, 1944. On that day,
Private Gandara's detachment came under devastating enemy fire from a strong
German force, pinning the men to the ground for a period of four hours. Private
Gandara voluntarily advanced alone toward the enemy position. Firing his machinegun from his hip as he moved forward, he destroyed three hostile machineguns before he was fatally wounded. Private Gandara's extraordinary heroism
and selflessness at the cost of his own life, above and beyond the call of duty, are in
keeping with the highest traditions of military service and reflect great credit upon
himself, his unit and the United States Army.*

JOE (not Joseph and no middle name or initial) GANDARA was born on April
25, 1924, to Mexican immigrants in Santa Monica, California. His mother's
maiden name was Orrantia. After three years of high school, Gandara went
to work in an aircraft assembly plant in Los Angeles. He enlisted in the army

84

on February 20, 1943, in Los Angeles and after basic infantry training volunteered for paratrooper school. His enlistment papers show that he was 68 inches in height and weighed only 132 pounds.

Gandara joined the 17th Airborne Division in England as the unit prepared for its jump into France in support of the D-Day invasion at Normandy. Early on the morning of June 6, 1944, Gandara boarded a C-47 transport of the 9th Air Force at Barkston Heath Airfield (Station 483), England, and soon jumped out into the dark skies behind Utah Beach on what was designated Drop Zone T. After three days of fighting, Gandara's company became pinned down by overwhelming German fire. Four hours passed, with the Americans sustaining more and more wounded and dead. Finally, Gandara charged forward against the German positions and destroyed three machine guns and their crews before he fell, mortally wounded.

Gandara was awarded the Distinguished Service Cross and the Purple Heart. He was buried in an American cemetery in France before being returned home in 1948 and buried at the foot of his mother's grave in Santa Monica's Woodlawn Cemetery (Block 7, Lot 34, Space A).

The hero paratrooper lay mostly unknown and unrecognized for nearly seventy years until the 2014 review of minority servicemen's records of those who had received the DSC to ensure that no prejudice had been shown to those deserving the Medal of Honor. In a White House ceremony on March 18, Gandara's niece, Miriam Theresa Adams of Lompoc, California, accepted the medal for her uncle. In accepting the medal, she said, "He was proud of his heritage, but he was an American."

Pres. Barack Obama said, "No nation is perfect, but here in America, we confront our imperfections and face a sometimes painful past, including the truth that some of these soldiers fought and died for a country that did not always see them as equal."

On June 4, 2014, in honor of the seventieth anniversary of the Normandy Invasion, the citizens of Amfreville, France, and paratroopers of the 82nd Airborne Division dedicated a monument and plaque to Granada near where he fell. The division commander, Maj. Gen. John W. Nicholson Jr., said, "Despite his young age when he died, he knew full well what would happen when he exposed himself. He knew he was likely to die and he did it anyway. He died protecting his comrades, but he also died to end the oppression of the French people and prevent the oppression of his countrymen. This cause and these people were worthy of his sacrifice. But that doesn't make the grieving we feel over his loss and thousands like him any less difficult. But we can remember. We can memorialize his sacrifice with this monument and our presence here today."

On November 4, 2016, the city of Santa Monica and the Los Angeles County Metropolitan Transportation Authority unveiled a plaque honoring Gandara at the 26th Street/Bergamot Metro Station in the neighborhood in which the Medal of Honor recipient had grown up. His great-niece, Hannah Adams, said, "I was honored to be with my mother at the White House to witness how a nation acknowledged the mistakes of the past, a nation that did not always appreciate the sacrifice of Americans of Mexican descent. Finally, our nation set the record straight. Gladly, we stand here today, a free and stronger nation because of our diversity."

★★★

21

Salvador J. Lara,
US Army

Company L, 180th Infantry Regiment, 45th Infantry Division

Aprilia, Italy, May 27–28, 1944

Date Presented: March 18, 2014

CITATION:

Private First Class Salvador J. Lara distinguished himself by acts of gallantry and intrepidity above and beyond the call of duty while serving as the Squad Leader of a rifle squad with 2d Platoon, Company L, 180th Infantry, 45th Infantry Division during combat operations against an armed enemy in Aprilia, Italy on May 27 and 28, 1944. On the afternoon of the 27th, Private First Class Lara aggressively led his rifle squad in neutralizing multiple enemy strongpoints and in inflicting large numbers of casualties on the enemy. Having taken his initial objective, Private First Class Lara noticed that the unit to his right was meeting stiff resistance from a large, well-entrenched enemy force in a deep ditch. Private First Class Lara quickly gathered three men and attacked a wide section of the enemy position, killing four, forcing fifteen others to surrender and causing two enemy mortar crews to abandon their weapons. His fearless and efficient performance enabled both his own unit and the unit to his right to continue to their objective. The next morning, as his company resumed the attack, Private First Class Lara sustained a severe leg wound, but did not stop to receive first aid. His company suffered heavy casualties as a result of withering machinegun fire coming from an enemy strongpoint on the right flank. After requesting permission to destroy the enemy machineguns armed only with a Browning Automatic Rifle, Private First Class Lara crawled alone toward the nearest machinegun. Despite his painful wound and the extreme dan-

ger of the task, he rose and fearlessly charged the nest, killing the crew members. Another machinegun opened fire on him, but he quickly neutralized this weapon with accurate fire from his Browning, killing three more of the enemy. His aggressive attack forced two other machinegun crews to flee their weapons. After rejoining his company, Private First Class Lara continued his exemplary performance until he captured his objective. Private First Class Lara's extraordinary heroism and selflessness above and beyond the call of duty are in keeping with the highest traditions of military service and reflect great credit upon himself, his unit and the United States Army.

SALVADOR J. LARA was born on July 11, 1920, to Mexican American parents in Riverside, California. Surviving relatives remember him as being "easy going, honorable, and faithful." Lara, whose nickname was "Chavo," attended three years of high school before going to work on nearby farms and orchards. He entered the army on July 29, 1942, and his enlistment record states that he was single, stood 68 inches tall, and weighed 172 pounds.

Upon the completion of his training, Lara joined the 45th Infantry Division, a former Oklahoma National Guard unit, as a replacement. The division went ashore on the Anzio Beachhead in January 1944, only to be met by heavy German resistance. Finally, in May the division began a breakout to drive toward Rome.

On May 27, Pfc. Lara, acting as a squad leader in a position usually held by a sergeant or staff sergeant, led his squad to destroy several enemy positions near Aprilia, Italy. He then led a team of three to attack another enemy stronghold on his right flank, killing four soldiers and capturing fifteen and their two mortar positions. The next day Lara's unit again met heavy resistance. Despite a serious leg wound, he grabbed a Browning Automatic Rifle and charged forward, neutralizing two German positions and killing their crews. Two other German machine gun crews hastily withdrew, leaving their heavy weapons behind. For his actions during the two-day battle, Lara received the Distinguished Service Cross.

Lara advanced in rank to staff sergeant as the 45th Infantry Division moved across Italy and France and on into Germany. When the war finally concluded, Lara remained in Europe as part of the occupation force in the 602nd Ordnance Armament Maintenance Battalion. He died on September 1, 1945, of what is listed as "not combat situation" causes. It is likely he was killed in some type of vehicle accident, but neither the official records nor his family provide any details. He is buried in the Lorraine American Cemetery and Memorial in Saint-Avold, France (Plot F, Row 17, Grave 33).

In a 2014 interview, his brother and niece stated that Lara's death had happened so long ago that they did not know much about his service or how he had died. The mostly forgotten Hispanic American hero remained obscure until minority DSC recipients were reviewed for an upgrade to the Medal of Honor. Alfonso Lara, eighty years old and Salvador's younger brother, accepted the medal from President Obama in a White House ceremony on March 18, 2014.

A sign recognizing Lara's accomplishments was dedicated on May 26, 2014, at the Ysmael Villegas Community Center in Riverside. The California Department of Veterans Affairs held a recognition ceremony for Lara, Pvt. Joe Gandara, and three other Hispanic Medal of Honor recipients on the west steps of the state capitol in Sacramento on May 27, 2014. A portion of Riverside's 91 Freeway has also been named in his honor.

★ ★ ★

22

Manuel Verdugo Mendoza,
US Army

Company B, 350th Infantry Regiment, 88th Infantry Division

Mt. Battaglia, Italy, October 4, 1944

Date Presented: March 18, 2014

CITATION:

For acts of gallantry and intrepidity above and beyond the call of duty while serving as a Platoon Sergeant with Company B, 350th Infantry, 88th Infantry Division during combat operations against an armed enemy on Mt. Battaglia, Italy on 4 October 1944. That afternoon, the enemy launched a violent counterattack preceded by a heavy mortar barrage. Staff Sergeant Mendoza, already wounded in the arm and leg, grabbed a Thompson sub-machinegun and ran to the crest of the hill where he saw approximately 200 enemy troops charging up the slopes employing flame-throwers, machine pistols, rifles, and hand grenades. Staff Sergeant Mendoza immediately began to engage the enemy, firing five clips and killing ten enemy soldiers. After exhausting his ammunition, he picked up a carbine and emptied its magazine at the enemy. By this time, an enemy soldier with a flame-thrower had almost reached the crest, but was quickly eliminated as Staff Sergeant Mendoza drew his pistol and fired. Seeing that the enemy force continued to advance, Staff Sergeant Mendoza jumped into a machinegun emplacement that had just been abandoned and opened fire. Unable to engage the entire enemy force from his location, he picked up the machinegun and moved forward, firing from his hip and spraying a withering hail of bullets into the oncoming enemy, causing them to break into confusion. He then set the machinegun on the ground and continued to fire until the gun jammed. Without hesitating, Staff Sergeant

Mendoza began throwing hand grenades at the enemy, causing them to flee. After the enemy had withdrawn, he advanced down the forward slope of the hill, retrieved numerous enemy weapons scattered about the area, captured a wounded enemy soldier, and returned to consolidate friendly positions with all available men. Staff Sergeant Mendoza's gallant stand resulted in thirty German soldiers killed and the successful defense of the hill. Staff Sergeant Mendoza's extraordinary heroism and selflessness above and beyond the call of duty are in keeping with the highest traditions of military service and reflect great credit upon himself, his unit and the United States Army.

MANUEL MENDOZA was born on June 15, 1922, in Miami, Arizona, to Julio and Guadalupe Verdugo Mendoza as the eldest of eleven children. According to his birth certificate, both his parents were born in Sonora, Mexico; his father worked as a miner and his mother as a housewife.

As a child, Mendoza moved with his family to Phoenix, where he completed only grammar school before dropping out to work on nearly farms and orchards to assist his family. On August 30, 1942, he married Alice Gaona, but the couple was together only a few weeks before Mendoza was drafted into the army on November 21. According to his enlistment papers, he stood 66 inches tall and weighed 130 pounds.

Mendoza began his active duty at Fort MacArthur, California, and upon completion of his training reported to the 88th Infantry Division as an infantryman. The 88th had been formed at Camp Gruber, Oklahoma, in July, 1942 as one of the US Army's first divisions in World War II to be composed of all draftees. The division deployed to North Africa, where the infantrymen trained before going into combat in the Italian Campaign in January 1944.

By the fall of 1944, Mendoza had advanced in rank to staff sergeant in charge of an infantry platoon. On October 4 his unit, while defending Mt. Battaglia, Italy, was hit by a German counterattack preceded by a heavy mortar barrage. Despite wounds from the mortars to an arm and leg, Mendoza grabbed a Thompson submachine gun and raced to the crest of the hill to face about 200 German soldiers advancing with automatic weapons, rifles, flamethrowers, and hand grenades. His withering fire killed thirty of the enemy and sent the remainder into a retreat so disorganized that they left many of their weapons behind as well as a wounded soldier who was taken prisoner.

Mendoza survived the battle and recovered from his wounds. The army awarded him the Distinguished Service Cross while his unit bestowed upon him the nickname "The Arizona Kid." He remained with the 88th Infantry Division in its drive northward through Italy. At war's end he returned to the United States and was honorably discharged as a technical sergeant on November 14, 1945, at Fort MacArthur.

The Hispanic American soldier returned to the Phoenix area and resided in Mesa, where he worked primarily as a self-employed truck driver and joined the Arizona Army National Guard. Full-time employment was hard to find for a poorly educated Mexican American, so on August 6, 1949, Mendoza reenlisted in the Regular Army and reported to Fort Ord, California. He later deployed to Korea and joined Company B, 27th Infantry Regiment, 25th Infantry Division. On October 28, 1951, Mendoza was again wounded, this time in his left hand, in the Battle of Sniper's Ridge near the Korean DMZ.

Following the truce in Korea, Mendoza, now a master sergeant, joined the 31st Infantry Division at Fort Carson, Colorado. He was discharged there on May 7, 1954, and returned to his Mesa home. Mendoza was known as a "jack of all trades" over the next few years as he worked in construction, farming, auto repair, and mining. His work ethic and leadership led to a position as a foreman at the Palo Verde Nuclear Generation Station west of Phoenix. He died on December 12, 2001, and is buried in Mesa's Mountain View Cemetery (Section B, Lot 50).

Mendoza rarely talked about his wartime experiences. His daughter, Sylvia Nandin, later recalled that she was about twelve years of age before she was even aware of her father's valor. Neither did the rest of the country know anything about the Arizona Kid until the DSC review that led to his upgrade to the Medal of Honor. On March 18, 2014, Pres. Barack Obama presented the medal to Mendoza's ninety-year-old widow, Alice, in the East Room of the White House.

Nandin said, "I do regret that my father did not live long enough to receive this award in person. However, I know he would have been exceptionally humbled by this highest of military awards."

Sen. John McCain (R-AZ) said, "I want to specifically recognize the late Master Sergeant Manuel V. Mendoza and his family. The men and women of Arizona are proud to count this American hero as one of their own, and we only wish this recognition came during his lifetime."

Mendoza has been inducted into the Arizona Veterans Hall of Fame. The building that houses the US Post Office in his birthplace of Miami is named in his honor.

KOREA

23

Baldomero Lopez,
US Marine Corps

Company A, 1st Battalion, 5th Marine Regiment, 1st Marine Division
Incheon, Korea, September 15, 1950
Date Presented: August 30, 1951

CITATION:

For conspicuous gallantry and intrepidity at the risk of his life above and beyond the call of duty as a Marine platoon commander of Company A, in action against enemy aggressor forces. With his platoon 1st Lt. Lopez was engaged in the reduction of immediate enemy beach defenses after landing with the assault waves. Exposing himself to hostile fire, he moved forward alongside a bunker and prepared to throw a hand grenade into the next pillbox whose fire was pinning down that sector of the beach. Taken under fire by an enemy automatic weapon and hit in the right shoulder and chest as he lifted his arm to throw, he fell backward and dropped the deadly missile. After a moment, he turned and dragged his body forward in an effort to retrieve the grenade and throw it. In critical condition from pain and loss of blood, and unable to grasp the hand grenade firmly enough to hurl it, he chose to sacrifice himself rather than endanger the lives of his men and, with a sweeping motion of his wounded right arm, cradled the grenade under him and absorbed the full impact of the explosion. His exceptional courage, fortitude, and devotion to duty reflect the highest credit upon 1st Lt. Lopez and the US Naval Service. He gallantly gave his life for his country.

BALDOMERO LOPEZ is the first marine and the first Hispanic American to earn the Medal of Honor in the Korean War. The photograph of him leading his platoon over the seawall at Inchon, minutes before he was killed in a manner that earned him his medal, has become one of the best-known and widely distributed images of the war.

Lopez was born on August 23, 1925, in Tampa, Florida, to a father, also named Baldomero, who had emigrated from the Asturias region of Spain as a young man, and Frances Reina, a Tampa native. He attended Hillsborough High School in Tampa, where he excelled in basketball and participated in the Junior Reserve Officer Training Corps. He maintained grades in the high Bs and low As while also working as a newspaper delivery boy. Considered a "scrawny kid," Lopez worked out during his final two years of school following the popular program of body builder Charles Atlas to be physically fit for military service. On July 8, 1943, shortly after graduating from high school, Lopez enlisted in the US Navy. A year later he was selected to attend the US Naval Academy at Annapolis, Maryland.

At the Naval Academy he entered an accelerated wartime program that produced officers in three rather than four years. With the nickname of "Lobo," Lopez was a popular midshipman. The academy's yearbook, *Lucky Bag*, described him as "one of the biggest hearted, best natured, fellows in the brigade." Commissioned a second lieutenant in the US Marine Corps on June 6, 1947, Lopez attended the basic officers course at Quantico, Virginia, before reporting to China, where he served in Tsingtao and Shanghai as a mortar section commander and a rifle platoon commander.

Back at Camp Pendleton, California, after his China tour, Lopez was promoted to first lieutenant on June 16, 1950, and volunteered to join the 5th Marine Regiment on the Korean Peninsula. His brother Jose later said, "He felt he was a Marine and Marines are trained to fight. He wanted to be a part of it."

The North Koreans had steadily pushed the Allied forces southward after their June 25, 1950, invasion of South Korea into what became known as the Pusan Perimeter in the southeastern part of the country. On September 15, 1950, Gen. Douglas MacArthur ordered an amphibious counterattack into the North Koran rear at Inchon.

Inchon Harbor had extreme high and low tides with a seawall protecting its harbor and defenses. The 5th Marine Regiment landed in the second wave with ladders to scale the seawall. Among the first over the top was 1st Lt. Lopez. He fired his rifle and then prepared to throw a hand grenade. Just as he pulled the grenade's pin, he was hit by automatic rifle fire to his chest and right shoulder, causing him to drop the activated explosive. With only seconds before it detonated in the midst of his platoon, Lopez crawled forward in an attempt to throw the grenade away from his marines. When he realized that his wounds did not leave him the strength to heave the grenade from their midst, Lopez pulled it under his body to shield his men from the blast.

A marine photographer snapped a picture of Lopez in the midst of ladders and followed by tightly grouped infantrymen just as he went over the wall and was struck by the enemy's bullets. The photo became an icon of the Inchon Invasion. Upon hearing the story and seeing the photograph, Jerry Thorp, a Scripps-Howard war correspondent, said that Lopez "died with the courage that makes men great."

Lopez's remains were returned to Florida for burial in Tampa's Centro Asturiano Memorial Park Cemetery (Section 57, Lot 1). On August 30, 1951, Sec. of the Navy Dan A. Kimball presented Lopez's Medal of Honor to his parents and brother Jose in a ceremony at the Pentagon.

Today the honor graduate of each US Marine Officers Basic Course company at Quantico receives the Lopez Award, which includes an engraving of the iconic photo of the young lieutenant going over the seawall at Inchon. Room 3021 in the Naval Academy's Bancroft Hall is dedicated to him and displays his photo and Medal of Honor citation. The US Navy's Military Sealift Command named a container ship (T-AK-3010) in his honor. A swimming pool across from Macfarlane Park in West Tampa, a Florida State Veterans nursing home in Land O'Lakes, and an elementary school in Seffner also carry his name. The Korean War Memorial at the Ed Radice Sports Complex in Tampa is dedicated to Lopez and contains an actual rock from the Inchon seawall.

***

24

Eugene Arnold Obregon,
US Marine Corps

Company G, 3rd Battalion, 5th Marine Regiment, 1st Marine Division

Seoul, Korea, September 26, 1950

Date Presented: August 30, 1951

CITATION:

For conspicuous gallantry and intrepidity at the risk of his life above and beyond the call of duty while serving with Company G, Third Battalion, Fifth Marines, First Marine Division (Reinforced), in action against enemy aggressor forces at Seoul, Korea, September 26, 1950. While serving as an ammunition carrier of a machine gun squad in a Marine Rifle Company which was temporarily pinned down by hostile fire, Private First Class Obregon observed a fellow Marine fall wounded in the line of fire. Armed only with a pistol, he unhesitatingly dashed from his covered position to the side of the casualty. Firing his pistol with one hand as he ran, he grasped his comrade by the arm with his other hand and, despite the great peril to himself, dragged him to the side of the road. Still under enemy fire, he was bandaging the man's wounds when hostile troops of approximately platoon strength began advancing toward his position. Quickly seizing the wounded Marine's carbine he placed his own body as a shield in front of him and lay there firing accurately and effectively into the hostile group until he himself was fatally wounded by enemy machine-gun fire. By his courageous fighting spirit, fortitude and loyal devotion to duty, Private First Class Obregon enabled his fellow Marines to rescue the wounded man and aided essentially in repelling the attack, thereby sustaining the highest traditions of the United States Naval Service. He gallantly gave his life for his country.

EUGENE OBREGON, a Southern California Hispanic, earned his Medal of Honor by saving the lives of his best friend, an Anglo Texan, and many others. Born on November 12, 1930, in Los Angeles, California, to Mexican American parents, Peter and Henrietta Obregon, the future hero attended Hollenbeck Junior High School and Theodore Roosevelt High School before enlisting at age seventeen in the Marine Corps on June 7, 1948. His high school classmates remember him as handsome with wavy hair; they said he "always had a lot of guts."

After completing boot camp at San Diego, Obregon reported to the Marine Corps Supply Depot in Barstow, California, where he served as a fireman. Upon the outbreak of the war on the Korean Peninsula, Obregon transferred to the First Marine Division and sailed westward on July 14, 1950. His unit arrived at Pusan, South Korea, on August 3 and engaged in combat along the Nakdong River a week later. On September 15 the division led the way in the amphibious landing at Inchon and then began fighting their way to Seoul.

Obregon was acting as an ammunition bearer for a machine gun on September 26 as his company fought through the streets of the South Korean capital. When they encountered heavy enemy fire, Obregon's best friend, Pfc. Bert M. Johnson, nineteen, an Anglo from Grand Prairie, Texas, was wounded. The Los Angeles Mexican American ran forward, armed only with a pistol that he fired with one hand while dragging his wounded friend off the road and bandaging his wounds with the other. A North Korean platoon counterattacked. Obregon grabbed Johnson's carbine and returned fire as he shielded his friend with his own body. His accurate fire broke up the enemy attack and saved the lives of his friend and other members of his platoon. He held his ground until he was mortally wounded.

Sec. of the Navy Dan A. Kimball presented Obregon's Medal of Honor to his mother and father at the Pentagon on August 30, 1951—the same ceremony in which Lt. Baldomero Lopez's parents received his award. Cpl. Bert Johnson, who had recovered from his wounds, was also in attendance. Obregon is buried in Calvary Cemetery near downtown Los Angeles, where many of the city's civic and business leaders, as well as Hollywood stars, are interred.

The Eugene A. Obregon Elementary School in Pico Rivera, California, is named in his honor. Parks outside the Marine Corps Logistics Base in Barstow and in Pico Rivera also bear his name as, does a street on Marine Corps Air Station Miramar and a highway interchange in East Los Angeles.

A monument honoring him stands in Pershing Square in downtown Los Angeles. The maritime prepositioning ship T-AK 3006 is named the USNS *PFC Eugene A. Obregon.*

★★★

25

Joseph Charles Rodriguez,
US Army

Company F, 17th Infantry Regiment, 7th Infantry Regiment
Muriye-ri, Korea, May 21, 1951
Date Presented: January 29, 1952

CITATION:
PFC Rodríguez distinguished himself by conspicuous gallantry and intrepidity at the risk of his life above and beyond the call of duty in action against an armed enemy of the United Nations. Rodriguez, an assistant squad leader of the 2d Platoon, was participating in an attack against a fanatical hostile force occupying well-fortified positions on rugged commanding terrain, when his squad's advance was halted within approximately 60 yards by a withering barrage of automatic weapons and small-arms fire from 5 emplacements directly to the front and right and left flanks, together with grenades which the enemy rolled down the hill toward the advancing troops. Fully aware of the odds against him, Sgt. Rodriguez leaped to his feet, dashed 60 yards up the fire-swept slope, and, after lobbing grenades into the first foxhole with deadly accuracy, ran around the left flank, silenced an automatic weapon with 2 grenades and continued his whirlwind assault to the top of the peak, wiping out 2 more foxholes and then, reaching the right flank, he tossed grenades into the remaining emplacement, destroying the gun and annihilating its crew. Sgt. Rodriguez' intrepid actions exacted a toll of 15 enemy dead and, as a result of his incredible display of valor, the defense of the opposition was broken, and the enemy routed, and the strategic strongpoint secured. His unflinching courage under fire and inspirational devotion to duty reflect highest credit on himself and uphold the honored traditions of the military service.

JOSEPH C. RODRIGUEZ fought in Korea, where he earned the Medal of Honor, and later served in the Vietnam War. He rose from the rank of private to sergeant 1st class and then from 2nd lieutenant to colonel in a thirty-year career in the US Army. Born on November 14, 1928, to Mexican American parents in San Bernardino, California, Rodriquez attended local schools before graduating from San Bernardino Valley College in the spring of 1950 with a degree in architecture. He was working with an architectural firm when he was drafted into the army on October 23, 1950. In an oral history interview in 2002, Rodriguez recalled that his father often reminded him of the strength that it took to get through hard times: "He raised me up saying, 'Son, you be a man. You be a man. You don't be afraid to die if it takes it.'"

After his induction at Fort Ord, California, Rodriguez reported for basic training at Fort Carson, Colorado, and was assigned to the 196th Regimental Combat Team. Upon completion of his training in February 1951, Rodriguez volunteered for Korea and sailed from Fort Lawton, Washington, to join the 7th Infantry Division as a replacement in Company F of the 17th Infantry Regiment. Three months later Rodriguez had advanced in rank to private 1st class, serving as an assistant squad leader in the company's second platoon.

On May 21, 1951, Company F was ordered to advance to and occupy high ground thirty miles north of the 38th Parallel near the village of Muriye-ri. The company tried three times to take the hill, only to be beaten back by machine-gun and small-arms fire as well as hand grenades rolled down the incline into the attacking Americans. Rodriquez's squad led the fourth assault. They, too, were stopped by withering fire and more hand grenades.

Rodriquez later recalled, "I felt something had to be done. I didn't even think about it. I just did it."

What Rodriquez did was grab an ammo bag of hand grenades and sprint uphill for sixty yards until he encountered the first enemy machine-gun position. He neutralized it with a hand grenade and then raced to the next machine gun amid bullets all around him and knocked that one out as well. Out of grenades, he turned downhill and ran to join his squad. Instead of seeking shelter, he gathered more grenades and went back up the hill. One after another he destroyed three more North Korean machine-gun nests. Fifteen enemy soldiers lay dead in his wake, and the others were in full retreat as F Company took control of the high ground.

A fellow squad leader in his platoon, Sgt. John J. Phelan Jr., of Tannersville, New York, later said of the battle, "I then noticed that Private First Class

Joseph Rodriguez was making his way up from the rear of the squad, mean-while picking up hand grenades from his squad members. After obtaining the grenades, Rodriquez left all cover and dashed 60 yards up the slope, yelling and throwing grenades with no regard for the murderous fire aimed at him."

Rodriquez survived the battle unscathed and was promoted to sergeant. His life as a combat infantryman, however, became no easier. A week later he was wounded so seriously by small-arms fire that he had to be evacuated to Japan for three months of rehabilitation. Upon recovery, he returned to his unit in the fall of 1951. He was restricted from further combat as he awaited the approval of his Medal of Honor.

On January 29, 1952, Pres. Harry Truman presented the Medal of Honor to Rodriquez in a White House Rose Garden ceremony. The president remarked that Rodriquez's medal citation was "among the most remarkable I have ever read."

Following the presentation, Rodriquez reported to his alma mater, San Bernardino Valley College, as a member of the Reserve Officer Training Corps staff. During this time he and his fiancé and later wife, Rose Aranda of Colton, California, appeared on the popular television quiz show *You Bet Your Life*, hosted by Groucho Marx, on April 24, 1952. Upon hearing Rodriguez say that he charged the hill in Korea because he was mad, Marx said, "You wiped out a whole army because you got mad? Joe, if I said anything tonight that you resent, I was just being facetious. . . . Well, I'm sure glad you're on our side. Rose, take good care of this fella. My advice is, don't ever make him mad—he's liable to wipe out Los Angeles!"

Rodriquez's superiors at Valley College encourage the Mexican American hero to seek a commission, and in 1953 he became a 2nd lieutenant in the army's Corps of Engineers. For the next twenty-eight years he served in a variety of assignments, including back to Korea and a tour in Vietnam during the war in Southeast Asia. However, he spent most of his career using his engineering skills and his Spanish fluency in Latin America with tours in the Panama Canal Zone, Puerto Rico, Bolivia, and Argentina. While on stateside assignments, he continued his education by taking classes at George Washington University, Florida State University, and Louisiana State University.

His final tour before retiring as a full colonel on December 31, 1980, was as the facilities engineer at Fort Bliss, Texas. Joe and Rose remained in El Paso after he retired, and he continued to serve his community as the director of the physical plant at the University of Texas at El Paso for ten years. One of his three children, Charles G. Rodriquez, graduated from the US Military Academy at West Point and rose to the rank of lieutenant general and adjutant general of the Texas National Guard.

Rodriguez died of an apparent heart attack on December 1, 2005. He is buried in Mountain View Cemetery in San Bernardino. A street near the Zaragoza International Bridge between Texas and Mexico at the southeast edge of El Paso is named in his honor.

★★★

26

Rodolfo Perez Hernandez,
US Army

Company G, 2nd Battalion, 187th Regimental Combat Team (Airborne)
Wontong-ni, Korea, May 31, 1951
Date Presented: April 12, 1952

CITATION:

Cpl. Hernandez, a member of Company G, distinguished himself by conspicuous gallantry and intrepidity above and beyond the call of duty in action against the enemy. His platoon, in defensive positions on Hill 420, came under ruthless attack by a numerically superior and fanatical hostile force, accompanied by heavy artillery, mortar, and machinegun fire which inflicted numerous casualties on the platoon. His comrades were forced to withdraw due to lack of ammunition but Cpl. Hernandez, although wounded in an exchange of grenades, continued to deliver deadly fire into the ranks of the onrushing assailants until a ruptured cartridge rendered his rifle inoperative. Immediately leaving his position, Cpl. Hernandez rushed the enemy armed only with rifle and bayonet. Fearlessly engaging the foe, he killed 6 of the enemy before falling unconscious from grenade, bayonet, and bullet wounds, but his heroic action momentarily halted the enemy advance and enabled his unit to counterattack and retake the lost ground. The indomitable fighting spirit, outstanding courage, and tenacious devotion to duty clearly demonstrated by Cpl. Hernandez reflect the highest credit upon himself, the infantry, and the US Army.

DESPITE SERIOUS head wounds, Rodolfo Hernandez charged into an enemy assault with nothing but an inoperative rifle and a fixed bayonet to earn his country's highest combat award. Born to Mexican American farm workers in Colton near Los Angeles on April 14, 1931, as one of eight children, Hernandez moved as a child with his parents to Fowler in the agricultural center of the San Joaquin Valley. His formal education ended after the eighth grade when he joined his parents in the vineyards and orchards as a laborer. "Rudy," as he was known to friends and family, later recalled that he "was small in size, but big in pride."

With his parents' permission, Hernandez volunteered for the army at age seventeen in 1948 because "jobs were hard to find and I wanted to be able to send a little money home." Upon completion of his basic training, he attended paratrooper school before joining the occupation forces in Germany. Shortly after the outbreak of the Korean War, Hernandez transferred to the 187th Regimental Combat Team (Airborne).

In the early-morning hours of May 31, 1951, Hernandez's company was defending the rain-soaked Hill 420 at Wontong-ni near the 38th Parallel when Chinese Communist forces—supported by artillery, mortar, and machine-gun fire—attacked G Company with a vastly superior numerical force. The soldiers held their ground until ordered to withdraw when they were nearly out of ammunition.

Years later, Hernandez said that artillery shrapnel had pierced his helmet and torn off a piece of his skull, exposing his brain. Grenade fragments had peppered most of his body. His rifle had jammed. In the interview with the *Fayetteville Observer* in 1986, Hernandez said, "I was hurt bad and getting dizzy. I knew the doctors could not repair the damage. I thought I might as well end it now."

Hernandez fixed his bayonet on his otherwise useless rifle, threw six grenades from his foxhole at the advancing enemy, and charged forward as he shouted, "Here I come!"

"Every time I took a step, blood rolled down my face. It was hard to see," he said in 1986. Although he suffered additional wounds from gunfire, Hernandez killed one enemy soldier after another with his bayonet before falling unconscious. His assault broke up the enemy advance and allowed his company to counterattack and retake Hill 420, where they found Hernandez surrounded by six dead bodies. Thinking that he, too, was dead, they loaded him into a body bag. Only when medic Ken Oates saw Hernandez move his fingers slightly did they realize he was still alive.

Hernandez was stabilized and evacuated to a hospital in South Korea. In 1976, Helen Ross, the wife of Donald K. Ross, who earned the Medal of Honor during the attack on Pearl Harbor in 1941, recorded Hernandez's experiences for a writer's contest sponsored by the Pacific Northwest Writer's Conference. In the article, Hernandez said, "A month after my last battle I finally drifted up to a semi-conscious state in a hospital in South Korea. I was like a newborn babe, completely helpless. In some ways I was even more dependent on others than a baby is."

Hernandez continued,

> Completely paralyzed on my right side and almost as bad on the left, I could neither talk nor swallow. Nor could I hear too well or think clearly. My bodily functions were beyond my control. And, though I could see, what I saw meant nothing to me. They told me later that I did one thing well. I could smile. In that last battle, a grenade tore away my helmet, a large part of my skull and a portion of my brain. It's tough to lose an arm or leg, but at least you know what you can or can't do about it. You know what is going on. Luckily, doctors can help people with brain damage, and miraculously different parts of the brain can be taught to take over new jobs. When I came to, I was unable to move my arms or legs. Tubes and bottles suspended over my bed should have told me that I was being fed intravenously. But I knew nothing, understood nothing. I didn't know what I wanted or needed. I didn't even realize at first that I was paralyzed. I lay there looking around, drifting in and out. I don't remember much about that hospital or the next one in Japan where I stayed until the middle of July, one-and-a-half months after the action. Finally I was sent to Letterman Hospital in San Francisco. There surgeons labored endlessly to repair damage to my skull, face, arm, leg and other parts of my mangled body. Surgeons must have dulled dozens of needles and scissors sewing and snipping threads for the tiny stitches inside and outside of my body which was pretty muscular. Damage to my brain was another thing. Most of my motor techniques had been interrupted. I had lost the simple abilities to move or talk. One of my ears had been damaged but I was lucky there. Hearing came back and I haven't had to wear a hearing aid. A few months after I learned to walk, I was told to get ready for a trip to Washington, DC. I still couldn't talk but my brother went with me and that helped. I felt pretty good in a smart

looking uniform. We went to the White House where President Truman decorated me with the Medal of Honor (April 12, 1952). After five long years of surgeons, doctors, nurses, therapists of many sorts and qualifications, there came another period of eight years of work and struggles to attain almost complete control of my body. I still don't have complete mastery of my right arm, but I've learned to write with my left and do most everything with one hand. I can use my right arm for a little leverage, but the hand is not much use. But, that's a small thing.

Volunteers in Fresno, California, built Hernandez a home near the veterans hospital where he continued to receive treatment. He never regained complete use of his right arm and spoke with difficulty, but once he was physically and mentally able, Hernandez studied business administration at Fresno City College for three years and then worked for the Veterans Administration in Los Angeles for seventeen years, counseling other wounded soldiers before retiring in Fayetteville, North Carolina, in 1979. At a Veterans Day parade in Morehead City, North Carolina, in 2007, he reunited with Keith Oates, the medic who had determined the wounded Hernandez to be still alive on the Korean battlefield so long ago.

Hernandez died of cancer and other ailments on December 21, 2013, at the Womack Army Medical Center at Fort Bragg, North Carolina. He is buried in Sandhills State Veterans Cemetery in Spring Lake, North Carolina (Section 4D, Plot 200).

A brass plaque in downtown Fort Myers, Florida, honors Hernandez's bravery. In 2013 Fort Bragg's Warrior Transition Battalion Complex was named in his honor. An exhibit in the Airborne and Special Operations Museum in Fayetteville depicts Hernandez's one-man bayonet charge.

★★★

27

Edward Gomez,
US Marine Corps

Company E, 2nd Battalion, 1st Marine Regiment, 1st Marine Division
Hill 749, Korea, September 14, 1951
Date Presented: July 6, 1952

CITATION:

For conspicuous gallantry and intrepidity at the risk of his life above and beyond the call of duty while serving as an ammunition bearer in Company E, Second Battalion, First Marines, First Marine Division (Reinforced), in action against enemy aggressor forces in Korea on September 14, 1951. Boldly advancing with his squad in support of a group of riflemen assaulting a series of strongly fortified and bitterly defended hostile positions on Hill 749, Private First Class Gómez consistently exposed himself to the withering barrage to keep his machine gun supplied with ammunition during the drive forward to seize the objective. As his squad deployed to meet an imminent counterattack, he voluntarily moved down an abandoned trench to search for a new location for the gun and, when a hostile grenade landed between himself and his weapon, shouted a warning to those around him as he grasped the activated charge in his hand. Determined to save his comrades, he unhesitatingly chose to sacrifice himself and, diving into the ditch with the deadly missile, absorbed the shattering violence of the explosion in his own body. By his stouthearted courage, incomparable valor and decisive spirit of self-sacrifice, Private First Class Gómez inspired the others to heroic efforts in subsequently repelling the outnumbering foe, and his valiant conduct throughout sustained and enhanced the finest traditions of the United States Naval Service. He gallantly gave his life for his country.

PFC. EDWARD GOMEZ willingly sacrificed his own life to save those of his fellow marines. Born on August 10, 1932, in Omaha, Nebraska, to Mexican American parents, Modesto and Matiana Gomez, as one of twelve children, the future hero attended the local high school. His brother Modesto described his sibling, nicknamed "Babe," as a "go-getter, an extrovert, and happy-go-lucky." Although only five feet one, Babe like to fight and participated in Golden Gloves matches.

Gomez occasionally had trouble with the local police and ended up spending a year in the state reform school at Kearney. He decided to turn his life around upon his release and, although only seventeen years old, convinced his father to allow him to join the Marine Corps on August 11, 1949. After basic training at San Diego, California, Gomez received additional training at Camp Pendleton, California. In 1951 he sailed to Korea as a replacement in the 1st Marine Division.

On September 14, 1951, Gomez was acting as an ammunition bearer for a machine gun in his company's assault against North Korean positions on Hill 749. After exposing himself several times to deliver ammo to his machine-gun crew, an enemy hand grenade landed near Gomez's team. Without hesitation, he grabbed the grenade and covered it with his body as he dove into a ditch. He died instantly, but the rest of his team was unharmed.

Gomez's remains were returned home, and he is buried in St. Mary's Cemetery in South Omaha. His grave is located 100 yards east of the main entrance. On July 6, 1952, Brig. Gen. Verne J. McCaul of the Glenview, Illinois, Naval Air Station presented the Medal of Honor to his parents at Omaha's Church of Our Lady of Guadalupe as the representative of the president.

As a boy, Babe Gomez and his family spoke Spanish in their rented home. He used to tell his mother that someday he would buy her her own house. His father, who continued to work at a meat packing plant, later proudly stated that his son had kept his word in that his military insurance had paid part of the cost of their new home.

When delivered to his parents, Gomez's personal effects contained a letter written shortly before the attack in which he died. "I am writing this on the possibility that I may die in this next assault," he wrote. "You will hear about it before getting this letter and I hope you don't take it too hard. I am not sorry I died because I died fighting for my country and that's the number one thing in everyone's life, to keep his home and country from being won over by such things as communism. I am very proud."

He concluded his letter with a request for his parents remember him to his siblings, "Remind the kids of me once in a while."

A school and street in Omaha are named in Gomez's honor. The South Omaha Boys Club contains the Edward Gomez Room, which displays Gomez's picture and citation along with a plaque. A mural of the Mexican American hero hangs in the Nebraska State Capitol in Lincoln, and his Medal of Honor is displayed in Omaha's Durham Museum.

★★★

28

Fernando Luis Garcia,
US Marine Corps

Company I, 3rd Battalion, 5th Marine Regiment, 1st Marine Division
Bunker Hill, Korea, September 5, 1952
Date Presented: October 25, 1953

CITATION:

Conspicuous gallantry and intrepidity at the risk of his life above and beyond the call of duty while serving as a member of Company I, Third Battalion, Fifth Marines, First Marine Division (Reinforced), in action against enemy aggressor forces in Korea on September 5, 1952. While participating in the defense of a combat outpost located more than one mile forward of the main line of resistance during a savage night attack by a fanatical enemy force employing grenades, mortars and artillery, Private First Class Garcia, although suffering painful wounds, moved through the intense hall of hostile fire to a supply point to secure more hand grenades. Quick to act when a hostile grenade landed nearby, endangering the life of another Marine, as well as his own, he unhesitatingly chose to sacrifice himself and immediately threw his body upon the deadly missile, receiving the full impact of the explosion. His great personal valor and cool decision in the face of almost certain death sustain and enhance the finest traditions of the United States Naval Service gave his life for his country.

PFC. FERNANDO GARCIA is the first native-born Puerto Rican to receive the Medal of Honor. Born on October 14, 1929, in Utuado, Puerto Rico, to Mr. and Mrs. German Garcia, he attended elementary and high school there. After graduating, he went to work as a file clerk with the Texas Company (later

Texaco) before entering the Marine Corps on September 19, 1951. Garcia completed boot training at Parris Island, South Carolina, in December and earned a promotion to private 1st class. After additional infantry training at Camp Pendleton, California, he sailed for Korea in March 1952 as a replacement in the 1st Marine Division.

On September 5, Garcia's company was defending Outpost Bruce about two kilometers forward of the main lines in the Bunker Hill area near Sejong in west-central Korea when it came under attack by a large force of Chinese Communists. The predawn battle continued for more than an hour. Garcia, although wounded, volunteered to go for additional ammunition from his platoon sergeant, S. Sgt. Floyd V. Wiley. Just as Garcia reached Wiley's position, a hand grenade landed between them. The Puerto Rican soldier shouted, "I'll get it," as he threw his body on the grenade just before it exploded.

The explosion knocked Wiley unconscious. When he came to, he found Garcia, but the Chinese were threatening the small American outpost. A short time later, Communists overran the marine position, forcing the survivors to withdraw without their dead. Garcia's body was never recovered.

On October 25, 1953, Garcia's parents were presented his medal in a ceremony in the Utuado City Hall. A memorial marker is in the Puerto Rico National Cemetery (Section MB-3) in Bayamon, Puerto Rico. His name is also on the wall of the Honolulu Memorial in the National Memorial Cemetery of the Pacific in Honolulu, Hawaii, a site that honors those missing in World War II, Korea, and Vietnam.

On February 5, 1959, the Marine Corps renamed its installation in Vieques, Puerto Rico, Camp Garcia. The camp closed in 2003. The US Navy commissioned the USS *Garcia* (DE-1040) on 1 December 21, 1964, as the first of the Garcia-class frigates. The DE-1040 was decommissioned on January 31, 1989, and transferred to Pakistan the same day. The ship was returned to the United States on January 13, 1994, and sold for scrap on March 29, 1994. American Legion Post 42 in Utuado is named in his honor, as is a low-income housing project in the same town. On November 11, 2008, the Puerto Rican government unveiled a portrait of Garcia in the Capitol Rotunda.

★★★

29

Benito Martinez,
US Army

Company A, 27th Infantry Regiment, 25th Infantry Division
Satae-ri, Korea, September 6, 1952
Date Presented: December 16, 1953

CITATION:

Cpl. Martinez, a machine gunner with Company A, distinguished himself by conspicuous gallantry and outstanding courage above and beyond the call of duty in action against the enemy. While manning a listening post forward of the main line of resistance, his position was attacked by a hostile force of reinforced company strength. In the bitter fighting which ensued, the enemy infiltrated the defense perimeter and, realizing that encirclement was imminent, Cpl. Martinez elected to remain at his post in an attempt to stem the onslaught. In a daring defense, he raked the attacking troops with crippling fire, inflicting numerous casualties. Although contacted by sound power phone several times, he insisted that no attempt be made to rescue him because of the danger involved. Soon thereafter, the hostile forces rushed the emplacement, forcing him to make a limited withdrawal with only an automatic rifle and pistol to defend himself. After a courageous 6-hour stand and shortly before dawn, he called in for the last time, stating that the enemy was converging on his position His magnificent stand enabled friendly elements to reorganize, attack, and regain the key terrain. Cpl. Martinez' incredible valor and supreme sacrifice reflect lasting glory upon himself and are in keeping with the honored traditions of the military service.

BENITO MARTINEZ was born to Mexican American parents, Francisco and Francisca Martinez, in Fort Hancock, Texas, on April 21, 1932. He attended elementary and high school in Fort Hancock before enlisting in the US Army on August 16, 1951. His enlistment documents state that his civilian trade or occupation was "student." Upon completion of his infantry training, Martinez joined the 25th Infantry Division in Korea as a replacement.

On September 5, 1952, Martinez and his company occupied a defensive position known as the Sandbag Castle near Satae-ri. Martinez and three other soldiers were assigned to Outpost Agnes—a forward early-warning listening post. Shortly after midnight the Chinese and North Koreans opened an artillery barrage on the Sandbag Castle. In the midst of the shelling, the Americans spotted enemy soldiers advancing to cut off the forward bunkers, including Outpost Agnes. Martinez ordered his three fellow soldiers to withdraw to the Sandbag Castle and stayed behind to meet the enemy attack. When his commander called him on a land line and told him to also abandon the listening post, Martinez replied that he thought he could delay the attack by continuing to man his machine gun.

Over the next six hours, Martinez, first with his machine gun and then with a Browning Automatic Rifle and a .45-caliber pistol, did stop the enemy. When his company was finally able to counterattack at dawn, they found Martinez dead and the hillside covered with enemy soldiers.

Martinez's remains were returned to Fort Hancock, where he was buried in the town ceremony with little fanfare. His veterans headstone, because his Medal of Honor had not yet been awarded, reflected only that he had received a Purple Heart. On December 16, 1953, the medal was presented to Martinez's mother in Washington, DC, by Sec. of the Army Robert T. Stevens. Nearly thirty-five years later, on July 3, 1987, Martinez's remains were moved to Fort Bliss National Cemetery in El Paso, where he received the ceremony and honors due to such a brave soldier. Brig. Gen. Donald Lionetti, the deputy commanding officer of Fort Bliss, said, "We are proud today, at long last to lay to final rest a true hero of the Southwest, a genuine hero of Mexican Americans everywhere."

This time Martinez got his Medal of Honor headstone. He is buried in Section B, Site 366A. The elementary school Martinez attended in Fort Stockton is named in his honor, and so is a similar institution in El Paso.

★★★

30

Ambrosio Guillen,
US Marine Corps

Company F, 2nd Battalion, 7th Marine Regiment, 1st Marine Division

Songuch-on, Korea, July 25, 1953

Date Presented: August 18, 1954

CITATION:

For conspicuous gallantry and intrepidity at the risk of his life above and beyond the call of duty while serving as a platoon sergeant of Company F, Second Battalion, Seventh Marines, First Marine Division (Reinforced), in action against enemy aggressor forces in Korea on July 25, 1953. Participating in the defense of an outpost forward of the main line of resistance, Staff Sergeant Guillen maneuvered his platoon over unfamiliar terrain in the face of hostile fire and placed his men in fighting positions. With his unit pinned down when the outpost was attacked under cover of darkness by an estimated force of two enemy battalions supported by mortar and artillery fire, he deliberately exposed himself to the heavy barrage and attacks to direct his men in defending their positions and personally supervise the treatment and evacuation of the wounded. Inspired by his leadership, the platoon quickly rallied and engaged the enemy force in fierce hand-to-hand combat. Although critically wounded during the course of the battle, Staff Sergeant Guillen refused medical aid and continued to direct his men throughout the remainder of the engagement until the enemy was defeated and thrown into disorderly retreat. Succumbing to his wounds within a few hours, Staff Sergeant Guillen, by his outstanding courage and indomitable fighting spirit, was directly responsible for the success of his platoon in repelling a numerically superior enemy force. His personal valor reflects the highest credit upon himself and enhances the finest traditions of the United States Naval Service. He gallantly gave his life for his country.

S. SGT. AMBROSIO GUILLEN received his Medal of Honor for actions taken only two days before the cease-fire that ended hostilities in the Korean War. He did this by leading his platoon in turning back an attack by a far numerically superior enemy force. Born on December 7, 1929, in La Junta, Colorado, to Mr. and Mrs. Pedro H. Guillen, he grew up in El Paso, Texas, where he went to school. His father claimed to have ridden as an aide-de-camp with Pancho Villa in the Mexican Revolution (1910–1920); his mother was a Mescalero Apache.

Guillen joined the Marine Corp at age eighteen and, after basic training at San Diego, served in the 6th Marine Regiment and at Naval Air Station Moffett Field, California. After additional training, he served a tour aboard the seaplane tender USS *Curtis*. Upon completion of his sea time, the Marine Corps selected him to be a drill instructor in the 2nd Training Battalion at the San Diego Recruit Depot. Guillen trained two groups of marines who earned Honor Platoon status. His commanding officer, Maj. Gen. John T. Walker, wrote in a Letter of Appreciation, "Your success in training these two platoons had demonstrated your outstanding ability as a leader."

The young marine soon proved that he was an outstanding leader on the battlefield as well as in training recruits. As a platoon sergeant, the now Staff Sergeant Guillen and his marines were in charge of the defense of a forward outpost near what would become the Demilitarized Zone (DMZ) near Songuch-on, Korea. In the early-morning hours of July 23, 1953, an estimated two enemy battalions, supported by mortar and artillery fire, attacked the outpost. With cease-fire negotiations nearing their fruition, the North Koreans and their Chinese allies wanted to occupy as much territory as possible before fighting ended.

From the beginning of the battle, Guillen continually exposed himself to the enemy ground and artillery fire as he organized the defense and directed the treatment and evacuation of the wounded. Guillen suffered severe wounds near the end of the battle, but he refused medical aid as he continued to lead and inspire his platoon. Finally, the bloodied enemy began an unorganized and disorderly retreat. Guillen's marines had held their ground. Unfortunately, Guillen died of his wounds a few hours later. Two days later the cease-fire ended the hostilities.

Guillen's body was escorted back home by his brother, Pfc. Ramon B. Guillen, who was serving in the theater with the army. He was buried in Fort Bliss National Cemetery (Section E, Grave 9171) in El Paso on October 20, 1953. On August 18, 1954, Sec. of the Navy Charles S. Thomas awarded Guillen's Medal of Honor to his parents in his Pentagon office.

Guillen Middle School and the Ambrosio Guillen Texas State Veterans Home in El Paso are named in his honor. A painting of the marine hero hangs in the lobby of the El Paso International Airport.

31

Joe Rodriquez Baldonado,
US Army

Company B, 1st Battalion, 187th Airborne Infantry Combat Team
Kangdong, Korea, November 25, 1950
Date Presented: March 18, 2014

CITATION:

Corporal Joe R. Baldonado distinguished himself by acts of gallantry and in-trepidity above and beyond the call of duty while serving as an acting machine gunner in 3d Squad, 2d Platoon, Company B, 187th Airborne Infantry Regiment during combat operations against an armed enemy in Kangdong, Korea on No-vember 25, 1950. On that morning, the enemy launched a strong attack in an effort to seize the hill occupied by Corporal Baldonado and his company. The platoon had expended most of its ammunition in repelling the enemy attack and the pla-toon leader decided to commit his 3d Squad, with its supply of ammunition, in the defensive action. Since there was no time to dig in because of the proximity of the enemy, who had advanced to within twenty-five yards of the platoon position, Corporal Baldonado emplaced his weapon in an exposed position and delivered a withering stream of fire on the advancing enemy, causing them to fall back in disorder. The enemy then concentrated all their fire on Corporal Baldonado's gun and attempted to knock it out by rushing the position in small groups and hurl-ing hand grenades. Several times, grenades exploded extremely close to Corporal Baldonado but failed to interrupt his continuous firing. The hostile troops made repeated attempts to storm his position and were driven back each time with ap-palling casualties. The enemy finally withdrew after making a final assault on Cor-poral Baldonado's position during which a grenade landed near his gun, killing him instantly. Corporal Baldonado's extraordinary heroism and selflessness at the cost of his own life, above and beyond the call of duty, are in keeping with the highest traditions of military service and reflect great credit upon himself, his unit and the United States Army.

CPL. JOE BALDONADO sacrificed his life in breaking up repeated enemy attacks and saving the lives of his platoon, though his actions went mostly unrecognized until he was finally awarded the Medal of Honor sixty-four years after his valor on a remote hill in Korea. Baldonado was born on August 28, 1930, in the Denver, Colorado, suburb of Aurora, to Ramon M. and Rebecca Rodriquez Baldonado. His Mexican American family of migrant workers moved in 1943 to Los Angeles and then a year later farther north to Gilroy, California, where the Baldonados worked in the garlic fields and fruit orchards. Baldonado dropped out before high school to join the workforce to help his parents.

In a 2017 interview, Baldonado's younger brother Charles said, "Joe was caring—a good guy and a good worker. He was only five foot four, but I looked up to him. He appeared much larger. When he joined the army, he told my mother that he was going into the army to get some money so he could buy my mother a house."

Baldonado volunteered for the army in 1948 at age seventeen and was inducted at Santa Clara, California. After basic and infantry training at Fort Lewis, Washington, Baldonado reported to the 511th Airborne Infantry Regiment in Japan, where he completed parachute training, adding the silver jump wings to his uniform. The 511th ended their occupation duty in March 1949 and traveled by ship through the Panama Canal to New Orleans and then on to their new station at Fort Campbell, Kentucky. In early 1950, Baldonado participated in Operation Swarmer, the largest airborne exercise in army history to that time.

On August 1, 1950, the 187th Airborne Regiment, also stationed at Fort Campbell, was alerted for deployment to Korea. Soldiers, including Baldonado, were transferred from the 511th to the 187th to bring it to full strength. The 187th debarked from San Francisco on September 6–7, 1950, and arrived at the Inchon beachhead on September 22, 1950. They went immediately into combat and less than a month later made a combat parachute assault into an area near Sukchon and Sunchon, North Korea, on October 20 with the objectives of capturing fleeing government officials and liberating POWs. The combat jump allowed Baldonado to add a gold star to his jump wings.

On November 25, 1950, Baldonado was a machine gunner in his platoon tasked with the responsibility of defending Hill 171 near Kangdong. When the Chinese Communists attacked, Baldonado took up an exposed position to pour fire into the advancing ranks, breaking up their attacks for more than three hours. The enemy concentrated their fire on his position, allowing many of his fellow soldiers to make a safe withdrawal. Finally, an enemy hand grenade ended the Mexican American's life as the enemy overran the platoon's position.

When the Americans retook Hill 171, they could not find Baldonado's body, and he is still designated Missing in Action today. His family was awarded the Distinguished Service Cross, and his military insurance did help his mother buy a home. A brief mention of Baldonado's heroism is made in Roy E. Appleman's *Disaster in Korea: The Chinese Confront MacArthur* (Texas A&M University Press, 1989), but other than his name on the Honolulu Memorial in the National Memorial Cemetery of the Pacific in Hawaii—along with more than 28,000 MIAs from World War II, Korea, and Vietnam in the Courts of the Missing—he went unrecognized until the 2014 review upgraded his DSC to the Medal of Honor. His brother Charles accepted the award from Pres. Barack Obama on March 18, 2014, in a White House ceremony.

Both Denver and Gilroy rushed to claim Baldonado as their native son upon the announcement of his Medal of Honor. Colorado newspapers and television stations called Baldonado a "forgotten hero." In an interview with Denver's KUSA television station, University of Colorado Denver history professor Dr. Tom Noel said, "It's a typical story of a lot of Hispanics who gave their lives, who got lost in the war and aren't remembered often. Heaven knows how many forgotten Joe Baldonados there are."

Sen. Mark Udall (D-CO) said in a news release, "In giving his life to defend his country and protect his brothers in arms, Corporal Baldonado proved himself to be true hero. He gave his life so that others might live, and today we honor him and his family for his selfless service to our country."

★★★

32

Victor Hugo Espinoza,
US Army

Company A, 1st Battalion, 23rd Infantry Regiment, 2nd Infantry Division
Chorwon, Korea, August 1, 1952
Date Presented: May 18, 2014

CITATION:

Corporal Victor H. Espinoza distinguished himself by acts of gallantry and intrepidity above and beyond the call of duty while serving as an Acting Rifleman in Company A, 23d Infantry Regiment, 2d Infantry Division during combat operations against an armed enemy in Chorwon, Korea on August 1, 1952. On that day, Corporal Espinoza and his unit were responsible for securing and holding a vital enemy hill. As the friendly unit neared its objective, it was subjected to a devastating volume of enemy fire, slowing its progress. Corporal Espinoza, unhesitatingly and being fully aware of the hazards involved, left his place of comparative safety and made a deliberate one man assault on the enemy with his rifle and grenades, destroying a machinegun and killing its crew. Corporal Espinoza continued across the fire-swept terrain to an exposed vantage point where he attacked an enemy mortar position and two bunkers with grenades and rifle fire, knocking out the enemy mortar position and destroying both bunkers and killing their occupants. Upon reaching the crest, and after running out of rifle ammunition, he called for more grenades. A comrade who was behind him threw some Chinese grenades to him. Immediately upon catching them, he pulled the pins and hurled them into the occupied trenches, killing and wounding more of the enemy with their own weapons. Continuing on through a tunnel, Corporal Espinoza made a daring charge, inflicting at least seven more casualties upon the enemy who were fast retreating into the tunnel. Corporal Espinoza was quickly in pursuit, but the hostile fire from the opening prevented him from overtaking the retreating enemy. As a result, Corporal Espinoza destroyed the tunnel with TNT, called for more grenades from his company, and hurled them at the enemy troops until they were out of reach. Corporal Espinoza's incredible display of valor secured the vital strong point and took a heavy toll on the enemy, resulting in at least fourteen dead and eleven wounded. Corporal Espinoza's extraordinary heroism and selflessness above and beyond the call of duty are in keeping with the highest traditions of military service and reflect great credit upon himself, his unit and the United States Army.

CPL. VICTOR HUGO ESPINOZA earned his Medal of Honor in Korea by leading the way to capture Hill 266, known as "Old Baldy" because it had been denuded of vegetation by artillery and air strikes. Espinoza was born in El Paso, Texas, on July 25, 1928, to Amado and Altagracia Chavez Espinoza. His birth certificate states that both his parents were born in Mexico and that his father's occupation was laborer and his mother a housewife. Although he entered the army as Victor Hugo, Espinoza's birth certificate recorded his name as Ugo Espinoza. It was not until January 22, 1982, that Espinoza's aunt, Andrea G. Veloz, filed an amendment to the birth certificate to officially change the name.

Espinoza spent the first decade of his life in El Paso with his parents until the death of his mother in 1938. He then lived with his godmother and in foster care before moving to California, where he graduated from Lincoln High School in Los Angeles. He briefly worked for the City of Los Angeles before entering the army in November 1950.

In July 1952, Espinoza, now a corporal in the 2nd Infantry Division, joined his company in an assault to secure Hill 266 just north of the 38th Parallel near Chorwon. Old Baldy, one of eleven prominent features along the Allied lines, dominated the terrain in three directions and served as a crucial point for the American defense. Espinoza's company came under withering fire from small arms, machine guns, and mortars as they advanced up the hill. The enemy fire was so intense that it stopped the company's advance. Espinosa grabbed his rifle and grenades and crossed open ground to destroy a machine-gun crew, a mortar position, and two enemy bunkers. When he ran out of grenades, he went back for more and continued his attack. After he had expended those, he used Chinese grenades discarded by the retreating enemy to do even more damage. Then he found a tunnel connecting the Chinese defenses, which he destroyed as well. By the time Espinosa's company secured Old Baldy, he had killed fourteen enemy soldiers and wounded another eleven.

In an article in *Stars and Stripes* on August 31, 1952, Espinosa said, "We went from bunker to bunker. We knocked out mortars, machineguns, burp guns and everything they had."

Espinoza returned to El Paso after the war and was awarded the Distinguished Service Cross in a ceremony on Noel Field at Fort Bliss on April 29, 1953. He remained in the army and advanced to the rank of master sergeant before his discharge. He returned again to El Paso, where he worked for a while at the Dick Poe Toyota dealership cleaning and buffing automobiles. He then moved to San Gabriel, Texas. He returned to El Paso shortly before his death on April 17, 1986. He is buried in Fort Bliss National Cemetery (Section F, Site 1115).

In a June 2017 interview, Sonny Espinoza, Victor's nephew, said his uncle was a feisty, happy-go-lucky guy at five feet seven. Sonny remembers family baseball games with Victor and his three brothers, who were also veterans. "All four did what they had to do for their God and country," said Sonny.

Upon the completion of the Department of Defense review in 2014, Espinosa's DSC was upgraded to the Medal of Honor. The medal was presented to several members of his family, including his son, Tyronne, by Pres. Barack Obama in a White House ceremony on March 18, 2014.

On May 31, 2017, a gate at the new William Beaumont Medical Center at Fort Bliss was named in his honor.

★★★

33

Eduardo Corral Gomez,
US Army

Company I, 8th Cavalry Regiment, 1st Cavalry Division
Tabu-dong, Korea, September 3, 1950
Date Presented: March 18, 2014

CITATION:

*Sergeant Eduardo C. Gomez distinguished himself by acts of gallantry and intre-
pidity above and beyond the call of duty while serving with Company I, 8th Cavalry Regiment, 1st Cavalry Division during combat operations against an armed
enemy in Tabu-dong, Korea on September 3, 1950. That afternoon, while conducting combat patrol, Sergeant Gomez's company was ruthlessly attacked by a hostile
force which moved within seventy-five yards of the command post before it was
immobilized by rocket fire. However, an enemy tank and multiple enemy machineguns continued to rake the company perimeter with devastating fire. Realizing the
tank posed a serious threat to the entire perimeter, Sergeant Gomez voluntarily
crawled thirty yards across an open rice field vulnerable to enemy observation and
fire, boarded the tank, pried open one of the hatches on the turret and dropped
an activated grenade into the hull, killing the crew. Wounded in the left side while
returning to his position, Sergeant Gomez refused evacuation. Observing that
the tripod of a .30 caliber machinegun was rendered inoperable by enemy fire, he
cradled the weapon in his arms, returned to the forward defensive positions, and
swept the assaulting force with withering fire. Although his weapon overheated
and burned his hands and his painful wound still bled, Sergeant Gomez maintained his stand and, upon orders to withdraw in the face of overwhelming enemy
superiority, remained to provide protective fire. Sergeant Gomez continued to pour*

*accurate fire into the enemy ranks, exacting a heavy toll in casualties and retard-
ing their advance. Sergeant Gomez would not consent to leave his post for medical
attention until the company established new defensive positions. Sergeant Gomez's
extraordinary heroism and selflessness above and beyond the call of duty are in
keeping with the highest traditions of military service and reflect great credit upon
himself, his unit and the United States Army.*

EDUARDO CORRAL (Corrall in some documents) Gomez single-handedly
destroyed an enemy tank and then provided protective fire for his company's
withdrawal despite serious wounds in one of the earliest major battles of the
Korean War. He did not receive his Medal of Honor until 2014—nearly four
decades after his death. Gomez's remains lie today in an unmarked grave in
Mexico.

Born on October 28, 1919, in Los Angeles, California, Gomez spent most of
his early years living in Mexico with his parents. Gomez served in the army
during World War II and participated in the D-Day invasion of Normandy. He
also served in the occupation of Germany before his discharge. He reentered
the army on February 9, 1949, and by September 3, 1950, he had advanced in
rank to sergeant in the 1st Cavalry Division.

He was positioning his machine gun in a defensive position near Tabu-
dong, Korea, when a North Korean regiment, supported by tanks, attacked.
When one of the tanks threatened to break into the American perimeter,
Gomez ran through the incoming fire, climbed atop the enemy Russian-made
T-34 tank, opened the hatch, and threw in a hand grenade. The explosion
destroyed the tank crew and wounded the Mexican American with shrapnel.

Gomez ignored his wounds, refused medical treatment, and returned to his
machine gun to delay the enemy attack until his company had fully formed its
defenses. He fired so many rounds that the weapon overheated, burning his
hands. Yet he fought on. The awards system often works slowly in wartime,
and Gomez did not receive the Distinguished Service Cross until November
27, 1951, for his bravery. He remained in the service after the war and retired
as a master sergeant after more than twenty years of service. Gomez died on
January 29, 1972, in Cuajimalpa, Mexico, and is buried in the city's cemetery
(Plot 12, Row 21, Grave 43). The grave is not marked. However, as of the spring
of 2021, the Gomez's family and the Congressional Medal of Honor Society
are working with cemetery officials to erect a headstone.

Pres. Barack Obama awarded Gomez's Medal of Honor to his nephew, Pete Corrall (correct spelling) of Meiners Oaks, California, in 2014 after the review of minority DSCs. Other family members were also in attendance. In an interview with *Stars and Stripes* on March 17, 2014, Corrall recalled that his uncle, known as "Lalo" to his relatives and friends, was "a generous, good uncle; a loving man."

Rep. Julia Brownley (D-CA) said in a March 18, 2014, press release, "I'm constantly reminded of the sacrifices our service men and women, and their families, make for our country every day. I am so pleased that the President recognized and paid tribute to Sgt. Gomez for his bravery in Korea and his heroism in battle."

The California Department of Veterans Affairs held a recognition ceremony for Gomez and other Medal of Honor recipients on the west steps of the state capitol in Sacramento on May 27, 2014. Peter J. Gravett, the department's secretary, observed that these medals had been "a long time coming" and added, "I am most pleased that such a regrettable oversight is finally being addressed. These men fought for our country and their fellow soldiers with bravery, commitment, and patriotism and now their descendants can receive comfort in knowing they descend from authentic American heroes."

34

Juan Enrique Negron,
US Army

Company L, 1st Battalion, 65th Infantry Regiment, 3rd Infantry Division
Kalma-Eri, Korea, April 28, 1951
Date Presented: March 18, 2014

CITATION:

Sergeant Negron distinguished himself by extraordinary heroism in action against enemy aggressor forces in the vicinity of Kalma-Eri, Korea, on 28 April 1951. On that date, Sergeant Negron took up the most vulnerable position on his company's exposed right flank after an enemy force had overrun a section of the line. When notified that elements of the company were withdrawing, Sergeant Negron refused to leave his exposed position, but delivered withering fire at hostile troops who had broken through a road block. When the hostile troops approached his position, Sergeant Negron accurately hurled hand grenades at short range, halting their attack. Sergeant Negron held the position throughout the night, while an allied counter attack was organized and launched. After the enemy had been repulsed, fifteen enemy dead were found only a few feet from Sergeant Negron's position. The extraordinary heroism exhibited by Sergeant Negron on this occasion reflects great credit on himself and is in keeping with the finest traditions of the military service.

JUAN NEGRON earned his Medal of Honor fighting with the segregated 65th Infantry Regiment, composed mostly of Puerto Ricans. Negron, called "Kike" by his family and friends, was born on September 26, 1929, in Corozal, Puerto Rico, and graduated from Corozal High School in 1947 before enlisting in the army on April 27, 1948. His enlistment papers and other official army documents, including his Medal of Honor citation, list his name as Juan E. Negron. Negron is from his father; however in Spanish naming customs he is also recorded, including on his headstone, as Negron-Martinez to recognize his mother's lineage.

Negron joined the army at San Juan and completed his basic training at Camp Santiago before reporting to the 65th Infantry Regiment, nicknamed the "Borinqueneers" in recognition of the island's original inhabitants, the Taino Indians and Buccaneers. The 65th was the only Hispanic-segregated unit is the history of the US Army. At the outbreak of the Korean War, the regiment was attached to the 3rd Infantry Division and deployed to the combat zone where it was one of the first American units to meet the North Koreans on the battlefield.

Gen. Douglas MacArthur, commander in chief of the United Nations Command in Korea, said, "The Puerto Ricans forming the ranks of the gallant 65th Infantry give daily proof on the battlefields of Korea of their courage, determination, and resolute will to victory, their invincible loyalty to the United States and their fervent devotion to those immutable principles of human relations which the Americans of the Continent and of Puerto Rico have in common. They are writing a brilliant record of heroism in battle and I am proud to have them under my command. I wish we could count on many more like them."

On April 28, 1951, Negron's unit was attacked by a large enemy force near Kalma-Eri, Korea. With part of their line penetrated and in danger of being overrun, Negron took up a position to place accurate rifle fire on the advancing soldiers. When they got nearer, he broke up their formation with hand grenades. Negron enabled his company to safely withdraw and then continued to hold his ground through the night while his fellow soldiers prepared to counterattack. When the company retook their old position, they found fifteen dead in front of the surviving Puerto Rican hero. He was awarded the Distinguished Service Cross.

Negron remained on active duty after the war and during his twenty-three-year army career advanced in rank to sergeant major. He served in Vietnam with the 34th Engineer Battalion, in the army's Doctrine Command in the United States, and in the army's inspector general office in Thailand. After his retirement on March 31, 1971, he attended the University of Puerto Rico and graduated magna cum laude on December 17, 1974, with a bachelor of arts degree. He then became active in the island's education system and government. He died on March 29, 1996, and is buried in the Puerto Rico National Cemetery in Bayamon (Section J, Site 3180).

Upon the completion of the 2014 review of minority recipients of the DSC, Negron's award was upgraded to the Medal of Honor. On March 18, 2014, Pres. Barack Obama awarded the medal to Negron's daughter, Iris Nereida Negron-Febus, in a White House ceremony. She said that if her father were still alive "he would have been calling friends, organizing a party, and saying with pride he was a soldier. I am so proud and happy to be his daughter."

Negron-Febus, with Gilberto Rivera Santiago, self-published a book about her father, *My Dad My Hero*, in 2017. She wrote about the White House ceremony, saying, "Twenty-four soldiers got the Medal of Honor, and Dad was one of them. Many were sad and upset that it took too long, but not me. It was in God's right time and moment through all the hard times of the war. I read all the soldiers' names who got the Medal of Honor, and saw that all took a stand also to fight; no giving up. Even though some of them died on the battlefields beyond the call of duty, they knew why they made a stand for freedom; a price only soldiers know and their families who missed them could feel."

The Puerto Rico National Guard Readiness Center at Fort Buchanan is named in Negron's honor. A statue of him stands in his hometown of Corozal.

★★★

35

Mike Castaneda Pena,
US Army

Company F, 5th Cavalry Regiment, 1st Cavalry Division
Waegwan, Korea, September 4, 1950
Date Presented: March 18, 2014

CITATION:

Master Sergeant Mike C. Pena distinguished himself by acts of gallantry and intrepidity above and beyond the call of duty while serving as a member of Company F, 5th Cavalry Regiment, 1st Cavalry Division during combat operations against an armed enemy in Waegwan, Korea, on September 4, 1950. That evening, under cover of darkness and a dreary mist, an enemy battalion moved to within a few yards of Master Sergeant Pena's platoon. Recognizing the enemy's approach, Master Sergeant Pena and his men opened fire, but the enemy's sudden emergence and accurate, point blank fire forced the friendly troops to withdraw. Master Sergeant Pena rapidly reorganized his men and led them in a counterattack, which succeeded in regaining the positions they had just lost. He and his men quickly established a defensive perimeter and laid down devastating fire, but enemy troops continued to hurl themselves at the defenses in overwhelming numbers. Realizing that their scarce supply of ammunition would soon make their positions untenable, Master Sergeant Pena ordered his men to fall back and manned a machine gun to cover their withdrawal. He single handedly held back the enemy until the early hours of the following morning when his position was overrun and he was killed. Master Sergeant Pena's extraordinary heroism and selflessness at the cost of his own life, above and beyond the call of duty, are in keeping with the highest

traditions of military service and reflect great credit upon himself, his unit and the
United States Army.

MIKE PENA joined the army at age fifteen, fought for twenty-seven months
in the Pacific Theater in World War II, and then earned his Medal of Honor
as a platoon sergeant in Korea. Born on November 6, 1924, in Corpus Christi,
Texas, Pena came from a family of immigrants. His father's parents had immigrated to the United States from Mexico in 1891. His father, Miguel, born
in 1889, moved to Bay City, Texas, in about 1910 and worked as a farmer. On
December 6, 1913, he married Maria Castaneda, who had been born in San
Luis Potosi, Mexico, in 1892. According to immigration documents, she had
entered the United States at Brownsville, Texas, on April 18, 1913. The 1920
census records the Penas and their three children living in Corpus Christi,
where Miguel managed a bicycle shop.

The future hero was known as Miguel Jr. while growing up, but he enlisted
in the army under his official name of Mike Castaneda Pena. Some documents record his name as Michael, but both his Medal of Honor citation and
his headstone use Mike. Shortly after his birth, Mike's parents separated. His
mother returned to Bay City, where she married Santos Pena (no relation to
Miguel), who was born in Nuevo Leon, Mexico, in 1929. The couple had five
more children while Santos worked for the Texas Gulf Sulphur Company.
Mike attended school in the town of Gulf for six years before the plant closed
and the family moved to another Texas Gulf Sulphur plant at Newgulf. The
Pena family took up residence in nearby Boling.

Two months before his sixteenth birthday Pena listed 1921 as his birthdate
and volunteered for the US Army. His initial assignment was as a horse soldier
with the 1st Cavalry Division at Fort Clark, Texas. In February 1941 his unit
transferred to Fort Bliss, Texas, from where he participated in the Louisiana
Maneuvers and then on border patrol out of Sierra Blanca, Texas.

In 1943, Pena and the 1st Cavalry transitioned from horse-mounted cav-
alrymen to infantry foot soldiers and deployed to the Pacific Theater. The
1st landed at Brisbane, Australia, on July 26, 1943, and, after six months of intense jungle and amphibious training, went into combat against the Japanese
on New Guinea in January 1944. The next month Pena's unit assaulted Los
Negros Island in the Admiralty Islands, where the Mexican American received his first Purple Heart on March 3 for fragments to his face from a hand

grenade. Pena, now a sergeant and a squad leader, then participated in the Leyte-Samar Campaign before joining the attack on the island of Luzon. On February 3, 1945, Pena's regiment joined the "flying column" that penetrated 100 miles of Japanese-held territory to be the "First to Manila." In the month-long battle that followed to liberate the city, Pena earned his second Purple Heart when he was struck in the thigh by shrapnel on February 24. He recovered in time to join in the liberation of the Santo Tomas Internment Camp.

Pena returned to the United States in August 1945 to be assigned to the 807th Replacement Battalion at Fort Leonard Wood, Missouri. He was honorably discharged on October 3 and then reenlisted for three more years on the same day. He served briefly at Camp Cook, California, and at Camp Hood, Texas, before rejoining his old unit as a sergeant 1st class in the 1st Cavalry Division at Camp McGill near Yokosuka, Japan. In an interview with *Stars and Stripes* during maneuvers near Mount Fuji on November 21, 1948, Pena said of his platoon, "They're good boys and will make fine soldiers. They're a little inexperienced but I can make good men out of them. They take to this training, have a good spirit and take the cold, and rugged field life in their stride."

On August 31, 1949, Pena was promoted to master sergeant and transferred to Camp Carson, Colorado, the following December. His stay in Colorado was brief. Upon the outbreak of the Korean War, Pena reenlisted for six more years and volunteered to rejoin his old company in Japan. On July 18, 1950, Pena and the 1st Cavalry Division made an amphibious landing on the beach at Pohang-dong, Korea, and took up defensive positions along the Naktong River to defend the northwestern portion of the Pusan Perimeter against the North Korean Army. In the early-morning hours of September 4 in the midst of a rainstorm, a battalion of North Koreans attacked Pena's platoon's defensive position. Forced to withdraw, Pena rallied his platoon for a counterattack that retook the lost ground. The enemy continued their attack. With the platoon nearly out of ammunition, Pena ordered the men to once again withdraw. He gathered the remaining ammo and covered their withdrawal with a machine gun. Single-handedly he thwarted the North Korean attack while his platoon moved to safety. About daylight the enemy finally overran Pena's position and left him dead on the battlefield.

Pena was initially buried in the 1st Cavalry Division Cemetery at Taegu, Korea. His remains were repatriated to the United States where he was buried on June 13, 1951, in Cedarvale Cemetery (Section 8, Row 15) in Bay City, Texas, near his mother. He left behind a wife and two sons. The commander of Fort Bliss, Maj. Gen. John T. Lewis, presented his widow, Aurora, with her husband's Distinguished Service Cross and his third Purple Heart. An article in the *El Paso Herald-Post* stated simply, "Many lived because Mike Pena died."

Pena's DSC was upgraded to the Medal of Honor after the completion of the 2014 review. His son, Michael David Pena, a retired navy chief petty officer, accepted the medal from Pres. Barack Obama in a White House ceremony.

The Master Sergeant Mike Castaneda Pena Training Support Center at Fort Hood, Texas, the current home of the 1st Cavalry Division, is named in his honor. A portion of FM 1301 in Matagorda County, Texas, has been designated the Mike C. Pena Memorial Highway.

$\star\star\star$

36

Demensio Rivera,
US Army

Company G, 2nd Battalion, 7th Infantry Regiment, 3rd Infantry Division
Changyong-ni, Korea, May 23, 1951
Date Presented: March 18, 2014

CITATION:

*Private Demensio Rivera distinguished himself by acts of gallantry and intrepidity
above and beyond the call of duty while serving as an automatic rifleman with 2d
Platoon, Company G, 7th Infantry Regiment, 3d Infantry Division during combat
operations against an armed enemy in Changyong-ni, Korea on May 23, 1951.
Early that morning, a large hostile force emerged from a dense fog and viciously
attacked Private Rivera and his comrades. Private Rivera immediately responded
by firing with deadly accuracy until his weapon jammed. Without hesitating, he
threw his rifle down and began to engage the enemy with his pistol and grenades.
At one point, Private Rivera fearlessly crawled from his emplacement to engage an
infiltrating enemy soldier in fierce hand-to-hand combat. With only the sound of
footsteps and obscure shadows to guide his aim, Private Rivera held his position
against tremendous odds, inflicting numerous casualties on the enemy until he
found himself without ammunition of any kind except one grenade. Displaying
a peerless fighting spirit and an utterly selfless devotion to duty, Private Rivera
pulled the pin from his last grenade and calmly waited for the enemy to reach his
position. As enemy troops leaped inside his bunker, Private Rivera activated the
grenade with the full knowledge that it meant his almost certain death. When the
debris from the explosion had cleared, friendly forces recovered a severely wounded
Private Rivera and discovered the bodies of four dead or dying enemy soldiers surrounding him.*

Private Rivera's extraordinary heroism and selflessness above and beyond the call of duty are in keeping with the highest traditions of military service and reflect great credit upon himself, his unit and the United States Army.

DEMENSIO RIVERA earned his Medal of Honor less than four weeks after his eighteenth birthday and only a month after arriving on the Korean battlefield. Born on April 29, 1933, as the youngest of five children to Demensio and Delores Rivera in Cabo Rojo, Puerto Rico, he moved with his parents to New York City while still a child.

Rivera joined the army in New York on September 26, 1950, and after infantry training joined the 3rd Infantry Division in Korea as a replacement. Less than a month later his unit was attacked by a superior number of enemy troops. An article in the June 20, 1951, issue of *Stars and Stripes* reported,

> Rivera blasted away at them until his rifle jammed. He broke up the rifle and scattered the pieces. The Chinese kept coming. Rivera whipped out his .45 pistol and pecked away at them as they scrambled up to where he was. Finally he ran out of ammunition. Surrounded and cut off from the rest of his company, Rivera was not sure what to do next. A replacement with less than a month's combat experience, he hadn't been told exactly how one should handle a situation like this—but he knew he wasn't going to give up. The Reds came closer and then a couple jumped into his hole with him. There was a loud explosion. Rivera had waited with a grenade in his hand and he had pulled the pin just before the Chinese jumped into his dugout. "We found him there later with two dead Chinese on top of him," said Co. G commander Lt. Edward W. Rhodes "He seemed more dead than alive when we hauled him back to the aid station. We poured some blood back into him and sent him on back to the hospital. I hear he's in Japan now, and doing fine."

Rivera recovered from his wounds and was medically discharged back to New York. He was awarded the Distinguished Service Cross, which was approved on August 6, 1952. He lived out his final years in New York and died there on March 19, 1967. He is buried in Cementerio San Miguel Arcangel (Section C, Row K, Site 184) in Cabo Rojo, Puerto Rico.

The 2014 review upgraded Rivera's DSC to the Medal of Honor. His granddaughter, army sergeant Ashley Randall, accepted the medal on his behalf from Pres. Barack Obama in a White House ceremony on March 18, 2014. Randall said that her father had served in Vietnam, but she had not even heard of a grandfather who fought so heroically in Korea.

37

Miguel A. Rodriguez Vera,
US Army

Company F, 2nd Battalion, 38th Infantry Regiment, 2nd Infantry Division

Chorwon, Korea, September 21, 1952

Date Presented: March 18, 2014

CITATION:

Private Miguel A. Vera distinguished himself by acts of gallantry and intrepidity above and beyond the call of duty while serving as an automatic rifleman with Company F, 38th Infantry Regiment, 2d Infantry Division in Chorwon, Korea, on September 21, 1952. That morning, despite suffering from wounds inflicted in a previous battle, Private Vera voluntarily left the aid station to join his comrades in an attack against well-fortified enemy positions on a hill of great importance. When the assaulting elements had moved within twenty yards of the enemy positions, they were suddenly trapped by a heavy volume of mortar, artillery and small-arms fire. The company prepared to make a limited withdrawal, but Private Vera volunteered to remain behind to provide covering fire. As his companions moved to safety, Private Vera remained steadfast in his position, directing accurate fire against the hostile positions despite the intense volume of fire which the enemy was concentrating upon him. Later in the morning, when the friendly force returned, they discovered Private Vera in the same position, facing the enemy. Private Vera's noble intrepidity and self-sacrifice saved many of his comrades' lives. Private Vera's extraordinary heroism and selflessness at the cost of his own life, above and beyond the call of duty, are in keeping with the highest traditions of the military service and reflect great credit upon himself, his unit and the United States Army.

MIGUEL VERA, by virtue of his last name and the alphabetized list of 2014 upgrades of Distinguished Service Crosses, is the final Hispanic recipient of the Medal of Honor for actions during the Korean War. Vega was born on October 11, 1932 (some sources erroneously say May 3), in Adjuntas, Puerto Rico, as the youngest of five children. He joined the army at age seventeen and two years later was serving as a light weapons infantryman with the 2nd Infantry Division in Korea.

On September 21, 1952, Vera and his company were ordered to secure the right sector of a hill known as "Old Baldy" near Chorwon. Although wounded in an earlier attack, Vera refused further medical attention and rejoined his unit for a final assault against the objective. The company came under heavy artillery and mortar barrages as well as intense crossfire from automatic weapons. When the company was stopped and then forced back, Vera selflessly remained behind to successfully cover the withdrawal, sacrificing his life for his fellow soldiers. Vera was buried in the Utuado Municipal Cemetery in Utuado, Puerto Rico. His Distinguished Service Cross was approved on April 29, 1953. As a result of the 2014 review, Vera's DSC was upgraded to the Medal of Honor. His nephew, Jose (Joe) Rodriguez, a Marine Corps veteran, accepted the medal from Pres. Barack Obama in a White House ceremony on March 18, 2014. On November 20, 2014, Vera's remains were moved from Puerto Rico and reinterred in Arlington National Cemetery (Section 71, Site 258), a move that Rodriguez had been working on even before the announcement of the upgrade to the Medal of Honor.

In a March 11, 2014, interview published on the Department of Defense website, Rodriquez said that the family called Vera by the nickname of "Nando." Rodriquez continued,

> He showed me a lot of compassion and always talked to me about education and how proud he was that he was going into the Army. He watched over me like a father. Nando was a frustrated artist. He liked to draw cartoons and used to do drawings for the local newspaper. He told me he was going into the Army to see if he could further his education and to help his mother buy a house she could call her own. In those days, a military career was a way for a young man in Puerto Rico to prosper and get out of the country.
>
> I overheard my father talking about a letter he got from Nando saying how difficult it was in Korea. He had to adjust to the food, to the language barrier and especially to the cold weather. First time in his life that was in

weather below 70 degrees. He said what kept him going was his religious beliefs in God and the "esprit de corps" of the Puerto Ricans serving in the unit. The next thing I remember was my father receiving a package from Nando with an inexpensive Timex watch and Nando asking if my father would have it fixed. I remember my father walking on a Saturday, his only day off, to the town jeweler to have the watch fixed and he mailed it out to Nando two weeks later. Four weeks later we received the package back saying "deceased." My father didn't even know that Nando had been killed. It was the first time I saw my father cry. Nando was his baby brother and he always took care of him.

I often think about Nando's mission and what he accomplished, even after his death. He did buy that house with the money the government gave his mother. Later on in life, I gained a little more interest in what happened to my uncle Nando and found that he was awarded the Distinguished Service Cross. To me that was a "Wow!" And now that I am honored to receive the Medal of Honor for Nando, it makes me really proud for the family and for those who served, not only in Korea but also Vietnam, and were never recognized. My dream was not to get the Medal of Honor for Nando, but to have him buried in Arlington (National Cemetery). I always felt he should have been a candidate for the Medal of Honor. It makes me very proud to receive and accept the award for my uncle Nando. I only wish my father was alive to see this. I don't think he even fully understood the importance of the Distinguished Service Cross.

God bless the United States of American and all of our fallen heroes.

Rodriquez added details about his Uncle Nando in an interview with the Army News Service on November 24, 2014, saying, "He was just an awesome guy. He never had a bad word to say about anybody, and the most amazing thing about it was that I was just reminded by somebody who went up the hill with him, when he earned the medal, he was 5'4" and 135 pounds. I always knew that he was a special kind of guy, very fair, very humble."

VIETNAM

38

Daniel D. Fernandez,
US Army

Company C, 1st Battalion, 5th Infantry (Mechanized), 25th Infantry
  Division
Cu Chi, Hau Nghia Province, Republic of Vietnam, February 18, 1966
Date Presented: April 6, 1967

CITATION:
*For conspicuous gallantry and intrepidity at the risk of his life above and beyond
the call of duty. Sp4c. Fernández demonstrated indomitable courage when the
patrol was ambushed by a Viet Cong rifle company and driven back by the intense
enemy automatic weapons fire before it could evacuate an American soldier who
had been wounded in the Viet Cong attack. Sp4c. Fernández, a sergeant and 2
other volunteers immediately fought their way through devastating fire and exploding grenades to reach the fallen soldier. Upon reaching their fallen comrade
the sergeant was struck in the knee by machine gun fire and immobilized. Sp4c.
Fernández took charge, rallied the left flank of his patrol and began to assist in the
recovery of the wounded sergeant. While first aid was being administered to the
wounded man, a sudden increase in the accuracy and intensity of enemy fire forced
the volunteer group to take cover. As they did, an enemy grenade landed in the
midst of the group, although some men did not see it. Realizing there was no time
for the wounded sergeant or the other men to protect themselves from the grenade
blast, Sp4c. Fernández vaulted over the wounded sergeant and threw himself on
the grenade as it exploded, saving the lives of his 4 comrades at the sacrifice of his
life. Sp4c. Fernández's profound concern for his fellow soldiers, at the risk of his life*

above and beyond the call of duty, are in the highest traditions of the US Army and reflect great credit upon himself and the Armed Forces of his country.

DANIEL FERNANDEZ was the first Hispanic to earn the Medal of Honor in the Vietnam War. Born on June 30, 1944, to Jose I. and Lorinda G. Fernandez in Albuquerque, New Mexico, Daniel attended grammar school there before his family moved to Los Lunas, where he graduated from high school. As a boy, Fernandez helped his father farm alfalfa and chilies, raise rabbits and chickens, and care for fruit trees. He often talked of his dream of one day owning his own ranch and being a cowboy. Friends described him as "competent, unselfish, and cheerful."

After entering the US Army on November 28, 1962, Fernandez completed basic and advanced individual training at Fort Polk, Louisiana, and received the military occupation specialty of 11B—light weapons infantryman. He then reported to Company C, 1st Battalion (Mechanized), 5th Infantry Regiment of the 25th Infantry Regiment at Schofield Barracks, Hawaii. According to an article in the division newspaper *Tropic Lighting News* on November 24, 1966, "He used to joke with his friends that he was in the Army for three years because he had flipped a coin with his draft board, and lost. Actually he had enlisted for three years. While he was in the Army he wanted to be a good soldier. He spent hours at Schofield Barracks in Hawaii pouring over infantry handbooks."

The 25th Infantry Division began transferring to Vietnam in early 1965. Fernandez was initially attached to the 501st Aviation Battalion as a helicopter door gunner and deployed to the war zone in February. In June he rejoined Company C after their arrival in country. When he completed his twelve-month tour at the end of January 1966, Fernandez volunteered to extend his enlistment in the army and to remain in Vietnam with Company C for a second tour. Even though he was younger than many of his platoon mates, they looked upon him as a "father confessor" and called him "Uncle Dan" as they went to him with their troubles and complaints.

Early on the morning of February 18, 1966, Fernandez's platoon was patrolling near Cu Chi when a Viet Cong company took them under fire. The American point man fell dead from the first shots. Fernandez, his sergeant, and two others fought their way forward to recover their dead comrade. When the sergeant was wounded, the New Mexico soldier took charge. As they attempted to pull the sergeant to safety, a grenade landed in their midst. In an instant, Fernandez shouted "move out" and threw himself on the grenade just before it exploded.

The rest of the platoon fought their way forward to recover the dead, wounded, and survivors. According to the article in the *Tropic Lighting News*, Fernandez was still alive when they dragged him to an open area for helicopter extraction. He said, "It hurts" and "Can't breathe." A fellow soldier, who often attended Roman Catholic mass with Fernandez, told him to "make a good act of contrition" because no priest was present. Fernandez's last words were "I will."

Fernandez's body was returned home where a Requiem Mass was held for him at Los Lunas High School prior to his burial in Santa Fe National Cemetery (Section S, Grave 246). His name is on the Vietnam Veterans Memorial in Washington, DC (Panel 05E, Row 046).

On April 6, 1967, Pres. Lyndon Johnson presented Fernandez's Medal of Honor to his parents in a ceremony in the White House Rose Garden. He said,

> We have come here to the Rose Garden today to speak of a very brave young American who gave his life for us in Vietnam. Specialist 4 Daniel Fernandez earned his country's highest military honor by a classic act of courage and self-sacrifice. He threw himself across a live grenade that had been fired among his comrades. By that act, he saved the lives of four other Americans. Two of them are here with us today. Daniel Fernandez died before he was 22 years old. He was not yet born when other Americans crossed the Pacific in World War II. He was not yet in school when others went to fight for freedom in Korea. Yet today, and forever, he is joined to a legion of American heroes. Daniel Fernandez died as more than a hero in battle. He died a martyr in the search for peace.

Daniel's father, Jose, accepted the medal from the president and said,

> We accept this medal from his commander in chief with mixed feelings of grief, humility, and gratitude for the honor given our son and reiterate what we have so often said, that he was just a typical American boy and that there are many more like him all over this great United States of America. We are privileged to accept this honor for him and for all the people who have served and for those still serving country in the Armed Forces. We are proud of these men and women, and therefore, since Daniel cannot be here to receive this Medal of Honor in person we accept it in his behalf and in behalf of his fellow soldiers and the American people whom he served

and represented on the battlefield and in death. We humbly thank God and this Great Democracy who has given us such brave and unselfish men and women.

Los Lunas has honored its hometown hero with the Daniel D. Fernandez Intermediate School, the Daniel D. Fernandez Memorial Park, and Fernandez Street. The Los Lunas Veterans of Foreign War Post 9676 is also named for him. In 2009 students at the Daniel D. Fernandez School wrote a biography of him titled *Man of Honor: The Story of Daniel D. Fernandez*.

★★★

39

Euripides Rubio Jr.,
US Army

Headquarters and Headquarters Company, 1st Battalion, 28th Infantry
  Regiment, 1st Infantry Division
Ap Cha Do, Tay Ninh Province, Republic of Vietnam, November 8, 1966
Date Presented: July 11, 1968

CITATION:

*For conspicuous gallantry and intrepidity in action at the risk of his life above and
beyond the call of duty. Capt. Rubio, Infantry, was serving as communications
officer, 1st Battalion, when a numerically superior enemy force launched a massive
attack against the battalion defense position. Intense enemy machinegun fire raked
the area while mortar rounds and rifle grenades exploded within the perimeter.
Leaving the relative safety of his post, Capt. Rubio received 2 serious wounds as
he braved the withering fire to go to the area of most intense action where he distributed ammunition, re-established positions and rendered aid to the wounded.
Disregarding the painful wounds, he unhesitatingly assumed command when a
rifle company commander was medically evacuated. Capt. Rubio was wounded
a third time as he selflessly exposed himself to the devastating enemy fire to move
among his men to encourage them to fight with renewed effort. While aiding the
evacuation of wounded personnel, he noted that a smoke grenade which was intended to mark the Viet Cong position for air strikes had fallen dangerously close
to the friendly lines. Capt. Rubio ran to reposition the grenade but was immediately struck to his knees by enemy fire. Despite his several wounds, Capt. Rubio
scooped up the grenade, ran through the deadly hail of fire to within 20 meters of
the enemy position and hurled the already smoking grenade into the midst of the*

enemy before he fell for the final time. Using the repositioned grenade as a marker, friendly air strikes were directed to destroy the hostile positions. Capt. Rubio's singularly heroic act turned the tide of battle, and his extraordinary leadership and valor were a magnificent inspiration to his men. His remarkable bravery and selfless concern for his men are in keeping with the highest traditions of the military service and reflect great credit on Capt. Rubio and the US Army.

EURIPIDES RUBIO was the first native of Puerto Rico to be awarded the Medal of Honor and the first one from the island to do so for actions in the Vietnam War. He is also the only Puerto Rican commissioned officer recipient of the medal. He was born on March 1, 1938, to Euripides and Luisa M. Velazquez Rubio in Ponce, Puerto Rico, and attended grammar school and high school there before enrolling in the University of Puerto Rico at Santurce.

In March 1955, Rubio enlisted in the US Army National Guard at Fort Buchanan and in July 1956 transferred to the Air Force Reserve. He again changed services in December 1958 when he joined the Army Reserve. In March 1959 he went on active duty and attended the Provost Marshal General's School at Fort Gordon, Georgia. Upon graduation the following June, Rubio joined the 382nd Military Police Battalion in Germany, where he remained until October 1962. He then returned to the United States and went to Fort McPherson, Georgia, where he served in military police units until May 1964. He then reported to Fort Benning, Georgia, where over the next two years he attended the Infantry School and qualified as a paratrooper and pathfinder as he advanced in rank to captain. During his off-duty time, he enjoyed skydiving with his friends. After attending the US Army Jungle Training School in Fort Sherman, Canal Zone, Rubio joined the 1st Infantry Division in Vietnam on July 10, 1966.

On November 8, 1966, Rubio was the signal officer for the 1st Battalion, 28th Infantry Regiment of the 1st Infantry Division in Tay Ninh Province in the Republic of Vietnam when early that morning his unit came under a sustained attack by two Viet Cong regiments. Rubio left the relative safety of his headquarters post in the midst of the battle to rally the soldiers, to redistribute ammunition, and to render aid to the wounded. Despite suffering two serious wounds, he assumed command of a rifle company when its captain was wounded. Rubio was wounded a third time as he reorganized the company and led their defense. He finally fell mortally wounded when he picked up a smoke grenade and charged the enemy to mark their positions for air strikes. His cause of death is listed as "multiple gunshot wounds to his neck and chest."

Eighteen soldiers died alongside Rubio in the battle that is credited with killing more than 400 of the enemy. *The First Infantry Division in Vietnam: "The Big Red One,"* compiled by the Turner Publishing Company, details the fight, which it calls one of the division's major battles of the war. It also mentions the heroics of Rubio as well as details of the battle and a list of the casualties.

Rubio was returned to Puerto Rico and buried in Buxeda Memorial Park in Rio Piedras. On May 24, 1981, his remains were transferred to the Honor Section of Puerto Rico National Cemetery (Section HSA, Site 5) in Bayamon.

On July 11, 1968, Sec. of the Army Stanley R. Resor, accompanied by Gen. William C. Westmoreland, chief of staff of the US Army, presented Rubio's Medal of Honor to his widow Ileana; son Edgardo, four; and daughter Anaeli, three. Resor said, "No man deserves more to be called a hero." An Associated Press photograph released from the ceremony shows young Edgardo rendering a hand salute to General Westmoreland.

The United States Army Reserve Center, located in the Puerto Nuevo sector of San Juan, the US Department of Veterans Affairs Outpatient Clinic in Ponce, and American Legion Post 142 in San Juan are named in his honor. Capt. Euripides Rubio's name is also inscribed on the El Monumento de la Recordación (Monument of Remembrance), located in front of the capitol building in San Juan, which is dedicated to Puerto Rico's fallen soldiers. An oil portrait of Rubio hangs in the Capitol Rotunda. His name is on the Vietnam Veterans Memorial in Washington, DC (Panel 12E, Row 044).

★★★

40

Elmelindo Rodrigues Smith,
US Army

Company C, 2nd Battalion, 8th Infantry Regiment, 4th Infantry Division
Plei Trap Valley, Kontum Province, Republic of Vietnam, February 16, 1967
Date Presented: October 3, 1968

CITATION:

*For conspicuous gallantry and intrepidity at the risk of his life above and beyond
the call of duty. During a reconnaissance patrol, his platoon was suddenly engaged
by intense machinegun fire hemming in the platoon on 3 sides. A defensive perimeter was hastily established, but the enemy added mortar and rocket fire to the
deadly fusillade and assaulted the position from several directions. With complete
disregard for his safety, P/Sgt. Smith moved through the deadly fire along the
defensive line, positioning soldiers, distributing ammunition and encouraging his
men to repeal the enemy attack. Struck to the ground by enemy fire which caused a
severe shoulder wound, he regained his feet, killed the enemy soldier and continued
to move about the perimeter. He was again wounded in the shoulder and stomach
but continued moving on his knees to assist in the defense. Noting the enemy massing at a weakened point on the perimeter, he crawled into the open and poured
deadly fire into the enemy ranks. As he crawled on, he was struck by a rocket. Moments later, he regained consciousness, and drawing on his fast dwindling strength,
continued to crawl from man to man. When he could move no farther, he chose to
remain in the open where he could alert the perimeter to the approaching enemy.
P/Sgt. Smith perished, never relenting in his determined effort against the enemy.
The valorous acts and heroic leadership of this outstanding soldier inspired those*

remaining members of his platoon to beat back the enemy assaults. P/Sgt. Smith's
gallant actions were in keeping with the highest traditions of the US Army and
they reflect great credit upon him and the Armed Forces of his country.

ELMELINDO RODRIGUES SMITH was a professional soldier with nearly
fourteen years of service in the US Army when he earned his Medal of Honor
in the Republic of Vietnam in 1967. Born on July 27, 1935, in Honolulu, Hawaii, to Elmelindo T. and Emily Smith, he came from a mixed racial background. His father was the son of a Puerto Rican immigrant from Ponce who
had come to Hawaii to work in the sugarcane fields in 1899. His mother was
native Hawaiian of mixed Asian ancestry. The future hero considered himself
American, Hawaiian, and Hispanic Asian.

Smith grew up in Wahiawa, Hawaii, where he went to elementary school.
His mother later recalled that her son "had some misunderstandings" at Leile-
hua High School and dropped out in the ninth grade. She added, "But he was
a nice boy. He gave me no trouble and was very helpful. He was a quiet sort
of person." As soon as Smith was old enough, he enlisted in the US Army at
Honolulu on June 3, 1953. His mother agreed with the decision, saying, "I felt
the army would be good for him. He got an education, too."

After six months at the Hawaiian Infantry Training Center, Smith joined
the 1st Cavalry Division in Korea in December 1953—only a few months after
the truce had ended the hostilities there. Over the next dozen years, Smith
spent more than half his time overseas in Okinawa, back in Korea, and in
Italy. In between these tours, he served in his home islands of Hawaii and at
Fort Lewis, Washington. Smith proved to be a good soldier as he advanced in
rank to staff sergeant and earned the Good Conduct Medal, 3rd Award. Each
of these awards meant that he had served without any disciplinary infractions
for three years.

During his tour on Okinawa, Smith met a Hawaiian-born Japanese American, Jane, who was serving in the Women's Army Corps. They married, and,
by the time Smith joined the 4th Infantry Division at Fort Lewis in July of
1964, the couple had two daughters.

In November 1966, Smith deployed to Vietnam with the division's 2nd
Battalion, 8th Infantry Regiment, which conducted operations in the western Central Highlands along the border between Cambodia and Vietnam. They experienced intense combat against the North Vietnamese Army

in the mountains of Kontum Province. On February 16, 1967, Staff Sergeant Smith was leading his platoon in a reconnaissance patrol south of Landing Zone 501 in the Plei Trap Valley when it came under intense attack from NVA forces using small-arms fire, machine guns, rocket-propelled grenades, and mortars. Despite the fact that he was wounded early in the battle, Smith moved his men into a defensive perimeter, directed return fire, and redistributed ammunition. He continually exposed himself to the enemy fire as he led his platoon's defense and was struck twice more by small-arms fire and grenade fragments. After his final wound, which would ultimately be fatal, he remained exposed to defend the primary route of the enemy attack, enabling his platoon to finally force the enemy to retreat.

For his actions, Smith was posthumously promoted to sergeant 1st class and recommended for the Medal of Honor. He is buried in the National Memorial Cemetery of the Pacific in Honolulu (Section W, Site 151). His name is on the Vietnam Veterans Memorial in Washington, DC (Panel 15E, Row 051).

On October 3, 1968, Sec. of the Army Stanley R. Resor presented Smith's Medal of Honor to his widow, Jane, in a Pentagon ceremony. In attendance were the Smith's daughters, his mother, and Sen. Daniel K. Inouye and Rep. Patsy T. Mink of Hawaii. Secretary Resor concluded the ceremony by saying,

> Strength of character and courage are qualities we value in every aspect of American life. Nowhere are they more important than on the battlefield; nowhere are they more severely tested than on the battlefield. Sergeant Smith met that test in a way which surpasses all standards one can reasonably expect from men in uniform. In meeting the test, he joins a long and honored line of men whose concepts of duty, honor, and loyalty have shaped and strengthened the United States Army as an instrument of freedom. I consider myself merely the representative of a grateful nation in expressing its esteem for Sergeant Smith as he is today awarded the Medal of Honor.

Hawaii's Schofield Barracks post theater is named in his honor. The Sergeant E. Smith Community Garden is located across from Wheeler Army Airfield near Pearl Harbor.

41

Maximo Yabes,
US Army

Company A, 4th Battalion, 9th Infantry Regiment, 25th Infantry Division
Phu Hoa Dong, Binh Duong Province, Republic of Vietnam,
    February 26, 1967
Date Presented: October 31, 1968

CITATION:

*For conspicuous gallantry and intrepidity at the risk of his life above and beyond
the call of duty. 1st Sgt. Yabes distinguished himself with Company A, which was
providing security for a land clearing operation. Early in the morning the company
suddenly came under intense automatic weapons and mortar fire followed by a
battalion sized assault from 3 sides. Penetrating the defensive perimeter the enemy
advanced on the company command post bunker. The command post received
increasingly heavy fire and was in danger of being overwhelmed. When several enemy grenades landed within the command post, 1st Sgt. Yabes shouted a warning
and used his body as a shield to protect others in the bunker. Although painfully
wounded by numerous grenade fragments, and despite the vicious enemy fire on
the bunker, he remained there to provide covering fire and enable the others in the
command group to relocate. When the command group had reached a new position, 1st Sgt. Yabes moved through a withering hail of enemy fire to another bunker
50 meters away. There he secured a grenade launcher from a fallen comrade and
fired point blank into the attacking Viet Cong, stopping further penetration of the
perimeter. Noting 2 wounded men helpless in the fire swept area, he moved them to
a safer position where they could be given medical treatment. He resumed his accurate and effective fire, killing several enemy soldiers and forcing others to withdraw*

from the vicinity of the command post. As the battle continued, he observed an en-
emy machinegun within the perimeter which threatened the whole position. On his
own, he dashed across the exposed area, assaulted the machinegun, killed the crew,
destroyed the weapon, and fell mortally wounded. 1st Sgt. Yabes' valiant and self-
less actions saved the lives of many of his fellow soldiers and inspired his comrades
to effectively repel the enemy assault. His indomitable fighting spirit, extraordi-
nary courage and intrepidity at the cost of his life are in the highest military tradi-
tions and reflect great credit upon himself and the Armed Forces of his country.

MAXIMO YABES saw his first combat as an infantryman in the Korean
War, but it was not until he had been a professional soldier for more than
fifteen years and attained the rank of 1st sergeant that he earned his Medal
of Honor in Vietnam. Born on January 29, 1932, to a Filipino father and an
Anglo mother in Lodi, California, Yabes moved at an early age to Oakridge,
Oregon, where he attended primary and secondary schools.

Some might question Yabes being included as "Hispanic." Spanish was the
official language of the Philippines until 1937. More importantly, the Congressional Medal of Honor Society includes Yabes with other Hispanic recipients.

The *Register Guard* of Eugene, Oregon, published an in-depth story about
Yabes on February 27, 1994, that included interviews with many of his boyhood friends. They recalled him as being "a sparkplug" and "a little go-devil
all the time." Although only five feet six and 140 pounds, Yabes ran track and
played on the Oakridge High School basketball team. He constantly told jokes
and found humor in nearly everything. Despite begin voted class president,
Yabes had to drop out of high school in 1950 to provide financial assistance to
his widowed mother when his father was killed in a shipyard accident.

On August, 20, 1951, Yabes entered the US Army at Eugene. After infantry
training at Fort Lewis, Washington, he served at Fort Ord, California, and
then completed airborne training at Fort Benning, Georgia. Following a tour
as a paratrooper at Fort Campbell, Kentucky, he reported to Japan in January
1953. Two months later he joined the 187th Parachute Infantry Regiment on
the Korean Peninsula, where he earned his first award—the Combat Infantryman Badge.

After he completed his tour in Korea, where he attended the Noncommissioned Officers Academy of the 1st Cavalry Division, Yabes continued to serve
in airborne units at Fort Campbell, in Germany, and at Fort Bragg, North
Carolina. He returned to Korea in 1960 and then reported to Fort Carson,

Colorado, in 1962, where he graduated from the Leadership and Mountain Training School. There he met his future wife, Janis, whom he married in 1964. Yabes transferred to the 25th Infantry Division in Hawaii in March 1965 and deployed with the unit to Vietnam in early 1966.

Yabes arrived at Cu Chi as sergeant 1st class. On February 12, 1967, the army promoted him to 1st sergeant. After only a brief party with his fellow NCOs to "wet down" the new stripes with beer, Yabes assumed the top sergeant position in Company A, 4th Battalion, 9th Infantry Regiment. Two weeks later his unit was given the mission of protecting a squad of army engineers whose assignment was to build a road between Phu Hoa Dong and a nearby plantation. Late in the afternoon of February 25, Company A moved into a night defensive position. Shortly after midnight mortar rounds began landing in the perimeter, followed by a ground attack by a Viet Cong regiment. Early in the fight, a hand grenade landed in the company command post position. Yabes shouted a warning and then shielded his fellow soldiers from the blast with his body. Although painfully wounded, he grabbed his rifle and return fire so the command group could move to a safer position. He continued to assist wounded comrades and to return fire until he spotted an enemy machine gun that threatened the entire perimeter. Without hesitation he charged the machine gun, killing its crew and ending the enemy attack before he fell from a final mortal wound. Twenty-three American soldiers died alongside Yabes. More than 100 Viet Cong were killed.

Yabes's body was returned to Denver, where he was buried in Fort Logan National Cemetery (Section R, Site 369). His name is on Panel 15E, Line 102, of the Vietnam Veterans Memorial in Washington, DC.

Sec. of the Army Stanley Resor, accompanied by Gen. William Westmoreland, presented Yabes's Medal of Honor to his widow on October 31, 1968, in a ceremony at the Pentagon. Janis returned to Colorado and operated a beauty salon in Boulder until 1972, when she enlisted in the US Army Reserve as a clerk. She told the *Denver Post*, "I just feel like it's a personal obligation." Janis served for three years in the reserves and later spent twenty-three years as the postmaster in Eldorado Springs, Colorado.

Like his boyhood friends, those soldiers who served with Yabes remembered him well when interviewed for the 1994 article in the *Register-Guard*. One recalled that he was "a crisp, spit-and-polish career soldier, but his heart was golden and he would give you anything. He was a father figure, oozed confidence, cocky, comical, and adaptable. . .a soldier's soldier who was smart, tough, fearless, a sergeant who backed his men, and a soft touch to soldiers who needed a few bucks." Another simply said, "He was one hell of a soldier."

A street, Yabes Court, is named for him in the Fort Carson housing area, as is an avenue in El Paso, Texas. His name is on a stone monument in the Garden of Valor at Schofield Barracks, Hawaii. The city of Oakridge, Oregon, built a memorial to him in Greenswater Park that features a flagpole, fountain, and a bronze bust of Yabes set on a granite pedestal. His Medal of Honor citation is engraved on its base.

★★★

42

Alfredo Gonzales,
US Marine Corps

Company A, 1st Battalion, 1st Marine Regiment, 1st Marine Division
Hue City, Thua Thien Province, Republic of Vietnam, January 31, 1968
Date Presented: October 31, 1969

CITATION:
*For conspicuous gallantry and intrepidity at the risk of his life above and beyond
the call of duty while serving as platoon commander, 3d Platoon, Company A. On
31 January 1968, during the initial phase of Operation Hue City, Sgt. Gonzalez'
unit was formed as a reaction force and deployed to Hue to relieve the pressure on
the beleaguered city. While moving by truck convoy along Route No. 1, near the
village of Lang Van Lrong, the Marines received a heavy volume of enemy fire. Sgt.
Gonzalez aggressively maneuvered the Marines in his platoon, and directed their
fire until the area was cleared of snipers. Immediately after crossing a river south of
Hue, the column was again hit by intense enemy fire. One of the Marines on top of
a tank was wounded and fell to the ground in an exposed position. With complete
disregard for his safety, Sgt. Gonzalez ran through the fire-swept area to the assistance of his injured comrade. He lifted him up and though receiving fragmentation
wounds during the rescue, he carried the wounded Marine to a covered position
for treatment. Due to the increased volume and accuracy of enemy fire from a fortified machine gun bunker on the side of the road, the company was temporarily
halted. Realizing the gravity of the situation, Sgt. Gonzalez exposed himself to the
enemy fire and moved his platoon along the east side of a bordering rice paddy to
a dike directly across from the bunker. Though fully aware of the danger involved,
he moved to the fire-swept road and destroyed the hostile position with hand*

grenades. Although seriously wounded again on 3 February, he steadfastly refused
medical treatment and continued to supervise his men and lead the attack. On 4
February, the enemy had again pinned the company down, inflicting heavy casual-
ties with automatic weapons and rocket fire. Sgt. Gonzalez, utilizing a number of
light antitank assault weapons, fearlessly moved from position to position firing
numerous rounds at the heavily fortified enemy emplacements. He successfully
knocked out a rocket position and suppressed much of the enemy fire before falling
mortally wounded. The heroism, courage, and dynamic leadership displayed by
Sgt. Gonzalez reflected great credit upon himself and the Marine Corps, and were
in keeping with the highest traditions of the US Naval Service. He gallantly gave
his life for his country.

ALFREDO GONZALES was the first Hispanic marine to earn the Medal of
Honor in the Vietnam War. "Freddy" Gonzales, as he was known to family
and friends, was born on May 23, 1946, in Edinburg, Texas, to Andres Cantu
and fifteen-year-old Dolia Gonzales, whose relatives in the Rio Grande Valley dated back to before there was a border between Mexico and Texas and
included Native Americans who predated the arrival of the Spanish. Cantu
abandoned Dolia before Freddy's birth and never played a role in his life. Although he went by the name of Freddy Cantu as a boy, he entered the Marine
Corps as Alfredo Gonzales and listed his father as "deceased" on enlistment
forms. Neither his future Veterans Administration grave marker nor his joint
marker with his mother contain any reference to Cantu.

The facts about the early lives of many Medal of Honor recipients are often
sparse or missing altogether. With the passage of time, memories fade and wit-
nesses die. Not so with Alfredo Gonzales. Texas and New Mexico journalist
John W. Flores spent sixteen years researching Gonzales and interviewing
those who knew him. Flores's book, *Marine Sergeant Freddy Gonzales: Vietnam
Hero*, is one of the most complete accounts of a recipient of the medal.

Flores writes that Dolia worked as a waitress in local cafes and toiled in the
nearby fields and orchards to support her son. Freddy attended Sam Houston
and Lamar elementary schools, Edinburg Junior High School, and Edinburg
High School. When not in school, Gonzales joined his mother or neighbors as
a farm worker. At age seven he worked as a "water boy," and as he grew older
he picked cotton, cabbage, carrots, beans, and citrus in the fertile Rio Grande
Valley. Waitressing and farm wages were low, however, and Dolia and her son
did not own an automobile until he was nearly out of high school.

Those who knew Gonzales as a boy describe him as having a temper, as being a tough kid who backed down from no one—but also as a quiet guy who never looked for trouble. Although small, he was solidly built and played football for the Edinburg Bobcats. His coach, Fred Akers, who went on to great success as the football coach at the University of Texas, was influential in the future of this marine. While in high school, Gonzales often told his mother that someday he wanted to be a high school coach like Akers.

Dolia recalls that she took her son to the movies to see *The Sands of Iwo Jima*, starring John Wayne as marine sergeant John Stryker, when he was still in grammar school. During the film, he leaned over and said, "Mom, I'm going to become a Marine sergeant someday, just like that."

When Gonzales graduated from high school in 1965, he had no desire to remain in the Valley as a farm worker. As the only child of a single mother, Gonzales did not have to worry about being drafted, but like many young men, he looked for adventure and opportunity. The Marine Corps offered both. Dolia was not happy about Freddy's plans to enlist in the Marine Corps and told him so. He responded, "Mom, they are the best. The toughest. If I am going to fight in a war, I want to be with guys like that. You know I can't afford college this coming semester this fall. And I do not want to keep working in the fields. I am in shape right now, and I can make basic training without any trouble."

Within days of his graduation, he went to San Antonio where he enlisted in the Marine Corps Reserves on June 3. On July 6 he was discharged from the reserves and enlisted in the regular corps to report to Marine Recruit Depot in San Diego for basic training. After graduating on September 22, he reported to Camp Pendleton for infantry training.

Gonzales graduated on October 25 and had a brief home leave back to Edinburg. On December 10 he boarded the USS *Weigel* in San Diego bound for Okinawa, where he joined the 1st Reconnaissance Company of the 1st Marine Division as a rifleman. In February 1966 he again departed by ship en route to Vietnam, where he began his tour with the 4th Marine Regiment of the 3rd Marine Division. Gonzales immediately earned the friendship of his fellow marines and the respect of his sergeants and officers. His friends described him as a "serious guy" who listened and learned. One of his commanders said that the Rio Grande Valley marine could "smell danger." During his thirteen-month tour, Gonzales advanced from private 1st class to corporal and then to lance corporal. Except for a bout of malaria and a minor shrapnel wound, he survived his first tour in the war mostly intact.

Gonzales flew home in January 1967 for a thirty-day leave before reporting to the 2nd Marine Division at Camp Lejeune, North Carolina, where he instructed recruits in counter-guerrilla techniques. He thought about going to college and becoming a coach, about asking a young woman in Edinburg to marry him, and about earning enough money to build his mother a new house. Other thoughts crossed his mind as well as he received letters from Vietnam about casualties in his old platoon.

His decision was made easier when he received a "Dear John" letter from his Edinburg girlfriend. In May he volunteered for a second tour in Vietnam. He stopped briefly at the replacement center at Camp Pendleton, where he was promoted to sergeant on July 1. On July 25 he departed for Vietnam, where he joined the 3rd Platoon, A Company, 1st Battalion, 1st Marine Regiment, 1st Marine Division as a squad leader.

By February 1968, Gonzales was an "old salt" with more than twenty-one months of infantry combat experience. Because of casualties and rotations, he often acted as his platoon commander in the absence of a senior NCO or officer.

On January 31, 1968, Gonzales was acting as platoon commander when his unit was ordered to move to Hue to reinforce units in the city fighting the communist Tet Offensive. When the convoy came under fire near the village of Lang Van Lrong, Gonzales took charge and drove the enemy back. When they were again ambushed farther down the road, Gonzales received shrapnel wounds carrying a wounded marine to safety. Despite the wounds, he then destroyed a machine-gun bunker with hand grenades.

Gonzales refused to be evacuated. On February 1 his company was ordered to advance into Hue to secure the Thua Thien Province headquarters. The marines were experienced jungle fighters, but they were not trained for urban warfare, which entailed fighting street to street, house to house. After two days of intense combat, Gonzales was wounded for the second time. Once again he refused medical treatment. The next day his company suffered heavy casualties from North Vietnamese Army forces using rocket-propelled grenades and machine guns. Gonzales led the attack against the NVA, which was located in Saint Joan of Arc Catholic Church. Using multiple light antitank weapons (LAWs), the marine sergeant silenced most of the enemy positions before a rocket-propelled grenade struck him in mid-body, nearly cutting him in half. He lived long enough for a corpsman, a fellow Catholic, to administer morphine and to whisper the Lord's Prayer in his ear.

Gonzales's body was returned to Edinburg, where, after a day lying in state at his mother's home, he was buried in Hillcrest Memorial Park Cemetery. His name is on the Vietnam Veterans Memorial in Washington, DC (Panel 37E, Row 21).

On October 31, 1969, Vice Pres. Spiro Agnew presented Gonzales's Medal of Honor to his mother. Gonzales's hometown, county, state, corps, and country have bestowed many honors on the marine hero. In Edinburg, there is a road, an elementary school, and an American Legion Post named in his honor. His old high school annually presents the Alfredo Gonzales Athletic Award. A veterans home in nearby McAllen also bears his name, as does Alfredo Gonzales Boulevard at Camp Lejeune, Gonzales Hall at Marine Corps Headquarters in Quantico, and Alfredo Gonzales Dining Hall at the Corpus Christi Naval Air Station. The Museum of South Texas History in Edinburg has a permanent display of his uniform and medals.

The USS *Gonzales* (DDG-66), a guided missile destroyer, was launched by the US Navy on February 18, 1995. Dolia was at the ceremony and for many years after attended the ship's changing of command as well as return from deployments and other ceremonies. She wrote letters to crew members and is known as "the Mother of the *Gonzales*."

★★★

43

Carlos James Lozada,
US Army

Company A, 2nd Battalion, 503rd Infantry Regiment, 173rd Airborne
  Brigade
Dak To, Kontum Province, Republic of Vietnam, November 20, 1967
Date Presented: November 18, 1969

CITATION:

For conspicuous gallantry and intrepidity in action at the risk of his life above and beyond the call of duty. Pfc. Lozada, US Army, distinguished himself at the risk of his life above and beyond the call of duty in the battle of Dak To. While serving as a machine gunner with 1st platoon, Company A, Pfc. Lozada was part of a 4-man early warning outpost, located 35 meters from his company's lines. At 1400 hours a North Vietnamese Army company rapidly approached the outpost along a well-defined trail. Pfc. Lozada alerted his comrades and commenced firing at the enemy who were within 10 meters of the outpost. His heavy and accurate machine-gun fire killed at least 20 North Vietnamese soldiers and completely disrupted their initial attack. Pfc. Lozada remained in an exposed position and continued to pour deadly fire upon the enemy despite the urgent pleas of his comrades to withdraw. The enemy continued their assault, attempting to envelop the outpost. At the same time enemy forces launched a heavy attack on the forward west flank of Company A with the intent to cut them off from their battalion. Company A was given the order to withdraw. Pfc. Lozada apparently realized that if he abandoned his position there would be nothing to hold back the surging North Vietnamese soldiers and that the entire company withdrawal would be jeopardized. He called for his comrades to move back and that he would stay and provide cover for them. He made this decision realizing that the enemy was converging on 3 sides of his position and only meters away, and a delay in withdrawal meant almost certain death. Pfc. Lozada continued to deliver a heavy, accurate volume of suppressive fire against the enemy until he was mortally wounded and had to be carried during the withdrawal. His heroic deed served as an example and an inspiration to his comrades throughout the ensuing 4-day battle. Pfc. Lozada's actions are in the highest traditions of the US Army and reflect great credit upon himself, his unit, and the US Army.

CARLOS JAMES LOZADA earned his Medal of Honor in one of the major battles of the Vietnam War, only the second Puerto Rican to do so in the conflict. Born on September 6, 1946, in Caguas, Puerto Rico, he moved at an early age to the Bronx, New York, with his parents. Lozada grew up in the Melrose projects of the South Bronx as a streetwise kid who never backed down from a fight. He enjoyed playing stickball with his friends and did well at Roosevelt High School in Brooklyn.

In his teens Lozada began dating a girl in his high school named Linda. They married shortly after they graduated. With a desire to fulfill his military obligation, and with the specific goal of earning veterans benefits so he could attend college after his service, Lozada enlisted in the US Army on August 15, 1966. Upon completion of basic training at Fort Jackson, South Carolina, and advanced infantry training at Fort Gordon, Georgia, Lozada graduated from the Airborne School at Fort Benning, Georgia, and earned the silver parachute wings of an army paratrooper. In addition to the training and prestige of being "airborne," the qualification paid him an extra $55 per month in jump pay.

After a brief home leave to the Bronx, Lozada said goodbye to Linda and his one-week-old daughter, Yvette. He arrived in Vietnam on June 11, 1967, and was assigned to the 173rd Airborne Brigade where he carried his squad's M-60 machine gun that he affectionately named "Linda" in honor of his wife. He wrote regularly to Linda. In a letter on September 9, 1967, he said, "I don't think you'll ever know how much I've enjoyed being with you and now we're married . . . When I get back to the World there will be many a good times . . . Can't you just see it, you, Yvette, and I walking down the street . . . We're clean as can be and we have a beautiful little girl in the prettiest baby dress money can buy . . . I'll see to it . . . You have given me so much to live for . . . love, understanding, patience . . . me and you will be together to be old and gray . . . and much in love."

On November 19, the 173rd and other US forces were engaged in intense combat in the Central Highlands against an enemy offensive near Dak To. The next day Lozada and three other troopers occupied an early-warning outpost forward of his company's defensive position at the base of Hill 875. In the early afternoon a North Vietnamese Army company rapidly approached the outpost. Lozada opened up with his machine gun, killing at least twenty enemy soldiers and breaking up their initial advance. The NVA reorganized and resumed their attack against the outpost and the rest of the company to cut them off from support from the remainder of the battalion. When the company began to withdraw to better positions, Lozada ordered his fellow soldiers to pull back, saying, "Go on, I'll hold them off."

And Lozada did indeed hold the enemy back to save his comrades. He continued to fire his machine gun until he was killed by multiple fragmentation wounds. Lozada's fellow paratroopers recovered his body. He is buried in the Long Island National Cemetery in East Farmington, New York (Section T, Site 2295). His name is on the Vietnam Veterans Memorial Wall in Washington, DC (Panel 30E, Row 045), as well as on the Monument of Remembrance, dedicated to Puerto Rico's fallen soldiers and situated in front of the capitol building in San Juan. An oil painting of Lazada also hangs the Capitol Rotunda. On November 21, 1987, with members of his old unit in attendance, the Bronx dedicated the Carlos J. Lozada Playground.

Vice Pres. Spiro Agnew presented Lazada's Medal of Honor to his widow, Linda, in a ceremony in the White House on November 18, 1969. Linda and Yvette later moved to Florida. She never remarried. Twenty years after the death of her husband, a reporter from the *New York Daily News* interviewed her. In the article, which appeared on October 11, 1987, Linda said, "I wish I was there when he got hurt. I wish I was there. It's just . . . Oh, poor thing. I try to imagine how he must have felt. All those people shooting at him. It must have been horrible. All those people trying to hurt him. Nobody should have to go through that. Sometimes I wish I could have been there to shoot at them. That's how angry I am because they shot my husband."

★★★

44

Hector Santiago-Colon,
US Army

Company B, 5th Battalion, 7th Cavalry Regiment, 1st Cavalry Division
Quang Tri Province, Republic of Vietnam, June 28, 1968
Date Presented: April 7, 1970

CITATION:

Sp4c. Santiago-Colon distinguished himself at the cost of his life while serving as a gunner in the mortar platoon of Company B. While serving as a perimeter sentry, Sp4c. Santiago-Colon heard distinct movement in the heavily wooded area to his front and flanks. Immediately he alerted his fellow sentries in the area to move to their foxholes and remain alert for any enemy probing forces. From the wooded area around his position heavy enemy automatic weapons and small-arms fire suddenly broke out, but extreme darkness rendered difficult the precise location and identification of the hostile force. Only the muzzle flashes from enemy weapons indicated their position. Sp4c. Santiago-Colon and the other members of his position immediately began to repel the attackers, utilizing hand grenades, anti-personnel mines and small-arms fire. Due to the heavy volume of enemy fire and exploding grenades around them, a North Vietnamese soldier was able to crawl, undetected, to their position. Suddenly, the enemy soldier lobbed a hand grenade into Sp4c. Santiago-Colon's foxhole. Realizing that there was no time to throw the grenade out of his position, Sp4c. Santiago-Colon retrieved the grenade, tucked it in to his stomach and, turning away from his comrades, absorbed the full impact of the blast. His heroic self-sacrifice saved the lives of those who occupied the foxhole with him, and provided them with the inspiration to continue fighting until they had forced the enemy to retreat from the perimeter. By his gallantry at the cost of his life and in the highest traditions of the military service, Sp4c. Santiago-Colon has reflected great credit upon himself, his unit, and the US Army.

SPEC. HECTOR SANTIAGO-COLON was the third Puerto Rican to be awarded the Medal of Honor in the Vietnam War and the second soldier to have a military installation named for him on his native island. Born on December 20, 1942, to Pablo M. Santiago and Pertonila Colon in the Salinas suburb of Las Mareas, he grew up as one of twelve siblings who worked in the sugarcane fields that surrounded his neighborhood. He was a strong young man who often walked ten miles to visit his grandmother. Friends describe him as being ambitious, humble, and willing to help anyone in need. He graduated from Salinas High School, where he participated on the track team. He then moved to New York City for better job opportunities.

Once in the United States, he determined that he wanted to become a member of the NYC's police department and that his best chance of being accepted was to be a military veteran. He was inducted into the US Army on May 23, 1967, and reported to Fort Jackson, South Carolina, for basic and advanced infantry training. On his enlistment papers he listed his race as "Negro." While on leave after completing his training, he became engaged to his childhood sweetheart. He and Rosita planned to marry when he returned from Vietnam.

Santiago-Colon arrived in Vietnam on October 23, 1967, and was assigned to the 7th Cavalry Regiment of the 1st Cavalry Division. Early in his tour he was wounded and evacuated to Japan for treatment. When he recovered, he was given the option of returning to a stateside assignment or rejoining his unit in Vietnam. Santiago-Colon replied that he was not finished with what he had come to do and that his old company and fellow soldiers needed him.

On June 28, 1968, Santiago-Colon was occupying a foxhole with several other soldiers defending against an attack by a large North Vietnamese Army force. In the midst of explosions, automatic weapons, and small-arms fire, an enemy soldier managed to crawl near enough to the Americans to toss a hand grenade into the foxhole. Realizing that there was no time to throw the grenade out of the defensive position, Santiago-Colon covered it with his body and absorbed its entire impact, saving the lives of his fellow soldiers. He died instantly from multiple fragmentation wounds.

Santiago-Colon's body was returned to Puerto Rico, where he was buried in the Salinas Municipal Cemetery. Pres. Richard Nixon awarded Santiago-

Colon's Medal of Honor to his parents in a White House ceremony on April 7, 1970.

In July 1975, the Puerto Rican National Guard renamed Camp Salinas near his birthplace to Camp Santiago. His name is on the Monument of Remembrance in front of the island's capitol building in San Juan, and a painting of the Vietnam hero hangs in the building's rotunda. A fitness center at the Sand Hill Training Center at Fort Benning also bears his name. Santiago-Colon's name is on the Vietnam Veterans Memorial (Panel 54W, Line 013) in Washington, DC.

45

Jay R. Vargas,
US Marine Corps

Company G, 2nd Battalion, 4th Marine Regiment, 9th Marine
 Amphibious Brigade
Dai Do, Quang Tri Province, Republic of Vietnam, April 30–May 2, 1968
Date Presented: May 14, 1970

CITATION:

*For conspicuous gallantry and intrepidity at the risk of his life above and beyond
the call of duty while serving as commanding officer, Company G, in action against
enemy forces from 30 April to 2 May 1968. On 1 May 1968, though suffering from
wounds he had incurred while relocating his unit under heavy enemy fire the
preceding day, Maj. Vargas combined Company G with two other companies
and led his men in an attack on the fortified village of Dai Do. Exercising expert
leadership, he maneuvered his marines across 700 meters of open rice paddy while
under intense enemy mortar, rocket and artillery fire and obtained a foothold in 2
hedgerows on the enemy perimeter, only to have elements of his company become
pinned down by the intense enemy fire. Leading his reserve platoon to the aid of his
beleaguered men, Maj. Vargas inspired his men to renew their relentless advance,
while destroying a number of enemy bunkers. Again wounded by grenade fragments, he refused aid as he moved about the hazardous area reorganizing his unit
into a strong defense perimeter at the edge of the village. Shortly after the objective
was secured, the enemy commenced a series of counterattacks and probes which
lasted throughout the night but were unsuccessful as the gallant defenders of Company G stood firm in their hard-won enclave. Reinforced the following morning,
the marines launched a renewed assault through Dai Do on the village of Dinh*

To, to which the enemy retaliated with a massive counterattack resulting in hand-to-hand combat. Maj. Vargas remained in the open, encouraging and rendering assistance to his marines when he was hit for the third time in the 3-day battle. Observing his battalion commander sustain a serious wound, he disregarded his excruciating pain, crossed the fire-swept area and carried his commander to a covered position, then resumed supervising and encouraging his men while simultaneously assisting in organizing the battalion's perimeter defense. His gallant actions uphold the highest traditions of the Marine Corps and the US Naval Service.

CAPT. JAY R. VARGAS was the first and only Hispanic American marine officer to earn the Medal of Honor in the Vietnam War. He was born in Winslow, Arizona, on July 29, 1938, to Manuel S.J. Vargas and Maria Teresa Sandoni. The senior Vargas was a Hispanic immigrant, and his mother an Italian one, having arrived from Italy in about 1917. Jay Vargas was named Manuel S.J. Vargas at birth but used the name Jay R. for most of his life, officially changing it in 1973. He never explained just why he finally made the change, nor did he respond to conjecture that Jay R. was derived from "Jr."

Vargas came from a patriotic family. Three of his brothers preceded him in the Marine Corps, with Angelo fighting on Iwo Jima and Frank on Okinawa in World War II and Joseph serving in Korea.

After graduating from Winslow High School, where he was an All-State baseball player, Vargas attended Arizona State University with an athletic scholarship and twice received All-Conference honors. He received a bachelor of science degree in education in 1962 and went on to play baseball in the minor leagues for the Class AA affiliate of the Los Angeles Dodgers. After a year his coaches determined that he could not hit the slider, and he was cut from the team. Vargas was devastated with the decision but still had a lifelong ambition to fall back on—to be a marine like his brothers. He enlisted in the Marine Corps on December 16, 1962, and graduated from the Officers Basic Course at Quantico in June 1963 as a 2nd lieutenant assigned to the 5th Marine Regiment, where he was an infantry platoon commander and rifle company executive officer. In 1964 he was a member of the 3rd Marine Division on Okinawa when he had his first encounter with recipients of the Medal of Honor. Upon entering the office of Brig. Gen. Raymond G. Davis, a Korean War medal recipient, to deliver a message, Vargas found the general in conference with four other wearers of the distinctive Medal of Honor blue ribbon—Carl Sitter, Reginald Myers, William Barber, and Louis Wilson. Vargas would later say that at the time had no idea that four years later he would become a member of their special club.

By 1968 he had risen in rank to captain in command of G Company, 2nd Battalion, 4th Marine Regiment in the northern part of South Vietnam near the DMZ. On March, 18, 1968, Vargas's company was participating in a battalion assault against elements of three North Vietnamese Army battalions in the heavily fortified village of Vinh Quan Thuong in Quang Tri Province. While two of the marine rifle companies advanced on the objective from the east, G Company, mounted on tanks and amphibian tractors, approached from the north. As the column moved across more than a mile of rice paddies and sand dunes, it came under increasingly intense rocket, artillery, and small-arms fire that stalled three of Vargas's seven tracked vehicles. He directed his men to dismount and then led them on foot through heavy enemy fire to penetrate the enemy's defensive lines, personally killing one enemy soldier as his company advanced and engaging the North Vietnamese in close combat, often hand-to-hand fighting. At the end of the battle, there were 127 North Vietnamese soldiers dead and 4 captured. Vargas received the Silver Star, the third-highest valor decoration, for his actions.

Six week later, on April 30, G Company floated down the Cua Viet River in tank-bearing boats to an area near the village of Dai Do, located fifteen kilometers south of the DMZ. Here they joined three other marine companies. G Company went ashore a kilometer southeast of the village and immediately began receiving fire. Despite being wounded, Vargas stayed in the field.

The next day he led an advance across 700 meters of open rice paddies toward the enemy positions. When they became pinned down by machine-gun fire, Vargas took charge of a few volunteers and charged forward. By the time he reached the enemy machine guns, he stood alone to neutralize the positions, personally killing eight North Vietnamese Army soldiers. He later recalled that they had had no choice but to attack right up the middle of the enemy defenses. Even though his fellow marines fell dead or wounded in the advance, Vargas went on alone, saying, "I couldn't stop. The adrenaline wouldn't let me."

Vargas secured the village and had begun preparing defensive positions when an NVA counterattack pushed the surviving marines into a Vietnamese graveyard. Surrounded, the marines survived only by the support of gunships, artillery, and naval gunfire. Still the NVA did not withdraw. On May 2 they attacked the survivors of G Company and other battalion units. In the fight

Vargas, although again hit by enemy shrapnel, exposed himself time after time as he pulled wounded marines, including his battalion commander, from the kill zone to more secure areas for medical treatment. When the battle finally concluded, 800 NVA soldiers and 72 marines lay dead—and Vargas was recommended for the Medal of Honor.

On May 14, 1970, Pres. Richard Nixon presented the medal to Vargas and eleven other marines, soldiers, sailors, and airmen in a White House ceremony in the East Room. President Nixon said,

> The Medal of Honor has been described many times, and there are no words that can add to the grandeur of that medal, what it means to those who receive it. I will simply say today that as we think of this great country of ours—particularly in this room, where we see the pictures of President Washington and Martha Washington, who, incidentally, were the only First Family that never lived in this house; it wasn't built until after their term—as we think of the beginning of this country 190 years ago, we think of it as the land of the free. We should all be reminded that it could not be the land of the free if it were not also the home of the brave. Today we honor the brave men, the men who, far beyond the call of duty, served their country magnificently in a war very far away, in a war which is one, many times, not understood and not supported by some in this country. I simply want to say to those who receive the medal and to those who are your families, that there are millions of your countrymen who today honor you as I have the privilege of representing them by presenting this medal to you. I believe also as I stand here, that as time goes on, millions more of your countrymen will look back at the experience that you have participated in and they will reach the conclusion that you served the cause of the land of the free by being brave, brave far beyond the call of duty; so brave that you received the very highest award that this Nation can provide.

A few months before the ceremony, Vargas's mother had died. He was very proud of her Italian heritage and often reminded those who called him Hispanic that he was also one-half Italian. His request that "M. Sandoni Vargas" be engraved on the back of his medal was approved by President Nixon and showed the valor of a son in battle and his lasting love for his mother.

Vargas remained in the corps after the ceremony and advanced in rank to colonel before his retirement to San Diego in 1992. During those years, he completed the Amphibious Warfare School, the Maine Command and Staff College, and the National War College. He also earned a master of arts degree in education from the United States National University in San Diego while on active duty. His assignments included command of the 7th Marine Regiment at Camp Pendleton, Naval ROTC instructor at the University of New Mexico, head of the Operations Branch at Marine Corps Headquarters, and the G-4 of the 1st Marine Amphibious Force.

After his retirement Vargas served as the secretary of the California Department of Veterans Affairs from 1993 to 1998. On July 9, 2001, he was appointed to the position of regional veterans liaison for the US Department of Veterans Affairs and remained in his position until January of 2009. Both during and after this time there, he led workshops for school administrators and teachers to introduce a free Congressional Medal of Honor Society curriculum that stresses qualities essential to a democracy. He also often speaks to veterans about their rights and encourages those suffering from depression or suicidal thoughts to seek help. In his speeches he relates the lessons he learned from his brothers that he calls the Three Golden Rules that he has followed all his life—both in and outside the Marine Corps. Number One is "Always set a good example; set your standards high." Number Two is "Take care of your men; regardless of peacetime or combat." And Number Three is "Never ask a Marine to do something you wouldn't do yourself."

Vargas has been honored by the American Academy of Achievement as an "extraordinary leader, a visionary and pioneer who has helped shape our world." He has received the National Collegiate Athletic Association's Commemorative Plaque for his contributions to college sports and his country. Vargas Field at the Winslow Ball Park is also named in his honor.

★★★

46

Jose Francisco Jimenez,
US Marine Corps

Company K, 3rd Battalion, 7th Marine Regiment, 1st Marine Division
South of Da Nang, Quang Nam Province, Republic of Vietnam,
   August 28, 1969
Date Presented: August 6, 1970

CITATION:

*For conspicuous gallantry and intrepidity at the risk of his life above and beyond
the call of duty while serving as a Fire Team Leader with Company K, Third Battalion, Seventh Marines, First Marine Division in operations against the enemy
in the Republic of Vietnam on 28 August 1969. On that date Lance Corporal
Jimenez' unit came under heavy attack by North Vietnamese Army soldiers concealed in well-camouflaged emplacements. Lance Corporal Jimenez reacted by
seizing the initiative and plunging forward toward the enemy positions. He personally destroyed several enemy personnel and silenced an antiaircraft weapon.
Shouting encouragement to his companions, Lance Corporal Jimenez continued
his aggressive forward movement. He slowly maneuvered to within ten feet of
hostile soldiers who were firing automatic weapons from a trench and, in the face
of vicious enemy fire, destroyed the position. Although he was by now the target of
concentrated fire from hostile gunners intent upon halting his assault, Lance Corporal Jimenez continued to press forward. As he moved to attack another enemy
soldier, he was mortally wounded. Lance Corporal Jimenez' indomitable courage,
aggressive fighting spirit and unfaltering devotion to duty upheld the highest traditions of the Marine Corps and of the United States Naval Service. He gallantly
gave his life for his country.*

ACCORDING TO HIS Medal of Honor citation, Jose Jimenez "gallantly gave his life for his country." This is not entirely accurate in that the Mexican hero was not an American citizen; it would be more accurate to say that he "gallantly gave his life for his adopted country and his fellow marines." He was born in Mexico City on March 20, 1946, to Francisco R. Cruz and Basilia Jimenez. His father died soon after his birth, and his mother moved to Morelia, Michoacan, Mexico, where he attended grammar school.

When Jimenez was ten, he journeyed with his mother to Eloy, Arizona, where he attended elementary school in Red Rock, Arizona and then graduated from Santa Cruz Union High School in Eloy. Jimenez, known as "Pancho" or "Jo Jo" to his friends, was popular with his fellow students in high school and was elected president of the Future Farmers of America. He excelled in working with livestock and found employment on a nearby ranch.

When Jimenez graduated from high school, he saw many of his friends either volunteering or being drafted into the military. As a noncitizen, he had no such obligation but told his mother, "This country has given us so much, and I must give something back."

His employer, rancher Lester Kinney, recommended that Jimenez join the Marine Corps and told him, "You are a good man and you should go with the best."

Jimenez enlisted in the Marine Corps Reserve in Phoenix on June 7, 1968, and transferred to the regular corps on August 12. He completed boot camp at the Marine Corps Recruit Depot in San Diego the following October and advanced infantry training at Camp Pendleton, California, in December. On February 27, 1969, he joined the 1st Marine Division in Vietnam. He performed well in the field and earned promotion to lance corporal in charge of a fire team on June 16.

On August 28, three companies of the 3rd Battalion, 7th Marine Regiment, were conducting a search-and-destroy mission twenty-nine miles south of the city of Da Nang when they encountered a large North Vietnamese Army force. Jimenez, aware that his company was in grave danger due to the heavy enemy fire, advanced alone and killed five and destroyed an antiaircraft position and a machine-gun emplacement before being mortally wounded by small-arms fire. Six more marines from his company were killed in the battle, two earning the Navy Cross and two more receiving the Silver Star.

In a letter dated September 2 to Jimenez's mother, 1st Lt. T. B. Edwards III, the company commander, informed her that her son had received last rites by a Catholic chaplain and that a memorial mass had been dedicated to his honor. Lieutenant Edwards concluded, "Jose Francisco was an excellent Marine. His 'happy' character and bravery were qualities he had that we all admired. He understood his mission here in Vietnam and he had great devotion to the Marine Corps and to his country. Perhaps these words are of some comfort to you; please know that those of us who knew him, feel his absence and we too, as you do, feel the loss of a good son and a good Marine."

Basilia Jimenez had her son buried in the Panteon Municipal Cemetery in Morelia, Mexico, near other members of her family. His name is on the Vietnam Veterans Memorial in Washington, DC (Panel W18, Line 2).

Pres. Richard Nixon awarded Jimenez's Medal of Honor to his mother on August 6, 1970. A short time later the Veterans Administration shipped his headstone to his mother's home in Arizona. She was financially unable to send the marker to her son's grave site in Mexico, so she stored it under her bed. It remained there for the next seventeen years before volunteers raised funds to ship it to Morelia. On November 11, 1987, Jimenez's Medal of Honor headstone was finally erected.

After Basilia Jimenez died in 2010 and was buried in Glendale, Arizona, her daughter Pilar began a campaign to bring her brother's remains back to the United States. On January 17, 2017, Jimenez was interred next to his mother in the Glendale Memorial Park Cemetery (Block 17, Section 2, Lot T). A bust of the marine hero is in the Eloy Veterans Center.

47

Emilio Alberto De La Garza Jr.,
US Marine Corps

Company E, 2nd Battalion, 1st Marine Regiment, 1st Marine Division
South of Da Nang, Quong Nam Province, Republic of Vietnam,
   April 11, 1970
Date Presented: September 9, 1971

CITATION:

For conspicuous gallantry and intrepidity at the risk of his life above and beyond the call of duty while serving as a machine gunner with Company E, Second Battalion, First Marines, First Marine Division, in the Republic of Vietnam on April 11, 1970. Returning with his squad from a night ambush operation, Lance Corporal De La Garza joined his Platoon commander and another Marine in searching for two enemy soldiers who had been observed fleeing for cover toward a small pond. Moments later, he located one of the enemy soldiers hiding among the reeds and brush. As the three Marines attempted to remove the resisting soldier from the pond, Lance Corporal De La Garza observed him pull the pin on a grenade. Shouting a warning, Lance Corporal De La Garza placed himself between the other two Marines and the ensuing blast from the grenade, thereby saving the lives of his comrades at the sacrifice of his own. By his prompt and decisive action, and his great personal valor in the face of almost certain death, Lance Corporal De La Garza upheld and further enhanced the finest traditions of the Marine Corps and the United States Naval Service.

THE FATHER OF Emilio Albert De La Garza Jr. was born in Austwell on the Texas Gulf Coast in 1920 and later moved to Laredo, where he worked as a furniture upholsterer. In 1941 he married Carmen C. Castaneda and enlisted in the army two years later. De La Garza served in North Africa and in the Po River Campaign in Italy before his discharge in 1947. He and Carmen then moved to Northwest Indiana where Emilio Sr. went to work at Inland Steel. Emilio Jr. was born on June 23, 1949, in East Chicago, Indiana, and graduated from E. C. Washington High School there in 1968.

After graduation, he married his high school sweetheart, Rosemary Rejon, and went to work in the same steel mill that employed his father. Emilio Jr. and Rosemary had a daughter, Renee, before he joined the Marine Corps on February 4, 1969, in Chicago. After boot camp at the Marine Corps Recruit Depot in San Diego, he completed infantry training at Camp Pendleton. The corps promoted him to private 1st class on July 1, 1969, and ordered him to Vietnam, where he arrived on July 28.

De La Garza began his tour as an ammo carrier in Company H, 2nd Battalion, 3rd Marine Regiment, 3rd Marine Division. On September 29, he was reassigned to the 1st Marine Division when the 3rd Division began rotating out of country in the initial withdrawal of US troops from the war zone. He was promoted to lance corporal on February 1, 1970.

On April 11, De La Garza was a machine gunner in the 3rd Platoon of E Company, 2nd Battalion, 1st Marine Regiment, conducting a squad-size patrol four miles south of Da Nang. When De La Garza spotted a Viet Cong hiding in a pond, he went into the water with a knife to capture the enemy soldier. As he dragged the VC to the shore, the enemy soldier pulled the pin on a concealed grenade. De La Garza shouted a warning to his fellow marines and placed himself to absorb the grenade's blast. Mortally wounded, his bravery saved the lives of several members of his squad.

De La Garza is buried in Saint John–Saint Joseph Catholic Cemetery in Hammond, Indiana. He was survived by his wife and daughter, his parents, and his brother Guadalupe, who would later serve seven years in the Marine Corps. De La Garza's name is on the Vietnam Veterans Memorial in Washington, DC (Panel 12W, Line 121). Vice Pres. Spiro T. Agnew presented his Medal of Honor to his family on September 9, 1971, in a ceremony at the Executive Office Building adjacent to the White House.

American Legion Emilio De La Garza Jr. Post 508 and Ivy Tech Community College's Emilio De La Garza Jr. Campus in East Chicago, Indiana, are named in his honor. Euclid Avenue in the city was also renamed for the marine hero. On Memorial Day, 2011, the Edward P. Robinson Community Veterans

Memorial in Munster, Indiana, dedicated a memorial plaque to De La Garza. In attendance was former navy corpsman Sam Lyles of Birmingham, Alabama, who had been with De La Garza when he was killed.

Renee Lugo, De La Garza's only child, also attended the Memorial Day ceremony. In interviews at the time she said that her mother and father had met in Hawaii in April 1970 for a mid-tour R&R. Two days after she returned home to East Chicago, she was notified that her husband had been killed shortly after he returned to Vietnam. Renee said that she did not remember her father because she was only two years old when he died but added, "I know the type of man he was. It doesn't surprise me that he did what he did. At the same time, it's just hard not having him here to see me grow up, to see his three granddaughters, and, you know, to be with my mom."

⋆⋆⋆

48

Miguel Hernandez Keith,
US Marine Corps

Combined Action Platoon 1-3-2, Combined Action Company 1-3,
  1st Combined Action Group, III Marine Amphibious Force
Quang Ngai Province, Republic of Vietnam, May 8, 1970
Date Presented: September 15, 1971

CITATION:

*For conspicuous gallantry and intrepidity at the risk of his life above and beyond
the call of duty while serving as a machine gunner with Combined Action platoon
1-3-2. During the early morning L/Cpl. Keith was seriously wounded when his
platoon was subjected to a heavy ground attack by a greatly outnumbering enemy
force. Despite his painful wounds, he ran across the fire-swept terrain to check the
security of vital defensive positions and then, while completely exposed to view,
proceeded to deliver a hail of devastating machinegun fire against the enemy. Determined to stop 5 of the enemy soldiers approaching the command post, he rushed
forward, firing as he advanced. He succeeded in disposing of 3 of the attackers
and in dispersing the remaining 2. At this point, a grenade detonated near L/Cpl.
Keith, knocking him to the ground and inflicting further severe wounds. Fighting
pain and weakness from loss of blood, he again braved the concentrated hostile fire
to charge an estimated 25 enemy soldiers who were massing to attack. The vigor of
his assault and his well-placed fire eliminated 4 of the enemy soldiers while the remainder fled for cover. During this valiant effort, he was mortally wounded by an
enemy soldier. By his courageous and inspiring performance in the face of almost
overwhelming odds, L/Cpl. Keith contributed in large measure to the success of*

his platoon in routing a numerically superior enemy force, and upheld the finest
traditions of the Marine Corps and of the US Naval Service.

AT THE AGE OF EIGHTEEN, Miguel Hernandez Keith was the youngest
Hispanic marine to earn the Medal of Honor in the Vietnam War. Keith was
born on June 2, 1951, in San Antonio, Texas, to Miguel and Delores Hernandez. The Hernandezes divorced a short time later, and Delores married Bobbie
G. Keith and moved with Miguel to Omaha, Nebraska. Keith legally adopted
Miguel, who would become known as Mike to his friends and as Michael to
his mother.

Delores Keith later recalled that her son was funny, rambunctious, and,
if she was about to admonish him, would disarm her with a smile. Miguel
attended North High School in Omaha, where he was known for his sense
of humor and his ability to play football, roller-skate, and dance. He was also
known for his strong will and his loyalty as a friend.

In December 1968, Keith dropped out of high school and enlisted in the
Marine Corps Reserves in Omaha on January 21, 1969. He was motivated by
a desire to serve his country and to follow in the footsteps of his stepfather,
who had also been a marine. On May 1, 1969, Keith transferred to the Regular Marine Corps and completed boot camp at the Marine Recruit Depot at
San Diego on July 17. He was promoted to private 1st class on August 1 and
completed infantry training at Camp Pendleton on September 18 and received
orders to Vietnam.

Delores Keith later recalled that she told her son that she did not want him
to go to Vietnam. He replied that he felt that he had a job to do and assured
her that he would make her proud.

Keith arrived in Vietnam on November 6, 1969; he was assigned to the 1st
Combined Action Group and was promoted to lance corporal on April 1, 1970.
On May 8 his platoon came under attack by a numerically superior force in
Quang Ngai Province. Although wounded early in the battle, Keith charged
forward with a machine gun, killing three of the enemy and stopping their advance. Wounded once more by grenade fragments, he nevertheless continued
to advance toward the center of the enemy formation containing more than
twenty-five soldiers. His attack forced them to retreat but not before wounding Keith for the third time, this time mortally.

Keith is buried in Omaha's Forest Lawn Cemetery (Plot 17 AL, Grave 444).
His name is on the Vietnam Veterans Memorial in Washington, DC (Panel

11W, Line 132). On September 15, 1971, Vice Pres. Spiro T. Agnew presented Keith's Medal of Honor to his family in a ceremony in the Executive Office Building adjacent to the White House. This is the same ceremony that honored Emilio De La Garza and three other marines.

Keith Hall, a barracks at Henderson Hall at the Marine Corps Headquarters in Arlington, Virginia, is named in his honor. A bronze plaque in its lobby recounts the young marine's bravery. The navy launched the USNS *Miguel Keith*, an Expeditionary Mobile Base, on May 10, 2021. Omaha's North High School presented an honorary diploma to Delores Keith for Miguel. A park on the corner of 30th and Y Streets in Omaha also bears his name. In 2015, Delores turned over her son's Medal of Honor and other decorations to park officials for display.

Delores Keith moved back to Texas after her son's death. Family friends said that she could not take the heartache of staying in Nebraska. In one of her final interviews, she said, "He didn't even get to see the world, to see anything. That's why I used to cry and I used to yell. I'd say, 'Why him? Why him?'"

★★★

49

Ralph Ellis Dias,
US Marine Corps

Company D, 1st Battalion, 7th Marine Regiment, 1st Marine Division
Que Son Mountains, Quang Nam Province, Republic of Vietnam,
  November 12, 1969
Date Presented: July 17, 1974

CITATION:

As a member of a reaction force which was pinned down by enemy fire while assisting a platoon in the same circumstance, Pfc. Dias, observing that both units were sustaining casualties, initiated an aggressive assault against an enemy machine-gun bunker which was the principal source of hostile fire. Severely wounded by enemy snipers while charging across the open area, he pulled himself to the shelter of a nearby rock. Braving enemy fire for a second time, Pfc. Dias was again wounded. Unable to walk, he crawled 15 meters to the protection of a rock located near his objective and, repeatedly exposing himself to intense hostile fire, unsuccessfully threw several hand grenades at the machinegun emplacement. Still determined to destroy the emplacement, Pfc. Dias again moved into the open and was wounded a third time by sniper fire. As he threw a last grenade which destroyed the enemy position, he was mortally wounded by another enemy round. Pfc. Dias' indomitable courage, dynamic initiative, and selfless devotion to duty upheld the highest traditions of the Marine Corps and the US Naval Service. He gallantly gave his life in the service to his country.

RALPH ELLIS DIAS was born on July 15, 1950, to Melvin and Anna Mae Dias in Indiana, Pennsylvania—the self-proclaimed "Christmas tree capital of the world." He attended Elderton Joint High School in nearby Shelocta before dropping out after two years. Dias enlisted in the Marine Corps at age seventeen on October 9, 1967. After completing boot camp at the Marine Corps Recruit Depot at Parris Island, South Carolina, in December, he transferred to Camp Lejeune, North Carolina, for infantry training.

Upon completion of his instruction at Camp Lejeune, Dias joined Company B, 1st Battalion, 28th Marine Regiment of the 5th Marine Division at Camp Pendleton, California, for further training. On April 28, 1969, he arrived in Vietnam as a member of the 1st Marine Division. Members of his platoon would later remember him as a quiet, soft-spoken marine.

While on patrol on the north slopes of the Que Son Mountains south of An Hoa on November 12, 1969, Dias's platoon went to support another platoon that was in heavy contact with a North Vietnamese Army company fighting from bunkers and trenches and supported by mortar fire. In the ensuing fight, an AH-1G Cobra gunship that was supporting the marines was shot down, killing its two-man crew. When Dias's platoon became pinned down with three dead marines and in danger of being overrun, he charged forward over an open area against the primary enemy machine-gun position, only to be seriously wounded by sniper fire. Despite his wound, he picked himself up and again charged the enemy machine gun, only to be wounded a second time. Unable to stand, he crawled forward throwing hand grenades. Just as his last grenade destroyed the machine-gun position, he was mortally wounded by another enemy rifle bullet. His heroism allowed his platoon to safely withdraw.

Dias is buried in Oakdale Cemetery in Leetonia, Ohio. His large black marble headstone contains his complete Medal of Honor citation. A Veterans Administration flat marker also is at the site. Dias's name is on the Vietnam Veterans Memorial in Washington, DC (Panel 16W, Line 063). In addition to his mother and father, he was survived by four sisters and three brothers—one of whom is a former marine.

Vice Pres. Gerald Ford awarded Dias's Medal of Honor to his mother in a ceremony at the Blair House on July 17, 1974. He was the fifty-sixth marine to be awarded the medal in the Vietnam War. A portion of Ohio State Route 344 in Leetonia is named in his honor. Dias's Medal of Honor, other awards, and photographs are on exhibit in the Massillon Museum in Massillon, Ohio.

50

Louis Richard Rocco,
US Army

Advisory Team 162, US Military Assistance Command, Vietnam

Northeast of Firebase Katum, Tay Ninh Province, Republic of
   Vietnam, May 24, 1970

Date Presented: December 12, 1974

CITATION:

Warrant Officer (then Sergeant First Class) Rocco distinguished himself when he volunteered to accompany a medical evacuation team on an urgent mission to evacuate 8 critically wounded Army of the Republic of Vietnam personnel. As the helicopter approached the landing zone, it became the target for intense enemy automatic weapons fire. Disregarding his own safety, WO Rocco identified and placed accurate suppressive fire on the enemy positions as the aircraft descended toward the landing zone. Sustaining major damage from the enemy fire, the aircraft was forced to crash land, causing WO Rocco to sustain a fractured wrist and hip and a severely bruised back. Ignoring his injuries, he extracted the survivors from the burning wreckage, sustaining burns to his own body. Despite intense enemy fire, WO Rocco carried each unconscious man across approximately 20 meters of exposed terrain to the Army of the Republic of Vietnam perimeter. On each trip, his severely burned hands and broken wrist caused excruciating pain, but the lives of the unconscious crash survivors were more important than his personal discomfort, and he continued his rescue efforts. Once inside the friendly position, WO Rocco helped administer first aid to his wounded comrades until his wounds and burns caused him to collapse and lose consciousness. His bravery under fire and intense devotion to duty were directly responsible for saving 3 of his fellow soldiers from certain death. His unparalleled bravery in the face of enemy fire, his complete disregard for his own pain and injuries, and his performance were far above and beyond the call of duty and were in keeping with the highest traditions of self-sacrifice and courage of the military service.

AS A YOUTH ON THE streets of East Los Angeles in 1954, Louis Richard Rocco was given the choice by a judge of joining the army or going to jail. Sixteen years later he was a career noncommissioned officer who earned the Medal of Honor in the Vietnam War.

Born in Albuquerque, New Mexico, on November 19, 1938, to a Spanish Italian father, Louis Rocco, and a Mexican American mother, Lita, Rocco, who always went by Richard, grew up in the suburb of Barelas with eight brothers and sisters. His father was often without work, and Richard stole potatoes and corn from the surrounding fields so his family would have something to eat. When he was ten years old, the Rocco family moved to the San Fernando Valley in California and then to Wilmington in South Los Angeles.

By the time he was thirteen, Rocco had joined a street gang and was constantly getting into fights and in trouble with the law. In a 2000 interview, he talked about his abusive, alcoholic father saying, "I hated being at home. I had a lot of problems, and I got kicked out of school I don't know how many times. Whenever a test or something could come up, I would act out or do something to get into trouble. That way, my secret could be kept."

Rocco was arrested for armed robbery at age sixteen and faced going to juvenile detention until he was twenty-one. While waiting at the courthouse for his sentencing, he wandered into an army recruiting office where he met a noncommissioned officer who listened to his story. The NCO then accompanied Rocco to court and convinced the judge to give him another chance. The judge ruled that if Rocco returned to school, obeyed curfew, shunned his gang, and stayed out of trouble, he could, with his parents' permission, join the army when he reached seventeen instead of going to jail.

On January 6, 1956, Rocco entered the US Army in Los Angeles and then completed basic training at Fort Ord, California. He then went to Fort Bragg, North Carolina, where he graduated from advanced infantry, airborne, and basic medical training before joining the 504th Parachute Infantry of the 82nd Airborne Division. He later said, "The army was what I needed. I didn't have structure. I didn't have discipline. I needed that desperately. I needed what the army had."

From Fort Bragg, Rocco transferred to Germany, where he served in the 11th Airborne Division as a field medic and in an evacuation hospital. While in Germany, he earned his high school equivalency diploma. In December 1960 he returned to the States and worked in the medical detachment of Letterman General Hospital at the Presidio of San Francisco, California. Eighteen months later he transferred to the army hospital at Fort MacArthur, California. There he found the recruiting NCO from Los Angeles who had saved him from jail recovering from injuries. Rocco took charge to ensure that his former mentor received special attention and constant care.

After a brief tour back in Germany, Rocco began his first tour in Vietnam as a Military Assistance Command (MACV) advisor to the South Vietnamese 7th Infantry Division operating out of My Tho near Saigon in November 1965. Following a stateside tour and another back in Germany, he went to Vietnam for a second time in November 1969 as an advisor to the South Vietnamese Airborne Division with MACV Advisory Team 162. He had by then advanced in rank to sergeant 1st class.

In an oral history interview on March 15, 1987, with the US Army Medical Department, Rocco talked about the actions that led to his Medal of Honor. He said,

> I was about a week away from my R&R. I was there seven or eight months and I was getting ready to go on R&R. We were making that push into Cambodia at that particular time. I was working with the 1st Cav. The 1st Cav was giving me helicopter support for the Vietnamese and we were in a joint operation throughout 3rd Corps and into Cambodia. And I was taking care of Vietnamese casualties, as well as American casualties. In a clearing station there on the border of Vietnam and Cambodia, was a place called Katum. And I had one medevac ship flying for me. And they were starting to get flooded with Vietnamese that were trying to leave the battle scene. So they just kept swarming the aircraft. And the pilots told me that unless I flew with them, and started sorting the people out, and keeping the rest of them off of the chopper, that they weren't going to fly for me no more. So I started flying medevac missions with them, and I, when we set down I'd go on, I'd check the wounded out and sort them out. And start medevacing them seriously, you know, going to the triage form of evacuation. In May of '70, got a call that they had some urgently wounded people. They were taking a lot of fire, taking a lot of casualties. And we called back

and asked to see where they were receiving fire from. And they told us they were receiving fires from north, south, and east. And that only left one approach into the LZ. And when we got there we were receiving fire from everywhere. As we started to hover down we were taking a lot of fire. So the advisors on the ground told us to get out of there. But by that time we were committed, and when we tried to get back the chopper just took intense fire and was shot down. And we hit an open field between the NVA and the South Vietnamese troop forces. The plane hit and it turned over on its side and started burning. And I, you know, at the time that we're being shot at we're shooting back. We, the 1st Cav used to carry 60's on their choppers. And myself and the medic were firing our 16's. We had the 60's out firing. When shot down, we had a case of grenades on board. And we had ammo on board. We hit. The aircraft caught fire. One of the pilots had received an AK round through his leg. Another, the other pilot had his arm ripped off. It was hanging. The medic had his back and hip broken, and his jaw completely ripped off. And one gunner was trapped in the chopper. The other one was in shock. So I pulled these guys and pulled them out of the helicopter and carried them to an open field, and put them behind a huge tree that was knocked down that offered protection. And I just ran back and forth across this, like a football field, and pulled them back. And after we were behind this tree later on the South Vietnamese came and took us into their perimeter. You could not get medevacs to come in. It was, we were under heavy fire for all that day and that night. We started calling in fire on our own position. The two companies were disseminated. They were, they had their dead just stacked like cord wood. So, on the second, they tried three attempts. Two helicopters got shot down trying to get us out. But they were able to get out of the fire zone. And on the second day they came in full force. They brought in what they call the Cobras. Had air strikes going. Just had everything available. They just brought in as much artillery, and air support as they could. While they were saturating the area they flew in a medevac behind the two Cobras. And through fire, they pulled us out. It turned out, later on we found out it turned out it was a regimental bunker complex. And they were armed to the teeth. They had a, they had a lot of firepower.

Rocco was evacuated back to the States with back injuries, a broken hip and a broken wrist, and burns to his face and hands. Following his recovery, he attended the first Physician's Assistance Course at the Academy of Health

Science at Fort Sam Houston, Texas. Upon graduation he received an associate's degree, an appointment as a warrant officer, and orders to report to the 101st Airborne Division at Fort Campbell, Kentucky.

On December 12, 1974, Pres. Gerald R. Ford presented the Medal of Honor to Rocco in a White House ceremony. Ford said, "This day is witness to the fact that the bravest of the brave still rise from among our people. That freedom and justice have survived and will survive. That peace is still our most precious and enduring goal. And that we—the American people—will forever cherish the noble ideals entrusted to us these past two centuries by our forefathers. These ideals do not sleep. They are not silent. They live among us here today."

Rocco retired from the army in 1978 as a chief warrant officer two and returned to his Albuquerque birthplace, where he went to work in the emergency room of the local Veterans Administration hospital. In 1983 he was named director of New Mexico's Veterans Service Commission. During his tenure, he established the Vietnam Veterans of New Mexico organization, opened a veterans center that provided peer counseling to Vietnam veterans, and started a shelter for the homeless, a nursing home for veterans, and a children's program that taught patriotism and courage. He also persuaded the New Mexico legislature and voters to waive tuition for all veterans at state colleges.

Rocco volunteered to go back on active duty in 1991 after the outbreak of the Gulf War. In an oral history interview with the US Army Medical Department on May 22 of that year, he explained his motivation to once again be in uniform. He said, "I kind of missed the military and at that particular time I thought that we were going to be in a full scale war in the Middle East and I felt that I could contribute in some way to the war effort. I felt that they needed experienced medics, experienced PA's, and that if I couldn't get to Saudi I could at least teach or talk to the medics here at Fort Sam."

After six months of recruiting and training medics and medical personnel, Rocco once again retired from active duty. When he returned home to Albuquerque, he met his fourth wife, Maria Chavez, and the couple relocated to San Miguel de Allende, Mexico, in 1992. They moved to San Antonio, Texas, in 1998 where Rocco continued to advise and council his fellow veterans and to promote antidrug programs in local schools.

In early 2002, Rocco was diagnosed with lung cancer, possibly from his exposure to Agent Orange in Vietnam, and died at age sixty-three the following October 19. He is buried in Fort Sam Houston National Cemetery (Section AI, Site 549). A youth center in San Antonio, a dining facility at Fort Sam Houston, and a park in Albuquerque are named in his honor. There is also a Louis Rocco chapter of the American GI Forum in Oklahoma City, and the Army Aviation Association of America (AAAA) offers a scholarship named in his honor.

Rocco was extremely modest about his Medal of Honor and seldom mentioned it to anyone. He was boastful, however, about his cooking skills and often bragged about winning the New Mexico Chili Cook-off. He also enjoyed working on cars and restoring vintage automobiles. He did his best to suppress his anger about how Vietnam veterans were treated when they came home, but in one of his final interviews, he said that he was at peace. He added, "I'm going to die. I don't want to die angry."

★★★

51

Roy Perez Benavidez,
US Army

Detachment B-56, 5th Special Forces Group (Airborne)
West of Loc Ninh, Republic of Vietnam, May 2, 1968
Date Presented: February 24, 1981

CITATION:

Master Sergeant (then Staff Sergeant) Roy P. Benavidez, United States Army, distinguished himself by a series of daring and extremely valorous actions on 2 May 1968 while assigned to Detachment B56, 5th Special Forces Group (Airborne), 1st Special Forces, Republic of Vietnam. On the morning of 2 May 1968, a 12-man Special Forces Reconnaissance Team was inserted by helicopters of the 240th Assault Helicopter Company in a dense jungle area west of Loc Ninh, Vietnam to gather intelligence information about confirmed large-scale enemy activity. This area was controlled and routinely patrolled by the North Vietnamese Army. After a short period of time on the ground, the team met heavy enemy resistance, and requested emergency extraction. Three helicopters attempted extraction, but were unable to land due to intense enemy small arms and anti-aircraft fire. Sergeant Benavidez was at the Forward Operating Base in Loc Ninh monitoring the operation by radio when these helicopters, of the 240th Assault Helicopter Company, returned to off-load wounded crew members and to assess aircraft damage. Sergeant Benavidez voluntarily boarded a returning aircraft to assist in another extraction attempt. Realizing that all the team members were either dead or wounded and unable to move to the pickup zone, he directed the aircraft to a nearby clearing where he jumped from the hovering helicopter, and ran approximately 75 meters under withering small arms fire to the crippled team. Prior to reaching the team's position he was wounded in his right leg, face, and head. Despite these painful injuries, he took charge, repositioning the team members and directing their fire to facilitate the landing of an extraction aircraft, and the loading of wounded and dead team members. He then threw smoke canisters to direct the aircraft to the team's position. Despite his severe wounds and under intense enemy fire, he carried and dragged half of the wounded team members to the awaiting aircraft. He then provided protective fire by running alongside the aircraft as it moved to pick up the remaining team members. As the enemy's fire intensified, he hurried to recover the body and classified documents on the dead team leader. When he reached the leader's body, Sergeant Benavidez was severely wounded by small arms fire in the abdomen and grenade fragments in his back. At nearly the same moment, the aircraft pilot was mortally wounded, and his helicopter crashed. Although in extremely critical condition due to his multiple wounds, Sergeant Benavidez secured the classified documents and made his way back to the wreckage, where he aided the wounded out of the overturned aircraft, and gathered the stunned survivors into a defensive perimeter. Under increasing enemy automatic weapons and grenade fire, he moved around the perimeter distributing water and ammunition to his weary men, reinstilling in them a will to live and fight. Facing a buildup of enemy opposition with a beleaguered team, Sergeant Benavidez mustered his strength, began calling in tactical air strikes and directed the fire from supporting gunships to suppress the enemy's fire and so permit another extraction attempt. He was wounded again in his thigh by small arms fire while administering first aid to a wounded team member just before another extraction helicopter was able to land. His indomitable spirit kept him going as he began to ferry his comrades to the craft. On his second trip with the wounded, he was clubbed from behind by an enemy soldier. In the ensuing hand-to-hand combat, he sustained additional wounds to his head and arms before killing his adversary. He then continued under devastating fire to carry the wounded to the helicopter. Upon reaching the aircraft, he spotted and killed two enemy soldiers who were rushing the craft from an angle that prevented the aircraft door gunner from firing upon them. With little strength remaining, he made one last trip to the perimeter to ensure that all classified material had been collected or destroyed, and to bring in the remaining wounded. Only then, in extremely serious condition from numerous wounds and loss of blood, did he allow himself to be pulled into the extraction aircraft. Sergeant Benavidez's' gallant choice to join voluntarily his comrades who were in critical straits, to expose himself constantly to withering enemy fire, and his refusal to be stopped despite numerous severe wounds, saved the lives of at least eight men. His fearless personal *leadership, tenacious devotion to duty, and extremely valorous actions in the face of overwhelming odds were in keeping with the highest traditions of the military service, and reflect the utmost credit on him and the United States Army.*

ALTHOUGH IT TOOK NEARLY twelve years for him to actually receive it, Roy Benavidez was the first US Army Special Forces enlisted soldier to earn the Medal of Honor in the Vietnam War. Born on August 5, 1935, in Lindenau near Cuero, Texas, as Raul Perez Benavidez, he later changed his first name to Roy. He said he did that after becoming angry at the way a drill sergeant shouted his first name as "Ra-oooool." Much about Benavidez's early life and military career is recorded in the two books he wrote, *The Three Wars of Roy Benavidez* and *Medal of Honor: A Vietnam Warrior's Story*.

The future hero's father, Salvador Benavidez Jr., was a native Texan whose ancestors had moved from Mexico to Texas in 1833 to receive a land grant. His relatives had fought on the side of Texas in its war for independence with Mexico. Salvador worked as a vaquero (cowboy) on neighboring ranches and as a sharecropper. Roy's mother, Teresa Perez, was a Yaqui Indian born in Monclova, Coahuila, Mexico.

In 1937, Roy's brother Rogelio was born; the same year that their father died of tuberculosis. Teresa and her two sons moved into Cuero, where she got a job as a domestic worker. She married Pablo Chavez about a year later, and although he was not cruel to his stepsons, he paid little attention to them.

At age five, Benavidez attended a local Spanish school to learn English before advancing to the regular school. The next year he entered St. Mary's Catholic School. A year later, when Roy was only seven, his mother also died of tuberculosis. His aunt and uncle, Nicholas and Isabel Benavidez, took Roy and Rogelio into their home in El Campo and raised them with their own eight children. Roy's grandfather Salvador lived nearby and often told him, "You are a Benavidez. You must always bring honor to that name." He also said, "People sometimes need help, and when they do you must help them."

Benavidez grew up as a self-described "tough, mean little kid" who was quick to anger and never hesitant to fight. As a youth he worked as a shoeshine boy and each fall joined his aunt, uncle, and cousins as migrant workers in the sugar beet fields of Colorado and the cotton fields of West Texas. He missed so much school time while working the fields that he dropped out when he was fifteen and went to work in a tire repair shop.

By 1952, Benavidez understood that with a lack of education and training his future was limited. He thought about going back to school but decided he was just too old to return to the classroom. Instead he joined the Texas National Guard. Benavidez found that army life suited him, and he enjoyed meeting people from different backgrounds and experiences. Twice he earned corporal stripes, only to lose them because of fighting and mouthing off to superiors. The highlight of his time with the National Guard was meeting World War II hero Audie Murphy, with whom he shared a small stature and a childhood of poverty. Benavidez later wrote, "Audie Murphy became my idol and role model."

At age nineteen Benavidez saw that there was no future on the farms and orchards where machines were rapidly replacing people. While the National Guard provided a part-time job, his only training had been as an infantry-man. In June 1954 he took a bus to Houston and enlisted in the regular army, knowing that he would be paid, housed, fed, and taught a trade. He had two ambitions: In hopes of someday becoming a Texas Ranger, he sought duty as a military policeman. As a result of wanting to be the best, he volunteered for airborne training.

He achieved neither. After basic training at Fort Ord, California, and then advanced infantry training at Fort Carson, Colorado—near where he had picked sugar beets as a migrant worker—he received orders to Korea as an infantryman. Although disappointed, Benavidez remained positive about being a soldier. He later wrote, "I saw it as my single chance to be successful. If I screwed up or if I succeeded it wasn't because I was brown or black or white. It was because of what was in me." He also enjoyed the travel and meeting other soldiers, including future baseball player and manager Billy Martin and country-western entertainer Faron Young.

After sixteen months in Korea with the 7th Infantry Division, Benavidez returned to the States in February 1957 for assignment to Fort Chaffee, Arkan-sas. He was there for only a short time with the most noteworthy event being his crossing paths with recent draftee Elvis Presley. Soon he was on his way to Germany for another sixteen-month overseas tour. He was then assigned to Fort Gordon, Georgia, and later to Fort Benning, where he served mostly as a driver to senior officers before being transferred to Fort Bragg, North Caro-lina. At Bragg he finally got the opportunity to attend jump school and in 1959 joined the 82nd Airborne Division, where he remained for the next six years.

In October 1965, Benavidez was ordered to Vietnam as an advisor to the Army of the Republic of Vietnam's 25th Infantry Division near Tam Ky. In early 1966 he was seriously wounded when he stepped on a land mine. Evacuated to Brooke Army Medical Center in San Antonio, Benavidez learned from his doctors that he would not be able to walk again. They were preparing his medical discharge. Benavidez convinced them to delay his discharge as he relied on his strong Catholic beliefs and inner will power to first crawl, then stand, and finally regain his mobility.

After a year of rehabilitation, he walked out of the hospital and returned to active duty with the 82d Airborne Division in July 1966. He then volunteered for Special Forces and after completing their courses went on training missions to Panama, Honduras, and Ecuador. The Green Beret sergeant hoped to continue to use his Spanish language skills with a permanent assignment to Venezuela. Instead he received orders to return to Vietnam for a second tour.

Benavidez arrived back in Southeast Asia in January 1968 and was assigned to the 5th Special Forces Military Assistance Command Studies and Observation Group (MACV-SOG). He joined Team B-56 operating out of Loc Ninh. The team's primary mission was to perform highly classified reconnaissance patrols across the border into Cambodia to determine North Vietnamese Army movement and troop strength. All of the Special Forces soldiers had what they called Alpha names to identify themselves on the radio. Benavidez soon became known as Tango Mike-Mike, "The Mean Mexican."

On May 2, 1968, Benavidez, now a staff sergeant, was sitting in the team's communications bunker in Loc Ninh when the radio erupted with shouts from a twelve-man patrol, composed up of three fellow Green Berets and nine Montagnard tribesmen. The team was deep in Cambodia and in danger of being overrun by a vastly superior NVA force. The radio operator pleaded, "Get us out of here! For God's sake, get us out!"

Benavidez grabbed a medical bag and, armed only with a knife, rushed to the helipad where an extraction helicopter was preparing to lift off.

When they reached a clearing near the team, Benavidez jumped from the helicopter only to be immediately hit by bullets and shrapnel in his legs and face. Despite the injuries, he found the patrol, all either dead or wounded. He began dragging the men to the clearing for extraction and retrieving classified documents and equipment. Just after he had most of the men on the chopper, he was shot in the back. About the same time, the chopper, which was skimming the ground to pick up more wounded, crashed onto the jungle floor.

The Mean Mexican gathered those still alive into a defensive perimeter as he coordinated air support. For the next six hours they held out in what became known as "six hours in hell." Benavidez suffered another gunshot wound to his leg. Near the end of the fight an NVA soldier penetrated the perimeter and stabbed Benavidez with his bayonet. The Mean Mexican wrestled the enemy soldier to the ground and killed him with his knife. When another extraction helicopter was finally able to land, Benavidez loaded the dead and wounded and then grabbed a rifle to kill two more NVA soldiers who were attempting to fire on the chopper.

Benavidez was the last man off the pickup zone and joined the dead and wounded in the cargo area of the helicopter. During the flight, he lost consciousness, appearing dead to initial examination staff at the evacuation hospital. A doctor was about to zip him into a body when Benavidez came to and managed to spit in his face. In the operating room doctors counted thirty-seven separate bullet, bayonet, and shrapnel wounds.

Once again Benavidez was transferred to Brooke Army Medical Center, where he remained for nearly a year as his wounds healed. During that time he was awarded the Distinguished Service Cross for his "six hours in hell." In May 1969 he again walked out of the hospital and reported to Fort Devens, Massachusetts, and then to Fort Riley, Kansas. His final assignment was at Fort Sam Houston, Texas, before he retired from active duty on September 10, 1976, and moved with his wife and three children back to El Campo.

Benavidez encountered fellow soldiers and officers, both before and after his retirement, who thought that he should have received the Medal of Honor. Several of his former officers began a campaign to upgrade his DSC but had no success. Some expressed concern that the army was not willing to admit that it had been conducting cross-border operations into Cambodia. However, the army was willing to review the recommendations but, following its own regulations, turned down a change of status five times because there was no "additional substantial information" provided. What this meant was that there was no information from a living witness to the battle.

A witness was finally found in an unusual way. On February 22, 1978, the *El Campo Leader News* ran a lengthy account of Benavidez's story. It was picked up by the Associated Press and republished worldwide. A hotel clerk in Australia put the article aside for a regular guest who visited from his home in the Fiji Islands. On his next trip to Australia, Brian T. O'Connor, the last remaining survivor of the twelve-man patrol read the article, contacted his old friend and teammate, and provided a lengthy statement supporting the upgrade to the Medal of Honor.

On February 24, 1981, Pres. Ronald Regan presented Roy P. Benavidez with the Medal of Honor in a Pentagon Courtyard ceremony. In his remarks, Reagan said, "If the story of his heroism were a movie script, you would not believe it."

President Reagan continued,

> Several years ago, we brought home a group of American fighting men who had obeyed their country's call and who had fought as bravely and as well as any Americans in our history. They came home without a victory not because they'd been defeated, but because they'd been denied permission to win. They were greeted by no parades, no bands, no waving of the flag they had so nobly served. There's been no "thank you" for their sacrifice. There's been no effort to honor and, thus, give pride to the families of more than 57,000 young men who gave their lives in that faraway war. As the poet Laurence Binyon wrote, "They shall grow not old, as we that are left grow old: Age shall not weary them, nor the years condemn. At the going down of the sun and in the morning we will remember them." Pride, of course, cannot wipe out the burden of grief borne by their families, but it can make that grief easier to bear. The pain will not be quite as sharp if they know their fellow citizens share that pain. There's been little or no recognition of the gratitude we owe to the more than 300,000 men who suffered wounds in that war. John Stuart Mill said, "War is an ugly thing, but not the ugliest of things. A man who has nothing which he cares about more than his personal safety is a miserable creature and has no chance of being free unless made and kept so by the exertions of better men than himself."

Benavidez returned home to speak often to schoolchildren on the importance of getting an education. He also spoke to civic, business, and military groups. In his talks he often said, "The real heroes are the ones who gave their lives for their country. I don't like to be called a hero. I just did what I was trained to do."

When the Social Security Administration began plans to cut disability payments to thousands of veterans and nonveterans in 1983, Benavidez testified before the House Select Committee on Aging to successfully preserve the benefits.

Benavidez died on November 29, 1998, at the age of sixty-three at Brooke Army Medical Center from respiratory failure and complications of diabetes. His body was escorted to St. Robert Bellarmine Catholic Church in El Campo, where he had married, where his three children were married, and where he had attended Mass. His body was then returned to Fort Sam Houston's main chapel for a public viewing followed by a Requiem Mass at San Fernando Cathedral in San Antonio. He was then buried in Fort Sam Houston National Cemetery (Section AI, Site 553).

Both the military and civilian sectors have further honored Benavidez. Bearing his name are the US Army Reserve Center in Corpus Christi; Artillery Training Area 67 at Fort Sill, Oklahoma; the National Guard Armory in El Campo; the Special Operations Logistic Complex at Fort Bragg; a conference room at the US Military Academy at West Point; and the USNS *Benavidez*. Also paying tribute with their names are American Legion Post 400 in San Antonio; a city park in Colorado Springs; elementary schools in Houston and San Antonio; and a recreation center in Eagle Pass, Texas. A GI Joe action figure, the Roy P. Benavidez Commemorative Edition, was released in 2001.

Benavidez's papers—including correspondence, photographs, military files and documents, and other memorabilia documenting his career—are on file in the Briscoe Center for American History at the University of Texas in Austin. His Medal of Honor is on display in the Ronald Reagan Presidential Library and Museum in Simi Valley, California.

★ ★ ★

52

Alfred Velazquez Rascon,
US Army

Headquarters Company, 1st Battalion, 503rd Airborne Infantry Regiment, 173rd Airborne Infantry Brigade

Long Khanh Province, Republic of Vietnam, March 16, 1966

Date Presented: February 8, 2000

CITATION:

Specialist Four Alfred Rascon distinguished himself by a series of extraordinarily courageous acts on March 16, 1966, while assigned as a medic to the Reconnaissance Platoon, Headquarters Company, 1st Battalion (Airborne), 503rd Infantry, 173rd Airborne Brigade (Separate). While moving to reinforce its sister battalion under intense enemy attack, the Reconnaissance Platoon came under heavy fire from a numerically superior enemy force. The intense enemy fire from crew-served weapons and grenades severely wounded several point squad soldiers. Specialist Rascon, ignoring directions to stay behind shelter until covering fire could be provided, made his way forward. He repeatedly tried to reach the severely wounded point machine-gunner laying on an open enemy trail, but was driven back each time by the withering fire. Disregarding his personal safety, he jumped to his feet, ignoring flying bullets and exploding grenades to reach his comrade. To protect him from further wounds, he intentionally placed his body between the soldier and enemy machine guns, sustaining numerous shrapnel injuries and a serious wound to the hip. Disregarding his serious wounds he dragged the larger soldier from the fire-raked trail. Hearing the second machine-gunner yell that he was running out of ammunition, Specialist Rascon, under heavy enemy fire crawled back to the wounded machine-gunner stripping him of his bandoleers of ammunition, giving

them to the machine-gunner who continued his suppressive fire. Specialist Rascon
fearing the abandoned machine gun, its ammunition and spare barrel could fall
into enemy hands made his way to retrieve them. On the way, he was wounded
in the face and torso by grenade fragments, but disregarded these wounds to re-
cover the abandoned machine gun, ammunition and spare barrel items, enabling
another soldier to provide added suppressive fire to the pinned-down squad. In
searching for the wounded, he saw the point grenadier being wounded by small
arms fire and grenades being thrown at him. Disregarding his own life and his
numerous wounds, Specialist Rascon reached and covered him with his body ab-
sorbing the blasts from the exploding grenades, and saving the soldier's life, but
sustaining additional wounds to his body. While making his way to the wounded
point squad leader, grenades were hurled at the sergeant. Again, in complete disre-
gard for his own life, he reached and covered the sergeant with his body, absorbing
the full force of the grenade explosions. Once more Specialist Rascon was critically
wounded by shrapnel, but disregarded his own wounds to continue to search and
aid the wounded. Severely wounded, he remained on the battlefield, inspiring his
fellow soldiers to continue the battle. After the enemy broke contact, he disregarded
aid for himself, instead treating the wounded and directing their evacuation. Only
after being placed on the evacuation helicopter did he allow aid to be given to him.
Specialist Rascon's extraordinary valor in the face of deadly enemy fire, his hero-
ism in rescuing the wounded, and his gallantry by repeatedly risking his own life
for his fellow soldiers are in keeping with the highest traditions of military service
and reflect great credit upon himself, his unit, and the United States Army.

ALFRED RASCON emigrated from Mexico, joined the US Army, earned the
Medal of Honor for his actions in Vietnam, received a college degree, achieved
an officer's commission, and served as the director of the US Selective Service
System. Rascon was born on September 10, 1945, in Chihuahua, Mexico, as
the only child of Alfredo and Andrea Rascon. Soon after his birth his family
moved to Oxnard, California, where they worked as laborers and became legal
permanent residents.

Rascon attended grammar and high school in Oxnard. He excelled in the
classroom, but with no money for college, he volunteered for the army in
October 1963. In testimony concerning "The Contribution of Immigrants to
America's Armed Forces" before the Senate Subcommittee on Immigration
on May 26, 1999, Rascon said,

... had my parents not made the difficult decision to immigrate from Mexico to the United States when I was a young boy, I would not be before you today. I am grateful for this opportunity from the committee to add to the dialogue on the contributions of immigrants to the U.S. military.

... So for this and for the many things you have done for immigrants, on behalf of immigrants across this Nation I want to thank you personally.

Although by birth immigrants are from other nations, they have served and continue to serve with pride and great distinction in the U.S. Armed Forces. The U.S. Military affords immigrants the opportunity to demonstrate their commitment to this great Nation, with some making the ultimate sacrifice, ... giving their lives.

When I began attending grade school in Southern California, I could not speak a word of English. I spent my youth wanting to assimilate into America. I gradually learned to speak English, even without an accent.... Learning English was a difficult task before me. Other than in school, Spanish was the language in my home and in the community.

Living near three military bases and watching conveys head for their port of debarkation on their way to the Korean War in the 1950's, I developed a fascination with the military. In fact, at the age of 7, I made a parachute and jumped off the roof of our home. Well, in military airborne jargon, my parachute had a total malfunction and I streamed in, resulting in a broken wrist.

As soon as I graduated from high school, at the age of 17, I joined the military. Being underage, I pressured my parents into signing the age waiver .... I volunteered to be a paratrooper, my first love.... As a legal permanent resident of this great country, I wanted to give back something to this country and its citizens for the opportunities it had given me and my parents.

After completing basic training at Fort Ord, California, Rascon was assigned to Fort Sam Houston, Texas, for medical training. He then graduated from the Airborne School at Fort Benning, Georgia, and reported in February 1964 to the Medical Platoon, Headquarters Company, 1st Battalion, 503rd Airborne Infantry Regiment, 173rd Airborne Brigade, stationed on Okinawa.

On May 5, 1965, Rascon and the 173rd Airborne arrived in Vietnam as the first major ground combat force of the US Army and were soon engaged with the enemy. Rascon suffered a minor wound early in his tour, earning his first Purple Heart. His second would not be so minor. In an interview by Kathy Kadane published in the October 2000 issue of *Vietnam* magazine, Racon recalled the events that led to his Medal of Honor. Rascon said,

I did not realize how big Operation Silver City was until later. I have a clear memory of traveling into the area, including a difficult crossing of the Song Be River on pontoons and rubber rafts. Others flew in by helicopter and established a landing zone from which the 173rd could operate. The mission was to insert us into War Zone D and to destroy MR-7 headquarters. This involved a thorough screening of the area.

We started out on March 9, searching the area. On March 14 and 15 we found large caches of weapons and rice. On the 15th, one bag that we found was booby-trapped, and two recon soldiers were wounded and extracted by helicopter. This was a scary event because when we found these materials, despite the fact that there could be other booby-traps, we were ordered to retrieve them and bring them back to the battalion area base. Then engineers would go back in and blow up everything we could not carry out.

That night, around 1 a.m., our encampment was shattered by the sound of mortars and artillery. We did not know if these were the "bad guys," or if we were the targets. By daybreak, we could hear the 2nd Battalion in a massive firefight. We later found out they were engaged with two reinforced battalions of the regular NVA. We learned that they were surrounded in an oval-shaped area about the size of a football field in the middle of dense jungle. They were being hit from all sides. But we were still sweeping the area. One company had found another large ammo cache, and it would have to be retrieved, so we did this. By midday, however, it was decided that B and C Companies would assist the 2nd Battalion. Later that afternoon, the recon patrol was told to take the lead, with A Company bringing up the rear.

The area was covered by dense jungle, so we had to work our way on narrow paths, which were enemy trails. We could hear the fighting from about 200 meters away when we came to a stretch where, to our left, was a burned-out, napalmed area; on the right, thick jungle; and ahead, a fork where two other trails met the trail we were on. At this location, we found piles of bandages and bodies of NVA soldiers that had been stacked up. We later learned that the 2/503 was putting it to the NVA, and as NVA were killed around the perimeter of the fighting, their bodies were being removed.

Moments later, the leader of the point squad, Sergeant Elmer R. "Ray" Compton, stopped the platoon, stating he had spotted the enemy setting up a machine-gun ambush in the heavy foliage ahead of us at the fork in the path, and that they were wearing dark green and khaki uniforms and had NVA pith helmets. After that, some things are blurred in my memory, they happened so fast. Within seconds of Compton's briefing, Pfc Neil Haffey, a grenadier, was brought forward and told to fire his M-79. As he did so, all hell broke loose. From what Haffey later told me, as he was firing his M-79, his projectile had not cleared his gun when they opened up on us. But Pfc William Thompson, an M-60 machine-gunner, somehow ended up lying on the edge of the trail. At that point, I was about 15 to 20 meters behind him with the main recon force.

Heavy weapons were being fired in both directions. I couldn't see what was happening up front. I remember somebody yelling "Doc!" so I started forward when Platoon Sergeant Jacob Cook said to me, "Doc, stay down or you're going to get killed. Don't go until we provide you cover fire." But I went forward anyway, crawling on my knees to the area where I heard yelling, toward the location of the point squad. Then I saw Thompson, who had been with the point squad, lying on the path. I saw that Haffey was much farther forward and to the side of the trail, seeking cover but trying to fire his M-79. However, everyone was pinned down with firing all around and hand grenades being thrown in all directions.

I could hear the NVA talking and yelling—I think they did not expect us, either. Both sides were trying to get in better fixed defensive positions. It was hell—tree limbs were falling from the machine-gun and hand-grenade explosions. I could hear Sergeants Lacuna and Cook yelling, trying to bring the remaining recon element up to outflank the enemy. However, the point squad was trapped and pinned down. It was weird—our two machine guns were up front. I don't know how this happened. Somebody said, "Send the machine guns up front," but they did not know that [machine-gunner Pfc Larry M.] Gibson was already up there, as well as Thompson. This ended up being fortunate—it kept everybody down, and it gave me cover fire. After a few tries, I made my way to Thompson. He was face down. I lay down between his legs and tried to find out where he was hit. Both of us were looking down machine-gun alley—I could see the gun that was shooting at us and the others. But I couldn't see or feel where Thompson was hit, so I crawled over him, turned around and put my back to the enemy fire. At this time, I could see out of the corner of my eye that Haffey, who was to the front ahead of me, was in a position where he was unable to fire his M-79, so he broke out his .45 pistol and started using that to counter the enemy. Incoming hand grenades were all over the place. I was hit by shrapnel and by gunfire in the hip—the bullet went up my spine and exited by my shoulder blade. I am only 5 feet 7 inches tall, but I managed to drag Thompson, who was over 6 feet, off the path, where I could examine him. By his wounds, I concluded quickly that he had been killed instantly.

I heard Gibson yelling for ammo. His assistant machine-gunner was not there—he was pinned down someplace else. But nobody could move forward. I crawled toward Gibson, who was on my right. He was yelling, "I need ammo!" I saw he was shot in the leg and was bleeding. I said, "You're shot!" Gibson yelled back at me, "Get away from me, Doc!" Gibson's concern was to maintain his suppressive fire on the enemy. I remembered that Thompson had two bandoleers of ammo wrapped around him. As Gibson was still putting down covering fire, I went back to Thompson and stripped the bandoleers off him and brought them back to Gibson, who at that time was almost out of ammo. He still didn't want any aid. He just wanted to keep firing at the NVA positions. As I left Gibson looking for other wounded, a hand grenade went over my head. It landed in front of Spec. 4 Jerry Lewis, a buddy of Haffey's. I didn't know until years later that Haffey had seen Lewis hit and killed instantly by the hand grenade and that Lewis was his best friend. At this point, Gibson, who had been able to reload, got the machine gun going again.

After Lewis was hit, I started looking for other wounded. I saw Haffey trying to place himself in a better position, but he was shot in the hip point-blank from about 3 meters by an enemy soldier. He later told me he remembered the guy looking at him and shooting him. I saw a number of hand grenades had been thrown within meters of him. I crawled over to him and threw myself on him, knocking him down. We both ended up getting hit by the shrapnel from the grenades. Haffey's only concern was to make sure that I could get back to Lewis to see how he was. I told Haffey I would go back to look at Lewis. I got back to Lewis, and immediately realized that the grenade had killed him instantly. After I left him, within a few seconds more hand grenades went off. One hit me in the face—that wound was the one that hurt the most! I thought my head spun around three times. The war stopped for me—everything was in slow motion. Blood was spurting out through my mouth. I thought my jaw was gone, and I was deathly afraid. I managed to pull myself together and remembered the other machine gun that had been abandoned on the trail. I was really afraid the M-60 and spare ammo would fall into the hands of the enemy, who were very close. Without much forethought, I made my way back to the trail. I grabbed the M-60, the spare barrel and two boxes of ammo. Strange to say, I was not hit that time by gunfire. I could hear everybody yelling: "Cover, Doc! Cover, Doc!"

At that point, I looked up and saw Sergeant Compton in a defensive position, firing. He knew he was already wounded, and as I made my way to him, I saw hand grenades thrown at him. I grabbed him and pushed him to the ground, but we both got nailed. Sergeant Compton wanted to continue his cover fire for the point squad. I could hear him still giving directions to the squad. Moments later, men from the rear had come up and were flanking the enemy, neutralizing the ambushers—I don't remember who this was. The only people who had really been nailed were members of the point squad up front, who had been the lead element. Without Compton's leadership, many members of the point squad would have been pushing up daisies.

Within a few moments, everything went quiet. The whole thing had taken only about 10 or 20 minutes. I remember just lying there. Then I started checking out who was wounded and giving instructions on how to get the wounded out to the landing zone. As we were coming out of the jungle, the 2/503 paratroopers came immediately to our aid, assisting with the medevacing and caring for our wounded.

I was helicoptered to a mini-triage area set up for the battalion. They stuck me on a sawhorse litter with my clothes still on and began examining me. I complained about my mouth, but nobody seemed to care! Then I was put on a helicopter and taken to the 93rd Field Evacuation Hospital in Long Binh.

Rascon was in such bad shape that a chaplain administered last rites to him when he arrived at the evacuation hospital. He continued his fight, this time against his own wounds, and was transferred to Johnson Army Hospital in Japan and then back to the States for further treatment. After a six-month recovery he was honorably discharged from active duty and placed in the reserves in May 1966.

Although he had been recommended for the Medal of Honor, the paperwork was misplaced, lost, or ignored at some level and he was awarded the Silver Star. Pres. Bill Clinton later said, "The request somehow got lost in a thicket of red tape."

Rascon was not overly bothered by the slight as he was looking forward rather than backward. He enrolled in college and graduated with a degree in business administration. He also completed the paperwork to become a naturalized US citizen. In 1970 he returned to active duty and attended the army's Infantry Officers Candidate School at Fort Benning and earned a commission as a 2nd lieutenant. He then served in various assignments in the States and overseas, including a second tour in Vietnam as an advisor in the US Military Assistance Command where he added the coveted Combat Infantryman Badge to the Combat Medic Badge that he had earned on his first tour.

In 1976, Rascon, now a captain, again left active duty to return to the reserves. That same year he was selected to be the US Army liaison officer to the Republic of Panama. He then worked for the Department of Justice's Drug Enforcement Administration and the Immigration and Naturalization Service and retired from the reserves in 1984.

During a 1985 reunion of the 173rd Airborne Brigade, Rascon's comrades learned that he never received the Medal of Honor. Ray Compton, Neil Haffey, and Larry Gibson, whose lives he had saved, sought to correct the oversight and began efforts for him to receive the recognition he deserved. With help from their congressmen and Pres. Bill Clinton, they convinced the Department of the Army to reopen the file.

On February 8, 2000, President Clinton presented Rascon the Medal of Honor in a ceremony held in the East Room of the White House. The president said,

> When the Medal of Honor was conceived in 1861, some Americans actually worried that it might be a bad thing, that the medals would be seen as somehow too aristocratic, and that there was no need for them in a genuinely democratic society. Today we award the Medal of Honor secure in the knowledge that people like Alfred Rascon have kept our democracy alive all these years. We bestow the medal knowing that America would not have survived were it not for people like him, who, generation after generation, have always renewed the extraordinary gift of freedom for their fellow citizens. Alfred was once asked why he volunteered to join and to go to Vietnam when he was not even a citizen. And he said, "I was always an American in my heart." Alfred Rascon, today we honor you, as you have honored us by your choice to become an American and your courage in reflecting the best of America. You said that you summoned your courage for your platoon because "you've got to take care of your people." That's a pretty good credo for all the rest of us as well.
>
> On behalf of all Americans, and especially on behalf of your platoon members who are here today, I thank you for what you mean to our country. Thank you for what you gave that day and what you have given every day since. Thank you for reminding us that being American has nothing to do with the place of your birth, the color of your skin, the language of your parents, or the way you worship God. Thank you for living the enduring American values every day. Thank you for doing something that was hard because no one else was there to do it. Thank you for looking out for people when no one else could be there for them.

On May 22, 2002, the US Senate confirmed Rascon as the tenth director of the Selective Service System. Rascon once again put on his uniform on September 1, 2002, to serve in Iraq and Afghanistan as a major and individual mobilization augmentee to the Surgeon General's Office. He retired from the military with the rank of lieutenant colonel and now makes his home in Laurel, Maryland.

On May 17, 2003, the Uniformed Services University of Health Sciences awarded Rascon the degree of Doctor of Medical Jurisprudence Honoris Causa. The army has renamed its training school for medics at Fort Campbell, Kentucky, the Alfred V. Rascon School of Combat Medicine. The post office in Savage, Maryland, also bears his name. Rascon has been honored by the American Immigration Lawyers Association and Foundation in Washington, DC, for his past contributions in the military. The Washington-based CATO Institute also honored him as a contributor to Hispanic Americans.

In his remarks when he presented Rascon his Medal of Honor, President Clinton said, "On that distant day, in that faraway place, this man gave everything he had, utterly and selflessly, to protect his platoon mates and the Nation he was still not yet a citizen of." Later Rascon said, with characteristic modesty, "I did it because I had to do it, and that's all there is to it." He said, "I don't consider myself a hero. Anybody in combat would do the same thing for their buddies and friends. We were all colorblind. We were all different nationalities. The important thing is that we were Americans fighting for America."

53

Humbert Roque Versace,
US Army

Detachment 52, Team 70, 5th Special Forces, Military Assistance
  Advisory Group
Thoi Binh District, An Xuyen Province, Republic of Vietnam,
  October 29, 1963–September 23, 1965
Date Presented: July 8, 2002

CITATION:

Captain Humbert R. Versace distinguished himself by extraordinary heroism during the period of 29 October 1963 to 26 September 1965, while serving as S-2 Advisor, Military Assistance Advisory Group, Detachment 52, Ca Mau, Republic of Vietnam. While accompanying a Civilian Irregular Defense Group patrol engaged in combat operations in Thoi Binh District, An Xuyen Province, Captain Versace and the patrol came under sudden and intense mortar, automatic weapons, and small arms fire from elements of a heavily armed enemy battalion. As the battle raged, Captain Versace, although severely wounded in the knee and back by hostile fire, fought valiantly and continued to engage enemy targets. Weakened by his wounds and fatigued by the fierce firefight, Captain Versace stubbornly resisted capture by the overpowering Viet Cong force with the last full measure of his strength and ammunition. Taken prisoner by the Viet Cong, he exemplified the tenets of the Code of Conduct from the time he entered into Prisoner of War status. Captain Versace assumed command of his fellow American soldiers, scorned the enemy's exhaustive interrogation and indoctrination efforts, and made three unsuccessful attempts to escape, despite his weakened condition which was brought about by his wounds and the extreme privation and hardships he was forced to endure. During his captivity, Captain Versace was segregated in an isolated pris-oner of war cage, manacled in irons for prolonged periods of time, and placed on extremely reduced ration. The enemy was unable to break his indomitable will, his faith in God, and his trust in the United States of America. Captain Versace, an American fighting man who epitomized the principles of his country and the Code of Conduct, was executed by the Viet Cong on 26 September 1965. Captain Versace's gallant actions in close contact with an enemy force and unyielding cour-age and bravery while a prisoner of war are in the highest traditions of the military service and reflect the utmost credit upon himself and the United States Army.

HUMBERT VERSACE was the first member of the US Army to be awarded the Medal of Honor for his actions while being held as a prisoner of war by the enemy. "Rocky," as he was known to his family and friends, was born in Honolulu, Hawaii, on July 8, 1937, to Humbert Joseph and Marie Versace. His father, an Italian American and 1933 graduate of West Point, was a career officer who served in both World War II and the Korean War.

Rocky's mother, Marie Teresa, was the daughter Rafael Rios, a Puerto Rican who immigrated to New York early in the twentieth century and mar-ried Marie Teresa Dowd, an American of Irish heritage. Marie was born in Brooklyn and after marrying Joseph Versace, the couple moved around the world on various military assignments. They had five children, with Rocky being the oldest. During her many moves with her family, she wrote for local newspapers as well as military publications. In 1957 she published her first book, *An Angel Grows Up*, using the pen name Tere Ríos. She followed with *Brother Angel* in 1963 and in 1965 with *The Fifteenth Pelican*, which was the basis for the 1960s Screen Gems television sitcom *The Flying Nun*, starring Sally Field. Rios dedicated the book to Rocky, who was a POW at the time, and to the children of the Vietnamese village he had assisted. Marie Versace was extremely proud of her Puerto Rican heritage and spent the last nine years of her life on the island.

Rocky's friends remember him as strong-willed with a firm sense of duty and moral responsibility—as well as being opinionated and headstrong. His brother, Stephen, said, "He could pretty much drive everybody crazy. There was no gray for Rocky and he lived that way. Right is right. Wrong is wrong."

Versace attended Gonzaga High School in Washington, DC, during his freshman and sophomore years. He then accompanied his parents to Ger-many, where he completed his junior year at Frankfurt American High

School. Concerned that the school would not make him sufficiently competitive for admission to West Point, he returned to the States and lived with his grandmother in Virginia, where he graduated from Norfolk Catholic High School. His efforts were successful, and he was appointed as a cadet in the military academy's class of 1959. At West Point, Versace, at six feet one and 185 pounds, excelled in sports, earning the Corps championship in wrestling for three years. Fellow classmate and Heisman Trophy–winner Pete Dawkins later said, "He was not fast, he certainly was not skilled, but he would never give up." Versace, a devote Catholic, was also known at the academy for his daily morning mass attendance at the post chapel.

Versace graduated from West Point in 1959 with a commission as a 2nd lieutenant in the armor branch. After attending the armor officer basic course at Fort Knox, Kentucky, he graduated from the airborne and Ranger schools at Fort Benning, Georgia, before reporting to the 1st Calvary Division in Korea, where he served as an M-48 tank platoon leader from March 1960 to April 1961.

On his return to the States, he joined the 3rd Infantry Regiment at Fort Myer, Virginia. The unit performed mostly ceremonial duties at Arlington National Cemetery and Washington, DC, and Versace soon became bored and yearned for the "real army."

He volunteered for Vietnam and attended advisor training at Fort Bragg, North Carolina; intelligence training at Fort Holabird, Maryland; and the Vietnamese language course at the Presidio of Monterey, California. He arrived in Southeast Asia on May 12, 1962. Versace initially served as an intelligence advisor at Xuan Loc in Long Kanh Province. In November 1962 he assumed the duties of the assistant intelligence officer advisor, 5th Army of Vietnam Division, in Bien Hoa. He also spent much time supporting local orphans and orphanages where the children called him "the Candyman" for the treats that he brought them. At the end of his one-year tour in May 1963, Versace extended for six months in-country because he believed in what he and his country were doing to support democracy in Vietnam. In a letter home the previous Christmas, he wrote, "I am convinced that your taxpayer's money is being put to a very worthy cause—that of freeing the Vietnamese people from an organized Communist threat aimed at the same nasty things all Communists want—at denying this country and its wonderful people a chance to better themselves."

After his extension, Versace joined Advisory Team 70 in the Mekong Delta as the team's intelligence officer. During this time he applied for acceptance at the Maryknoll Seminary in Ossining, New York, with the objective of becoming a priest and returning to Vietnam as a missionary. This ambition fit with Versace's beliefs because Maryknoll priests are known as the "Marines of the Catholic Church" for their reputation of moving into rough areas, living side by side with indigenous peoples, and learning the language. Their stated mission is to focus on "combating poverty, providing healthcare, building communities, and advancing peace and social justice."

Versace would never get the opportunity to become a missionary priest. On October 29, 1963, less than two weeks before he was to leave Vietnam, he made a liaison visit to Army Special Forces Team Detachment A-23. He decided to accompany the team and their Civilian Irregular Defense Group on an operation into the U Minh Forest, where they were ambushed by the 306th Main Force Viet Cong Battalion and overrun. Versace, who suffered multiple wounds to his leg; 1st Lt James N. "Nick" Rowe of McAllen, Texas; and Sgt. Daniel L. Pitzer of Spring Lake, North Carolina; were taken prisoner. The incident was of such importance that the November 1, 1963, issue of *Stars and Stripes* printed what little information was known at the time.

The prisoners were taken deep into the jungle where they were brutalized, provided little food or shelter, and exposed to constant propaganda. Versace resisted from the beginning, citing the rules of the Geneva Convention as he refused to reveal anything other than his name, rank, and serial number. He made his first of four unsuccessful escape attempts even before his leg wounds had healed. Fluent in Vietnamese and French, he constantly berated his captors. After nearly two years of captivity, the North Vietnam's "Liberation Radio" announced on November 26, 1965, that Versace had been executed in response to the death of three Communists in Da Nang. Versace's fellow prisoners would later report that the night before his execution they could hear him loudly singing "God Bless America" from his bamboo cage.

Upon notification of their son's fate, Versace's parents attempted to learn more details about their son's death. Marie Rios went to Paris in the late 1960s in an unsuccessful effort to see the North Vietnamese delegation as it arrived for peace talks. She later expressed her frustration and anguish in poems.

Little was known about Versace's brave resistance until Nick Rowe escaped on December 31, 1968. Rowe, who graduated from West Point a year after Versace, secured an appointment with Richard Nixon and briefed the president about the heroism of his fellow West Pointer. Nixon ordered that Versace be put in for the Medal of Honor, but the rising objections to the war in general and a long-term unofficial army policy of not decorating POWs resulted in only a Silver Star and a Purple Heart for the dead hero.

Versace's remains have never been recovered. His headstone is above an empty grave in Memorial Section MG-108 of Arlington National Cemetery. His name is inscribed on the Vietnam Veterans Memorial in Washington DC (Panel 01E, Row 033).

The public became more familiar with the Versace story when Rowe published *Five Years to Freedom* in 1971. Rowe continued to be an advocate and supporter of Versace until his assassination on April 21, 1989, by Filipino guerillas in Quezon City, where he was a colonel at the Joint US Military Advisory Group headquarters.

"Friends of Rocky Versace"—composed of family members, West Point graduates, and the Special Forces community—renewed efforts to secure the Medal of Honor for Versace in 1999. Legislation added by Congress to the 2002 Defense Authorization Act finally authorized the recognition that the heroic POW deserved. Pres. George W. Bush presented the Medal of Honor to Versace's surviving siblings in the East Room of the White House on July 8, 2002.

In his remarks, Bush said,

> I am honored to be a part of the gathering as we pay tribute to a true American patriot, and a hero, Captain Humbert "Rocky" Versace. Nearly four decades ago, his courage and defiance while being held captive in Vietnam cost him his life. Today it is my great privilege to recognize his extraordinary sacrifices by awarding him the Medal of Honor.
>
> One of his fellow soldiers recalled that Rocky was the kind of person you only had to know a few weeks before you felt like you'd known him for years. Serving as an intelligence advisor in the Mekong Delta, he quickly befriended many of the local citizens. He had that kind of personality. During his time there he was accepted into the seminary, with an eye toward eventually returning to Vietnam to be able to work with orphans.
>
> When Rocky completed his one-year tour of duty, he volunteered for another tour. And two weeks before his time was up, on October the 29th, 1963, he set out with several companies of South Vietnamese troops, planning to take out a Viet Cong command post. It was a daring mission, and an unusually dangerous one for someone so close to going home to volunteer for.
>
> After some initial successes, a vastly larger Viet Cong force ambushed and overran Rocky's unit. Under siege and suffering from multiple bullet

wounds, Rocky kept providing covering fire so that friendly forces could withdraw from the killing zone. Eventually, he and two other Americans, Lieutenant Nick Rowe and Sergeant Dan Pitzer, were captured, bound and forced to walk barefoot to a prison camp deep within the jungle. For much of the next two years, their home would be bamboo cages, six feet long, two feet wide, and three feet high. They were given little to eat, and little protection against the elements. On nights when their netting was taken away, so many mosquitoes would swarm their shackled feet it looked like they were wearing black socks. The point was not merely to physically torture the prisoners, but also to persuade them to confess to phony crimes and use their confessions for propaganda. But Rocky's captors clearly had no idea who they were dealing with. Four times he tried to escape, the first time crawling on his stomach because his leg injuries prevented him from walking. He insisted on giving no more information than required by the Geneva Convention and cited the treaty, chapter, and verse over and over again.

He was fluent in English, French and Vietnamese, and would tell his guards to go to hell in all three. Eventually the Viet Cong stopped using French and Vietnamese in their indoctrination sessions, because they didn't want the sentries or the villagers to listen to Rocky's effective rebuttals to their propaganda. Rocky knew precisely what he was doing. By focusing his captors' anger on him, he made life a measure more tolerable for his fellow prisoners, who looked to him as a role model of principled resistance. Eventually the Viet Cong separated Rocky from the other prisoners. Yet even in separation, he continued to inspire them. The last time they heard his voice, he was singing "God Bless America" at the top of his lungs.

On September the 26th, 1965, Rocky's struggle ended [with] his execution. In his too short life, he traveled to a distant land to bring the hope of freedom to the people he never met. In his defiance and later his death, he set an example of extraordinary dedication that changed the lives of his fellow soldiers who saw it firsthand. His story echoes across the years, reminding us of liberty's high price, and of the noble passion that caused one good man to pay that price in full.

Versace has been inducted into the Ranger and the Military Intelligence Halls of Fame. A memorial plaque to him is outside MacArthur Barracks at West Point, and the Rocky Versace Plaza, complete with a bronze statue, is in Alexandria, Virginia. His name is also on the Monument of Remembrances in front of the San Juan, Puerto Rico, capitol building.

$$\bigstar\bigstar\bigstar$$

54

Leonard Louis Alvarado,
US Army

Company D, 2nd Battalion, 12th Cavalry Regiment, 1st Cavalry
  Division (Airmobile)

Phuoc Long Province, Republic of Vietnam, August 12, 1969

Date Presented: March 18, 2014

CITATION:

Specialist Four Leonard L. Alvarado distinguished himself by acts of gallantry and intrepidity above and beyond the call of duty while serving as a Rifleman with Company D, 2d Battalion, 12th Cavalry, 1st Cavalry Division (Airmobile) during combat operations against an armed enemy in Phuoc Long Province, Republic of Vietnam on August 12, 1969. On that day, as Specialist Four Alvarado and a small reaction force moved through dense jungle en route to a beleaguered friendly platoon, Specialist Four Alvarado detected enemy movement and opened fire. Despite his quick reaction, Specialist Four Alvarado and his comrades were soon pinned down by the hostile force that blocked the path to the trapped platoon. Specialist Four Alvarado quickly moved forward through the hostile machinegun fire in order to engage the enemy troops. Suddenly, an enemy grenade exploded nearby, wounding and momentarily stunning him. Retaliating immediately, he killed the grenadier just as another enemy barrage wounded him again. Specialist Four Alvarado crawled forward through the fusillade to pull several comrades back within the hastily-formed perimeter. Realizing his element needed to break away from the hostile force, Specialist Four Alvarado began maneuvering forward alone. Though repeatedly thrown to the ground by exploding satchel charges, he continued advancing and firing, silencing several emplacements, including one enemy machine-

gun position. From his dangerous forward position, he persistently laid suppressive fire on the hostile forces, and after the enemy troops had broken contact, his comrades discovered that he had succumbed to his wounds. Specialist Four Alvarado's extraordinary heroism and selflessness at the cost of his own life, above and beyond the call of duty, are in keeping with the highest traditions of military service and reflect great credit upon himself, his unit and the United States Army.

BY VIRTUE OF alphabetization, Leonard Alvarado was the first Hispanic American to receive the Medal of Honor for actions in the Vietnam War following the military's reassessment of citations of those passed over for the honor because of their race or ethnicity. Alvarado was born on February 13, 1947, in Bakersfield, California, to Mexican Americans Leonard and Beatrice Alvarado. He graduated from East Bakersfield High School before entering the army on July 25, 1968.

After completion of basic and advanced infantry training, Alvarado arrived in Vietnam on January 21, 1969, and joined the 1st Cavalry Division. Over the next eight months, he advanced in rank to specialist 4 and earned the reputation of a proficient infantryman, receiving the Bronze Star, Air Medal, Army Commendation Medal with "V" device, Army Good Conduct Medal, and Combat Infantryman Badge.

In a February 24, 2014, interview with *Stars and Stripes*, Steve Koppenhoefer, his platoon leader in the summer of 1969, said, "He was the scariest guy I have ever seen. Alvarado was tall, maybe six feet four inches. He looked like a pretty regular guy when he wasn't in the bush. In the jungle, he had scimitar sideburns and coal-black eyes. He was intimidating. People in my platoon loved to tell stories about Alvarado."

On August 12, 1969, Alvarado's platoon maneuvered to assist a beleaguered American platoon in the jungle near Vic Duc Phong in Phuoc Long Province. Alvarado charged forward through machine-gun fire and was wounded by an enemy grenade. He killed the grenadier and, despite being again wounded, crawled forward to pull several comrades to safety. He silenced a machine-gun position with his M-60 machine gun, and he continued fighting even after he was knocked down repeatedly by exploding satchel charges.

In a posting on the Virtual Vietnam Veterans Wall, Lieutenant Koppenhoefer wrote,

I was Leonard's platoon leader beginning sometime in March of 1969 until his death on August 12th. His actions in the face of the enemy were always extraordinary. He was already a legend in our outfit. He never hesitated to go in the path of danger, as if it was his calling. Early in the fight on the night of August 12, he took his M60 machine gun and his ammo bearer and attacked the enemy unit that was attacking us, breaking up their attack and saving many lives, possibly including mine. When he was wounded, one of my sergeants and I went to pull him to safety and into the hands of our platoon medic. He was in our arms when he died, and I think we probably heard his last words. It was a privilege to have him in my platoon, and it would be the wish of any army that they could train all of their soldiers to be half what Alvarado was.

Alvarado posthumously received the Distinguished Service Cross. His name is on the Vietnam Veterans Memorial (Panel 19W, Line 7) in Washington, DC. Many friends and family members in Bakersfield wanted Alvarado buried in Arlington National Cemetery, but his mother, Beatrice, insisted he be laid to rest in his hometown. She said that she felt the army had him long enough and that she wanted him close to home where she could visit his grave often. Alvarado's grave is in Bakersfield's Greenlawn Memorial Park in the Holy Cross Section (Block 64, Lot D).

The Defense Authorization Act of 2014 approved the upgrade of twenty-four Distinguished Service Crosses, including Alvarado's, to the Medal of Honor. His daughter, Lenora, accepted the medal on his behalf from Pres. Barack Obama in a White House ceremony on March 18, 2014.

An exhibit of Alvarado's picture and Medal of Honor citation are in the Kern County Courthouse in Bakersfield. A portion of Renfro Road between Santa Fe Way and Reina Road in Bakersfield is named in his honor. The California Department of Veterans Affairs honored him with a Medal of Honor Recognition Ceremony on the west steps of capitol in Sacramento on May 27, 2014.

★★★

55

Jesus Santiago Duran,
US Army

Company E, 2nd Battalion, 5th Cavalry Regiment, 1st Cavalry Division
Border area between Ph Romeas Hek, Cambodia, and Tay Ninh,
    Republic of Vietnam, April 10, 1969
Date Presented: March 18, 2014

CITATION:

*Specialist Four Jesus S. Duran distinguished himself by acts of gallantry and intre-
pidity above and beyond the call of duty while serving as an acting M-60 machine
gunner in Company E, 2d Battalion, 5th Cavalry, 1st Cavalry Division (Airmobile) during combat operations against an armed enemy in the Republic of Vietnam on April 10, 1969. That afternoon, the reconnaissance platoon was moving
into an elaborate enemy bunker complex when the lead elements began taking concentrated ambush fire from every side. The command post was in imminent danger
of being overrun. With an M-60 machinegun blazing from his hip, Specialist Four
Duran rushed forward and assumed a defensive position near the command post.
As hostile forces stormed forward, Specialist Four Duran stood tall in a cloud of
dust raised by the impacting rounds and bursting grenades directed towards him
and thwarted the enemy with devastating streams of machinegun fire. Learning
that two seriously wounded troopers lay helplessly pinned down under harassing
fire, Specialist Four Duran assaulted the suppressive enemy positions, firing deadly
bursts on the run. Mounting a log, he fired directly into the enemy's foxholes, elimi-
nating four and cutting down several others as they fled. Specialist Four Duran
then continued to pour effective fire on the disorganized and fleeing enemy. Specialist Four Duran's extraordinary heroism and selflessness above and beyond the*

call of duty are in keeping with the highest traditions of military service and reflect
great credit upon himself, his unit and the United States Army.

JESUS DURAN was the third serviceman born in Mexico to receive the Medal of Honor for his actions in the Vietnam War. He was born on July 26, 1948, as the sixth of twelve children of Crescencio and Librida Duran in Juarez, Mexico. When Jesus was twelve years old, the family moved to Riverside, California, where he attended high school.

On May 13, 1968, Duran joined the army and, after completion of basic and advanced infantry training, was ordered to Vietnam. His widow, Alma Brigandi, said in a 2014 interview, "He just wanted to better himself, to do something for his country. By joining the service, he was able to become a US citizen."

As a rifleman and then a M-60 machine gunner with the Echo Company Reconnaissance Platoon of the 2nd Battalion, 5th Cavalry Regiment, Duran advanced in rank to specialist 4 and earned the Air Medal, Good Conduct Medal, and Combat Infantryman Badge. His acting platoon leader, Sgt. Michael Dehart of Troy, Ohio, remembered Duran as "a kid who had beautiful black hair and a great smile" and "a young man of character" in an interview with *Hispanic News Link* on March 21, 2014. Dehart added that Duran was a "petite" man who weighed in at 120 pounds and stood about five feet seven.

On April 10, 1969, Duran's reconnaissance platoon was conducting search operations along the South Vietnam and Cambodian border west of Tay Ninh and east of Ph Romeas Hek when they encountered a North Vietnamese Army bunker complex. Duran charged forward, firing his M-60 from the hip, and established a defensive position near the platoon's command post. He continued firing as the NVA focused their rifle and hand-grenade fire on him. He again ran forward to retrieve two seriously wounded members of his platoon. He then stood to fire into the enemy bunkers, killing four and forcing the remainder to retreat.

Duran received the Distinguished Service Cross before his discharge. He returned home and enrolled in Riverside City College, where he studied sociology. He then worked for a year for the Riverside County Probation Department and then three years as a corrections officer for the California Youth Authority at Chino. Family members remember him during this time as "very outgoing" and "much a part of the community."

Bad things, however, at times happen to good people. On February 17, 1977, Duran walked into a neighborhood bar just down the street from his home. For unknown reasons, a fellow patron pulled out a knife and began stabbing people, including Duran, who suffered a fatal heart wound. He is buried in Riverside's Olivewood Cemetery in the North Lawn Plot (Division 1, Space 3, Grave 64).

Duran's DSC was upgraded to the Medal of Honor after the review of minority records concluded in 2014. On March 18 of that year, Pres. Barack Obama presented the medal to Duran's daughter, Tina Duran-Ruvalcaba, in a White House ceremony. Alma Brigandi also attended the ceremony and afterward said that she hoped this honor would not only bestow honor on Jesus, but on the Hispanic community—whom she called a "patient people."

A portion of California State Route 91 in Riverside and the Specialist Jesus S. Duran Eastside Library are named in his honor. A gate at the William Beaumont Hospital at Fort Bliss, Texas, also bears his name. Riverside mayor Rusty Bailey spoke at a ceremony renaming the city's East Side Library in his honor and the Cass Blanc Library renaming for World War II Medal of Honor recipient Salvador J. Lara. He said, "Riverside is a city with a proud military history and a lasting commitment to its veterans. Honoring our latest Medal of Honor recipients this way demonstrates our gratitude for their service while keeping their memories at the forefront of our minds forever. Every time a young person walks into one of these libraries, they will be reminded of who these brave men were and inspired by their acts of heroism."

★★★

56

Santiago Jesus Erevia,
US Army

Company C, 1st Battalion (Airmobile), 501st Infantry Regiment,
101st Airborne Division (Airmobile)
Tam Ky, Quang Nam Province, Republic of Vietnam, May 21, 1969
Date Presented: March 18, 2014

CITATION:
*Specialist Four Santiago J. Erevia distinguished himself by acts of gallantry and
intrepidity above and beyond the call of duty while serving as a radio telephone
operator in Company C, 1st Battalion (Airmobile), 501st Infantry, 101st Airborne
Division (Airmobile) during [a] search and clear mission near Tam Ky, Republic
of Vietnam on May 21, 1969. After breaching an insurgent perimeter, Specialist
Four Erevia was designated by his platoon leader to render first aid to several
casualties, and the rest of the platoon moved forward. As he was doing so, he came
under intense hostile fire from four bunkers to his left front. Although he could
have taken cover with the rest of the element, he chose a retaliatory course of action. With heavy enemy fire directed at him, he moved in full view of the hostile
gunners as he proceeded to crawl from one wounded man to another, gathering
ammunition. Armed with two M-16 rifles and several hand grenades, he charged
toward the enemy positions behind the suppressive fire of the two rifles. Under very
intense fire, he continued to advance on the insurgents until he was near the first
bunker. Disregarding the enemy fire, he pulled the pin from a hand grenade and
advanced on the bunker, leveling suppressive fire until he could drop the grenade
into the bunker, mortally wounding the insurgent and destroying the fortification.
Without hesitation, he employed identical tactics as he proceeded to eliminate*

the next two enemy positions. With the destruction of the third bunker, Specialist
Four Erevia had exhausted his supply of hand grenades. Still under intense fire
from the fourth position, he courageously charged forward behind the fire emitted
by his M-16 rifles. Arriving at the very edge of the bunker, he silenced the occupant
within the fortification at point blank range. Through his heroic actions the lives of
the wounded were saved and the members of the Company Command Post were
relieved from a very precarious situation. His exemplary performance in the face
of overwhelming danger was an inspiration to his entire company and contributed
immeasurably to the success of the mission. Specialist Four Erevia's conspicuous
gallantry, extraordinary heroism, and intrepidity at the risk of his own life, above
and beyond the call of duty, were in keeping with the highest traditions of military
service and reflect great credit upon himself, his unit, and the United States Army.

SANTIAGO EREVIA was one of only three living veterans to receive the
Medal of Honor as a result of the 2014 congressional mandate that reviewed
applications for race bias. A total of twenty-four decisions were reversed in
the process.

Many sources claim that Erevia was born in 1946 in Nordheim, Texas, but
information provided by his granddaughter, Jessica Erevia, in 2016 states that
he was born on December 15, 1945, in Corpus Christi.

His Mexican American parents, Santiago and Raphaela Erevia, were laborers and moved at some point to Nordheim, where Santiago went to work in the
cotton fields. The young Erevia excelled in school but, with encouragement
from his father, dropped out of high school in the tenth grade to work full
time. Over the next four years he labored as a deliveryman and as a cook in
small restaurants in Texas and Nevada. In 1968 he was in the midst of a divorce
and facing the draft, so he volunteered for the army. He later said, "I joined the
army because I had no money to go to college and I wanted a better future. I
thought I could better myself."

Upon completion of basic and advanced infantry training, Erevia was sent
to Vietnam, where he joined the 101st Airborne Division. "Jesse," as he was
known to his fellow soldiers, saw the war up close on only his second day in
the field when a fellow soldier lost his leg after he stepped on a mine. By the
spring of 1968, Erevia had advanced in rank to specialist 4 and earned an Air
Medal, an Army Commendation Medal, and the Combat Infantryman Badge.
He also had been selected to be his platoon leader's radio-telephone operator.

His fellow infantrymen remember him as a quiet and unassuming soldier who did his job well.

On May 21, 1969, Erevia was tending the wounded from an attack against an enemy position when his platoon came under heavy fire from four bunkers. Erevia grabbed his M-16 and one belonging to a wounded man as well as several grenades and ran forward into the fire. In an interview with the Associated Press in 2014, Erevia said, "I thought I was going to get killed when I started to advance because when you fight battles like that you don't expect to live." In other interviews he said, "It was either do or die, I said, 'Well, if I'm going to die, I might as well die fighting.'"

But live he did as he went from bunker to bunker until all were destroyed and their occupants dead. Erevia was recommended for the Medal of Honor but instead received the Distinguished Service Cross. He later said that he thought that he received the DSC because he was not killed or seriously wounded in the battle. Others said he did not receive the Medal of Honor because of his ethnicity.

Erevia earned a promotion to sergeant before leaving active duty and returning to Texas where he joined the National Guard and served for another seventeen years. He also became a mail carrier for the US Postal Service and retired in 2002 after thirty-two years of service. During this time, he earned his high school equivalency diploma and took college courses.

On March 18, 2014, President Obama presented Erevia his long-overdue Medal of Honor in a White House ceremony. After the ceremony, Erevia, in his usual humble manner, said that there were many more soldiers more deserving of the medal than he. Santiago Erevia died in San Antonio from a heart attack on March 22, 2016, leaving behind his wife, Leticia, a daughter, and three sons—one of whom served in the war in Iraq. Erevia is buried in San Antonio's Fort Sam Houston National Cemetery (Section AD, Site 486). His Medal of Honor headstone states, "Hero to family and country."

The 101st Airborne Division honors Erevia with a display in its headquarters at McAuliffe Hall at Fort Campbell, Kentucky, and the Texas State Legislature passed House Resolution 2419 recognizing his receipt of the Medal of Honor. The National Society of Hispanic MBAs awarded Erevia its Brillante Award for Military Excellence.

$\bigstar\bigstar\bigstar$

57

Felix Modesto Conde-Falcon,
US Army

Company D, 1st Battalion, 505th Airborne, 82nd Airborne Division

Ap Tan Hoa, Lam Dong Province, Republic of Vietnam, April 4, 1969

Date Presented: March 18, 2014

CITATION:

Conde-Falcon distinguished himself by exceptionally valorous actions, April 4, 1969, while serving as platoon leader during a sweep operation in the vicinity of Ap Tan Hoa, Vietnam. Entering a heavily wooded section on the route of advance, the company encountered an extensive enemy bunker complex, later identified as a battalion command post. Following tactical artillery and air strikes on the heavily secured communist position, the platoon of Conde-Falcon was selected to assault and clear the bunker fortifications. Moving out ahead of his platoon, he charged the first bunker, heaving grenades as he went. As the hostile fire increased, he crawled to the blind side of an entrenchment position, jumped to the roof, and tossed a lethal grenade into the bunker aperture. Without hesitating, he proceeded to two additional bunkers, both of which he destroyed in the same manner as the first. Rejoined with his platoon, he advanced about one hundred meters through the trees, only to come under intense hostile fire. Selecting three men to accompany him, he maneuvered toward the enemy's flank position. Carrying a machine-gun, he single-handedly assaulted the nearest fortification, killing the enemy inside before running out of ammunition. After returning to the three men with his empty weapon and taking up an M-16 rifle, he concentrated on the next bunker. Within ten meters of his goal, he was shot by an unseen assailant and soon died of his

wounds. His great courage, his ability to act appropriately and decisively in ac-
complishing his mission, his dedication to the welfare of his men mark him as an
outstanding leader. Conde-Falcon's extraordinary heroism and devotion to duty,
at the cost of his life, were in keeping with the highest traditions of the military ser-
vice and reflect great credit upon himself, his unit, and the United States Army.

FELIX CONDE-FALCON was an army career noncommissioned officer with
more than six years of service when he earned his Medal of Honor in the Mekong Delta region of South Vietnam. Born on February 24, 1938, in Juncos,
Puerto Rico, he moved as a boy with his parents to Chicago, where he attended
public schools and then volunteered for the army in April 1963.

After basic and advanced infantry training, Conde-Falcon served at Fort
Bliss and Fort Hood, Texas, as an infantryman and as a drill instructor as he
advanced in rank to staff sergeant. While at Fort Hood, he met and married
a local woman Lydia Layton. The couple was stationed at Fort Bliss when
Lydia went into labor with their first child two months early. When doctors
told Conde-Falcon that they might be able to save only one, the mother or the
baby, Conde-Falcon showed the tenacity and refusal to give in that he would
later display on the battlefield. As his son would later recall, his father said,
"No, you're going to save them both."

The doctors were successful in saving Lydia and their son, and the couple
had another child at Fort Bliss before returning to Fort Hood, where they
bought a home before his departure for Vietnam. Conde-Falcon arrived in-
country on July 10, 1968, and joined the 1st Brigade of the 82nd Airborne
Division as a platoon sergeant. His soldiers later remembered him as "quite a
man and soldier." In battle he was always on the offense and moving forward.
When the fighting concluded, he was "a great guy, a jokester." Many of his men
said that he was "like a father" to them and was "always looking out for them
and trying to protect them."

Early in his tour, Conde-Falcon earned the Bronze Star with "V" device
for bravery under fire. On April 4, 1969, Conde-Falcon's unit encountered an
enemy battalion base camp. He pushed forward using a machine gun, a rifle,
and hand grenades to neutralize bunker after bunker as he protected his men
and killed the enemy. Nearing the final fortification, he fell mortally wounded
from small-arms fire. His remains were returned to Central Texas, where he is
buried in the Rogers Community Cemetery. He was posthumously promoted

to sergeant 1st class, and his family was awarded his Distinguished Service Cross. Conde-Falcon's name is on the Vietnam Veterans Memorial in Washington, DC (Panel 27W, Line 9).

At the time of his death, Conde-Falcon's children, Richard and Juanal, were aged three and one, respectively. They grew up without their father, and it was not until twenty years after his death that members of his platoon who were with him when he died were able to track them down and tell them about their father's heroics. When the 2014 review of minority DSCs authorized the Medal of Honor for Conde-Falcon, many of these veterans attended the White House ceremony on March 18, 2014, when Pres. Barack Obama presented the award to Richard in his father's stead. At the time, two of Conde-Falcon's grandchildren were serving in the US Armed Forces.

After the ceremony, Rep. John R. Carter (R-TX), whose district included Fort Hood, said, "There is no more deserving recipient of the Medal of Honor than Sgt. Felix Conde-Falcon. Despite a life cut short, this brave warrior's patriotism, valor, and commitment to serve reflect the very best of both America and Central Texas. May his legacy remind us of the values and freedoms we must never cease to defend."

On February 3, 2017, members of Conde-Falcon's old unit—the 1st Battalion, 505th Infantry Regiment—visited the Congressional Medal of Honor Museum aboard the USS *Yorktown* in Charleston Harbor, South Carolina, to present a plaque in his honor. According to an army news release, Lt. Yohan Silva, a platoon leader in the battalion, said, "It is important for our leaders to obtain a better perspective of historical leaders and their real-life actions. Educating ourselves about where we have been and what we should strive for in the future."

The battalion commander, Lt. Col. Marcus Wright, added, "With Conde-Falcon being the only Medal of Honor recipient from the 82nd during the Vietnam War, we want to be able to educate the paratroopers, celebrate Conde-Falcon's legacy in the battalion, and give the paratroopers more pride in the organization."

58

Candelario Garcia Jr.,
US Army

Company B, 1st Battalion, 2nd Infantry, 1st Brigade, 1st Infantry Division
Lai Khe, Republic of Vietnam, December 8, 1968
Date Presented: March 18, 2014

CITATION:
Sergeant Candelario Garcia distinguished himself by acts of gallantry and intrepidity above and beyond the call of duty while serving as an acting Team Leader for Company B, 1st Battalion, 2d Infantry, 1st Brigade, 1st Infantry Division during combat operations against an armed enemy in Lai Khe, Republic of Vietnam on December 8, 1968. On that day, while conducting reconnaissance, Sergeant Garcia and his platoon discovered communication wire and other signs of an enemy base camp leading into a densely vegetated area. As the men advanced, they came under intense fire. Several men were hit and trapped in the open. Ignoring a hail of hostile bullets, Sergeant Garcia crawled to within ten meters of a machine-gun bunker, leaped to his feet and ran directly at the fortification, firing his rifle as he charged. Sergeant Garcia jammed two hand grenades into the gun port and then placed the muzzle of his weapon inside, killing all four occupants. Continuing to expose himself to intense enemy fire, Sergeant Garcia raced fifteen meters to another bunker and killed its three defenders with hand grenades and rifle fire. After again braving the enemies' barrage in order to rescue two casualties, he joined his company in an assault which overran the remaining enemy positions. Sergeant Garcia's extraordinary heroism and selflessness above and beyond the call of duty are in keeping with the highest traditions of military service and reflect great credit upon himself, his unit and the United States Army.

CANDELARIO GARCIA earned his Medal of Honor in Vietnam, only to die a year before it was finally awarded forty-five years later. Born on February 26, 1944, to Mexican American parents Candelario and Josephine Flores Garcia in Corsicana, Texas, Garcia inherited a legacy of bravery. The Vietnam War hero's father had been killed in action a short time after his birth in France during World War II. Garcia, known as "Junior" or "Spider" to his friends, graduated from Corsicana High School in 1962. A classmate later recalled that everyone liked Garcia and enjoyed being around him.

Garcia joined the army on May 23, 1963, and trained as an infantryman. Five years later, after having reenlisted upon completion of his initial obligation, he was back serving his third tour in Vietnam. By then he had already earned the Silver Star, the Air Medal, and the Army Commendation Medal with "V" device and had advanced in rank to sergeant. On December 8, 1968, Garcia, called "Cid" by his fellow soldiers, neutralized two enemy machinegun bunkers and their defenders with his rifle and hand grenades to rescue two wounded comrades. He received the Distinguished Service Cross for his actions.

Upon the completion of his tour, Garcia was honorably discharged and returned to Corsicana. He worked at several jobs but spent most of his time caring for his ailing mother. Garcia maintained contact with several of his high school classmates through monthly dinners. He did not, however, talk about his experiences in Vietnam.

In an 2014 interview with the Dallas–Fort Worth CBS affiliate, Garcia's brother, Manuel Flores, said that the family knew little about Candelario's time in Vietnam other than that he earned lots of medals. Flores noted that Candelario was never the same after the war and said, "You may have built a soldier, but you took my brother. I remember when he went into the military and I remember when he came back. He never came back—part of him came back, the part I could visibly see, but the part where his mind was I didn't know anything about." Flores added that his brother suffered from alchoism and PTSD after the war.

Garcia died at age sixty-eight on January 10, 2013, at his residence in Corsicana, and his cremains were buried in the Dallas–Fort Worth National Cemetery (Section 17A, Site 57). His flat marker noted only his birth and death dates and that he had received the Purple Heart.

A year later, the 2014 review of minority DSCs upgraded his award to the Medal of Honor. At the family's request, Michael A. Grinston, the command sergeant major of the 1st Infantry Division, accepted the medal from Pres. Barack Obama in a White House ceremony on March 18, 2014. "It was a rare privilege and absolute honor to represent the Garcia family for the Big Red One," Grinston said after the ceremony. "It was a once-in-a-lifetime opportunity to see a chapter in our division's history rewritten to recognize an American hero long denied his rightful award."

With the family's permission, the Dallas–Fort Worth National Cemetery relocated Garcia's remains on June 12, 2014 to Section 107, Site 209. The upright headstone notes his Medal of Honor, Silver Star, Bronze Star, and Purple Heart.

On Memorial Day, May 30, 2016, a statue of Garcia was dedicated on the grounds of the Navarro County Courthouse in Corsicana. Mayor Chuck McClanahan said, "As we gather today, we do so in solidarity, paying tribute to so many, who have given their lives . . . the men and women that have made the ultimate sacrifice so that we may enjoy freedom. Today, while we memorialize, give thanks, and honor all soldiers, we also give special tribute to one of our own—Sergeant Garcia, who did portray selflessness and great courage . . . a task very few of us would attempt. He is an example we should all be willing to follow."

Rep. Joe Barton (R-TX) of the congressional district that includes Corsicana offered an apology to the family of Garcia during his address at the event. He said, "On behalf of the United States Congress, the American people, the United States Army, the United States Government, and the United States of America, I want to apologize to you personally that it's taken so long for your relative to receive the Medal of Honor. He should have received it while he was alive."

★★★

59

José Rodela,
US Army

Detachment B-36, Company A, 5th Special Forces Group (Airborne)
Phuoc Long Province, Republic of Vietnam, September 1, 1969
Date Presented: March 18, 2014

CITATION:

Sergeant First Class Jose Rodela distinguished himself by acts of gallantry and intrepidity above and beyond the call of duty while serving as the company commander, Detachment B-36, Company A, 5th Special Forces Group (Airborne), 1st Special Forces during combat operations against an armed enemy in Phuoc Long Province, Republic of Vietnam on September 1, 1969. That afternoon, Sergeant First Class Rodela's battalion came under an intense barrage of mortar, rocket, and machine gun fire. Ignoring the withering enemy fire, Sergeant First Class Rodela immediately began placing his men into defensive positions to prevent the enemy from overrunning the entire battalion. Repeatedly exposing himself to enemy fire, Sergeant First Class Rodela moved from position to position, providing suppressing fire and assisting wounded, and was himself wounded in the back and head by a B-40 rocket while recovering a wounded comrade. Alone, Sergeant First Class Rodela assaulted and knocked out the B-40 rocket position before successfully returning to the battalion's perimeter. Sergeant First Class Rodela's extraordinary heroism and selflessness above and beyond the call of duty are in keeping with the highest traditions of military service and reflect great credit upon himself, his unit and the United States Army.

BY VIRTUE OF the alphabetical listing of the Distinguished Service Cross upgrades in 2014, Jose Rodela is the last Hispanic American recipient of the Medal of Honor for actions during the Vietnam War. Born to Mexican American parents in Corpus Christi, Texas, on June 15, 1937, Rodela tired of the classroom and dropped out of Miller High School during his sophomore year.

In 1955, at age seventeen, he joined the army and found that he liked the order and discipline of the service and reenlisted after his initial tour. Over the next fourteen years, he served in infantry assignments in the United States and Korea. He also volunteered for airborne and Special Forces training and was a member of the Green Berets and a master parachutist with the rank of sergeant 1st class when he reported to Vietnam in 1969. Fellow soldiers recall that he was a serious, unassuming noncommissioned officer. Rodela never liked special attention. In a 2014 interview with the *NCO Journal* he said, "I don't like to be singled out. I never did and I still don't."

Rodela's job was to train raw Cambodian troops into an effective fighting unit. In the *NCO Journal* article he said, "I recruited them, I trained them, I took them to war. All of the others in that Special Forces company had companies of Vietnamese to train, but I was the only one with Cambodians. They turned out to be pretty good soldiers. I lucked out. They were my people. I trained them. It had taken me almost a month and a half to train these people and get them ready for war. That was my job. When my commander told me to go out, get myself some people and go to war, that's what I did."

On September 1, 1969, a day he remembers as being hot, sticky, and overcast, Rodela was acting as a company commander with the 3rd Battalion, 3rd Mobile Strike Force Command, in the steep, jungle-covered hills of Phuoc Long Province. "That day, we were after a battalion-sized North Vietnamese unit," Rodela recalls. "I had about 100 to 120 men, all Cambodians. It had just started to get daylight. We found these machinegun positions. They were surprised; they didn't know we were there—despite all the noise we were making walking through the jungle."

The enemy opened fire with mortars, machine guns, rockets, and small arms to initiate a battle that lasted eighteen hours. Despite nearly half the company being wounded or killed, the Cambodians held their ground and did not allow the enemy to overrun their positions. Rodela, despite wounds to his head and back, continuously moved around the battlefield rallying his troops, caring for the wounded, and directly engaging the enemy.

When the battle finally concluded, Rodela was evacuated to Fort Sam Houston, Texas, where, while recovering from his wounds, he was awarded the Distinguished Service Cross. He rejoined the Special Forces after his recovery and for the next five years advised and trained troops in Central and South America. He retired from the army in 1975 and worked for the US Postal Service in Corpus Christi and San Antonio. At age seventy-seven, in 2014, Rodela still managed to daily walk more than a mile from his San Antonio retirement home to a restaurant to have breakfast with his son Edmund, a Marine Corp veteran.

When the 2014 review board upgraded his DSC to the Medal of Honor, Rodela accepted it from Pres. Barack Obama in a White House ceremony on March 18, 2014. In an interview with the *San Antonio Express News*, Rodela expressed discomfort in being thrust into a spotlight he did not imagine or desire. He said, "I'm a little disturbed. I don't like it, but I go along with it because of service to my country. I really wish they had left me alone, but I'm here."

As of this writing in late 2020, Rodela is still living in San Antonio. He remains as modest as ever, saying, "Any member of the Army can do the same thing as I did. Just remember your training."

AFGHANISTAN

★ ★ ★

60

Leroy Arthur Petry,
US Army

Company D, 2nd Battalion, 75th Ranger Regiment

Paktya Province, Afghanistan, May 26, 2008

Date Presented: July 12, 2011

CITATION:

For conspicuous gallantry and intrepidity at the risk of his life above and beyond the call of duty: Staff Sergeant Leroy A. Petry distinguished himself by acts of gallantry and intrepidity at the risk of his life above and beyond the call of duty in action with an armed enemy in the vicinity of Paktya Province, Afghanistan, on May 26, 2008. As a Weapons Squad Leader with D Company, 2nd Battalion, 75th Ranger Regiment, Staff Sergeant Petry moved to clear the courtyard of a house that potentially contained high-value combatants. While crossing the courtyard, Staff Sergeant Petry and another Ranger were engaged and wounded by automatic weapons fire from enemy fighters. Still under enemy fire, and wounded in both legs, Staff Sergeant Petry led the other Ranger to cover. He then reported the situation and engaged the enemy with a hand grenade, providing suppression as another Ranger moved to his position. The enemy quickly responded by maneuvering closer and throwing grenades. The first grenade explosion knocked his two fellow Rangers to the ground and wounded both with shrapnel. A second grenade then landed only a few feet away from them. Instantly realizing the danger, Staff Sergeant Petry, unhesitatingly and with complete disregard for his safety, deliberately and selflessly moved forward, picked up the grenade, and in an effort to clear the immediate threat, threw the grenade away from his fellow Rangers. As he was releasing the grenade it detonated, amputating his right hand at the wrist and further injur-

ing him with multiple shrapnel wounds. Although picking up and throwing the live grenade grievously wounded Staff Sergeant Petry, his gallant act undeniably saved his fellow Rangers from being severely wounded or killed. Despite the severity of his wounds, Staff Sergeant Petry continued to maintain the presence of mind to place a tourniquet on his right wrist before communicating the situation by radio in order to coordinate support for himself and his fellow wounded Rangers. Staff Sergeant Petry's extraordinary heroism and devotion to duty are in keeping with the highest traditions of military service, and reflect great credit upon himself, 75th Ranger Regiment, and the United States Army.

LEROY PETRY is the first and, as of the end of 2020, the only Hispanic to earn the Medal of Honor in the Global War on Terrorism. Born on July 29, 1979, in Santa Fe, New Mexico, to an Anglo father, Larry, and a Mexican American mother, Lorella Tapia, Petry attended Santa Fe High School for two years. Although he was very active in sports and liked by his fellow students, Petry did poorly in the classroom and had to repeat his freshman year. He transferred to the private St. Catherine Indian School his sophomore year and became a good student. When he graduated in 1998, he enrolled in New Mexico Highlands University in Las Vegas and also worked with his father and grandfather maintaining vehicles for Pecos Public Transportation and painting signs for a local company.

Tiring of the boring jobs and influenced by a cousin who was a US Army Ranger, Petry enlisted in the army in Santa Fe in September 1999. He attended One Stop Infantry Training, the Airborne Course, and the Ranger Assessment and Selection Program, all at Fort Benning, Georgia, before reporting to 2nd Battalion, 75th Ranger Regiment at Fort Lewis (now Joint Base Lewis-McChord), Washington. He then returned to Fort Benning to attend Ranger School and earned the coveted black and gold tab.

With the attacks on the United States on September 11, 2001, Petry began a series of deployments with the 75th Rangers to fight the War on Terrorism. Over the next seven years, he served eight tours—two in Iraq and six in Afghanistan for a total of twenty-eight months. He acted as a grenadier, squad automatic rifleman, fire team leader, squad leader, operations sergeant, and weapons squad leader as he advanced in rank to staff sergeant.

On May 26, 2008, Petry and his unit were in eastern Afghanistan near the mountainous border with Pakistan. Pres. Barack Obama later described the action, saying,

Helicopters carrying dozens of elite Army Rangers race over the rugged landscape. And their target is an insurgent compound. The mission is high risk. It's broad daylight. The insurgents are heavily armed. But it's considered a risk worth taking because intelligence indicates that a top al Qaeda commander is in that compound. Soon, the helicopters touch down, and our Rangers immediately come under fire. Within minutes, Leroy—then a Staff Sergeant—and another soldier are pushing ahead into a courtyard, surrounded by high mud walls. And that's when the enemy opens up with their AK-47s. Leroy is hit in both legs. He's bleeding badly, but he summons the strength to lead the other Ranger to cover, behind a chicken coop. He radios for support. He hurls a grenade at the enemy, giving cover to a third Ranger who rushes to their aid. An enemy grenade explodes nearby, wounding Leroy's two comrades. And then a second grenade lands—this time, only a few feet away. Every human impulse would tell someone to turn away. Every soldier is trained to seek cover. That's what Sergeant Leroy Petry could have done. Instead, this wounded Ranger, this 28-year-old man with his whole life ahead of him, this husband and father of four, did something extraordinary. He lunged forward, toward the live grenade. He picked it up. He cocked his arm to throw it back.

The grenade exploded just as Petry released it, amputating, his right hand and spraying his body with shrapnel, but saving the lives of the other two Rangers. Petry remained focused as he placed a tourniquet on the remainder of his right arm. He later said that he knew that he had to remain calm and set the example for the young Rangers around him.

After the battle, Petry was evacuated to Germany and then to Darnall Army Medical Center at Fort Hood, Texas, for treatment. Fitted with a prosthetic hand, complete with a small plaque listing the names of Rangers killed in his regiment, Petry returned to active duty and again deployed to Afghanistan and was promoted to sergeant 1st class.

When President Obama presented Petry his Medal of Honor on July 12, 2011, in a ceremony in the East Room of the White House, he concluded his remarks by saying, "This is the stuff of which heroes are made. This is the strength, the devotion that makes our troops the pride of every American. And this is the reason that—like a soldier named Leroy Petry—America doesn't simply endure, we emerge from our trials stronger, more confident, with our eyes fixed on the future."

Petry remained in the army for three more years after receiving the medal but, because of lingering effects from his wounds and a desire to earn a college degree, he retired from active duty on July 29, 2014. At his retirement ceremony he was promoted to master sergeant and awarded the Legion of Merit. He resides in the Pacific Northwest with his wife, Ashley, and their four children.

Santa Fe has honored its hometown hero with a nine-foot-tall bronze and stainless steel statue at its city hall. The city's South Meadow Bridge over the Santa Fe River has also been rededicated in his name.

In an interview published in Fort Benning's newspaper, *The Bayonet*, shortly after receiving his Medal of Honor, Petry said, "The service is the greatest thing I've done. It's one of the greatest things you can do for your nation—selflessly serve and keep us free. I constantly thank veterans because they did that for me, and I grew up in a great nation."

SOURCES AND BIBLIOGRAPHY

BOOKS

Benavidez, Roy P., and John R. Craig. *Medal of Honor: A Vietnam Warrior's Story*. Washington, DC: Brassey's, 1995.

———. *The Three Wars of Roy Benavidez*. San Antonio, TX: Corona Publishing, 1986.

Boudonck, Greg. *Puertorriquenos Who Served with Guts, Glory, and Honor: Fighting to Defend a Nation Not Completely Their Own*. Columbia, SC: CreateSpace, 2014.

Broadwater, Robert P. *Civil War Medal of Honor Recipients*. Jefferson, NC: McFarland, 2007.

Caughey, John Walton, and Jack D.L. Holmes. *Bernardo de Galvez in Louisiana, 1776–1783*. Gretna, LA: Firebird Press, 1999.

Chavez, Thomas. *Spain and the Independence of the United States*. Albuquerque: University of New Mexico Press, 2002.

Donovan, Frank R. *The Medal: The Story of the Medal of Honor*. New York: Dodd, Mead, 1962.

Duffy, James P. *Lincoln's Admiral: The Civil War Campaigns of David Farragut*. New York: Wiley, 1997.

Flores, John W. *Marine Sergeant Freddy Gonzales: Vietnam Hero*. Jefferson, NC: McFarland & Company, 2014.

Ford, Nancy Gentile. *Americans All: Foreign Born Soldiers in World War I*. College Station: Texas A&M University Press, 2001.

Gomez, Laura. *Manifest Destinies: The Making of the Mexican American Race*. New York: New York University Press, 2007.

Gonzales, Manuel G. *Mexicanos: A History of Mexicans in the United States.* Bloomington: Indiana University Press, 1999.

Jacobs, Bruce. *Heroes of the Army: The Medal of Honor and Its Winners.* New York: W. W. Norton, 1956.

———. *Korea's Heroes: The Medal of Honor Story.* New York: Berkley Publishing, 1961.

Johnson, John Allen. *California Valor: Charles Harold Gonsalves.* Bloomington, IN: Trafford Publishing, 2004.

Jordan, Kenneth N. *Forgotten Heroes: 131 Men of the Korean War Awarded the Medal of Honor, 1950–1953.* Atglen, PA: Schiffer Publishing, 1995.

———. *Heroes of Our Time: 231 Men of the Vietnam War Awarded the Medal of Honor, 1964–1972.* Atglen, PA: Schiffer Publishing, 2004.

———. *38 Highly Decorated Marines in World War II, Korea, and Vietnam.* Atglen, PA: Schiffer Publishing, 1997.

———. *433 Men of World War II Awarded the Medal of Honor, 1941–1945.* Atglen, PA: Schiffer Publishing, 1996.

Kastelc, Laurie, ed. *Man of Honor: The Story of David Fernandez.* Bloomington, IN: AuthorHouse, 2009.

Long, George, Raymond L. Collins, and Gerard F. White. *Medal of Honor Recipients, 1863–1994.* 2 vols. New York: Facts on File, 1995.

Matovina, Timothy M. *The Alamo Remembered: Tejano Accounts and Perspectives.* Austin: University of Texas Press, 1995.

McDonald, L. Lloyd. *Tejanos in the 1835 Texas Revolution.* Gretna, LA: Pelican Publishing, 2009.

Mikaelian, Allen. *Medal of Honor: Profiles of America's Military Heroes from the Civil War to the Present.* New York: Hyperion, 2002.

Morin, Raul. *Among the Valiant: Mexican-Americans in World War II and Korea.* Alhambra, CA: Borden Publishing, 1963.

Murphy, Edward F. *Heroes of World War II.* Novato, CA: Presidio Press, 1990.

———. *Korean War Heroes.* Novato, CA: Presidio Press, 1992.

———. *Vietnam Medal of Honor Heroes.* Novato, CA: Presidio Press, 1997.

Neal, Charles M., Jr. *Valor across the Lone Star State: The Congressional Medal of Honor in Frontier Texas.* Austin: Texas State Historical Association, 2002.

Negron-Febus, Iris N., and Gilberto Rivera Santiago. *My Dad; My Hero: This Is Your Life.* Columbia, SC: CreateSpace, 2017.

Oropeza, Lorena. *Fighting on Two Fronts: Latinos in the Military.* Washington, DC: National Park Service, 2015.

Owens, Ronald J. *Medal of Honor: Historical Facts and Figures.* Paducah, KY: Turner Publishing, 2004.

Proft, Robert J. *United States of America's Congressional Medal of Honor Recipients: Their Official Citations.* Columbia Heights, MN: Highland House, 2007.
Ramirez, Jose A. *To the Line of Fire: Mexican Texans and World War I.* College Station, TX: Texas A&M University Press, 2009.
Rowe, James N. *Five Years to Freedom.* New York: Little, Brown, 1971.
Samora, Julian, and Patricia Vandel Simon. *A History of the Mexican People.* South Bend, IN: University of Notre Dame Press, 1977.
Schott, Joseph D. *Above and Beyond: The Story of the Congressional Medal of Honor.* New York: G. P. Putnam's Sons, 1963.
Sinton, Starr, and Robert Hargis. *World War II Medal of Honor Recipients.* Vol. 1, *Navy and USMC.* Oxford, UK: Osprey, 2003.
———. *World War II Medal of Honor Recipients.* Vol. 2, *Army and Air Corps.* Oxford, UK: Osprey, 2003.
Takaki, Robert. *Double Victory: A Multicultural History of America in World War II.* Boston: Little, Brown, 2000.
Thompson, Jerry. *Vaqueros in Blue and Gray.* College Station: Texas A&M University Press, 2000.
Tillman, Barrett. *Heroes: US Army Medal of Honor Recipients.* New York: Berkley Group, 2006.
Turner Publishing, comp. *The First Infantry Division in Vietnam: "The Big Red One," 1965–1970.* Nashville, TN: Turner Publishing, 1993.
Zamora, Emilio. *The World War I Diary of Jose de la Luz Saenz.* College Station: Texas A&M University Press, 2014.

PERIODICALS

Hide, Michele A. "On the Front Lines." *Hispanic* 6, no. 7 (August 1993): 34.
Kadine, Kathy. "Alfred Rascon: A Case of Forgotten Valor during the Vietnam War." *Vietnam.* October 2000.
Mink, Michael. "The Mother of the USS *Gonzales.*" *Norfolk Flagship.* August 19, 2009. https://www.militarynews.com/norfolk-navy-flagship/news/quarterdeck/the-mother-of-the-uss-gonzalez/article_f9c3ceeo-fd52-50c2-8e81-65202b4cb6ae.html.
Smith, Philip R., Jr. "Amigos: Americans All." *Soldiers* 26, no. 9 (September 1971): 22–26.
Thomas, Richard L. "Rest in Peace." *Leatherneck* 71 (July 1988): 38.
Villahermosa, Gilberto. "America's Hispanics in America's Wars." *Army.* September 2002. http://www.valerosos.com/HispanicsMilitary.html.

US GOVERNMENT DOCUMENTS

National Park Service. *Hispanics and the Civil War: From Battlefield to Home-front.* Washington, DC: US Department of the Interior, 2011.

Naval History and Heritage Command, Bureau of Naval Personnel Diversity Directorate. *Hispanics in the United States Navy.* Washington DC, Chief of the Bureau of Naval Personnel, 2010.

Office of the Assistant Secretary of Defense for Personnel and Readiness. *Population Representation in the Military Services, Fiscal Year 2010 Summary Report.* Washington DC: US Department of Defense, 2010.

Office of the Deputy Assistant Secretary of Defense for Military Manpower and Personnel Policy. *Hispanics in America's Defense.* Washington DC: US Department of Defense, 1990.

INDEX

ABOUT THE AUTHOR

MICHAEL LEE LANNING is the author of more than two dozen nonfiction books on military history, sports, and health. More than 1.1 million copies of his books are in print in fifteen countries, and editions have been translated into twelve languages. He has appeared on major television networks and the History Channel as an expert on the individual soldier on both sides of the Vietnam War.

The New York Times Book Review declared Lanning's *Vietnam 1969–1970: A Company Commander's Journal* to be "one of the most honest and horrifying accounts of a combat soldier's life to come out of the Vietnam War." The *London Sunday Times* devoted an entire page to review his *The Military 100: A Ranking of the Most Influential Military Leaders of All Time.* According to the *San Francisco Journal,* Lanning's *Inside the VC and NVA* is "a well-researched, groundbreaking work that fills a huge gap in the historiography of the Vietnam War."

A veteran of more than twenty years in the US Army, Lanning is a retired lieutenant colonel. During the Vietnam War he served as an infantry platoon leader, reconnaissance platoon leader, and an infantry company commander. In addition to having earned the Combat Infantryman's Badge and the Bronze Star with "V" device with two oak leaf clusters, Lanning is Ranger-qualified and a senior parachutist.

Lanning was born in Sweetwater, Texas, and is a 1964 graduate of Trent High School. He has a BS from Texas A&M University and an MS from East Texas State University. He currently resides in Lampasas, Texas.

BOOKS BY MICHAEL LEE LANNING

The Only War We Had: A Platoon Leader's Journal of Vietnam
Vietnam 1969-1970: A Company Commander's Journal
Inside the LRRPs: Rangers in Vietnam
Inside Force Recon: Recon Marines in Vietnam (with Ray W. Stubbe)
The Battles of Peace
Inside the VC and NVA: The Real Story of North Vietnam's Armed Forces
    (with Dan Cragg)
Vietnam at the Movies
Senseless Secrets: The Failures of US Military Intelligence, from
    George Washington to the Present
The Military 100: A Ranking of the Most Influential Military Leaders of All Time
The African American Soldier: From Crispus Attucks to Colin Powell
Inside the Crosshairs: Snipers in Vietnam
Defenders of Liberty: African Americans in the Revolutionary War
Blood Warriors: American Military Elites
The Battle 100: The Stories behind History's Most Influential Battles
Mercenaries: Soldiers of Fortune, from Ancient Greece to Today's Private
    Military Companies
The Civil War 100: The Stories behind the Most Influential Battles, People, and
    Events in the War Between the States
The Revolutionary War 100: The Stories behind the Most Influential Battles,
    People, and Events of the American Revolution
Double T Double Cross: The Firing of Coach Mike Leach
At War with Cancer (with Linda Moore-Lanning)
Tours of Duty: Vietnam War Stories
Tony Buzbee: Defining Moments
Texas Aggies in Vietnam: War Stories
The Veterans Cemeteries of Texas
Dear Allyanna: An Old Soldier's Last Letter to His Granddaughter
The Court Martial of Jackie Robinson
The Blister Club: The Extraordinary Story of the Downed American Airmen
    Who Escaped to Safety in World War II

CPSIA information can be obtained
at www.ICGtesting.com
Printed in the USA
JSHW011204150322
23718JS00002B/6